Successful Leasing and Selling of Retail Property

While a great deal of care has been taken to provide accurate and current information, the ideas, suggestions, general principles, and conclusions presented in this book are subject to local, state, and federal laws and regulations, court cases, and any revisions of same. The reader is thus urged to consult legal counsel regarding any points of law—this publication should not be used as a substitute for competent legal advice.

Executive Editor: Wendy Lochner
Project Editor: Chris Christensen
Copy Editor: Patricia Stahl
Interior Design: Edwin Harris
Cover Design: Vito Depinto
Indexer: Rita Tatum

© 1989, 1984, 1980 by Longman Group USA Inc. and Grubb & Ellis Company
Published by Longman Financial Services Publishing, a division of Longman Financial Services Institute, Inc.

All rights reserved. The text of this publication, or any part thereof, may not be reproduced in any manner whatsoever without written permission from the publisher.

Printed in the United States of America.

89 90 91   10 9 8 7 6 5 4 3 2 1

Library of Congress Cataloging in Publication Data
Main entry under title:
Successful leasing and selling of retail property / Grubb & Ellis Company. — 3rd ed.
    p. cm.
    Includes index.
    ISBN 0-88462-110-3
    1. Selling—Stores.   2. Building leases.   3. Real estate business.
I. Grubb & Ellis Company.
HD1393.26.S76S83 1988
333.33'6'0688—dc19
                                      88-17545
                                          CIP

Successful Leasing and Selling of Retail Property

Developed by
Real Estate Education Company
in cooperation with
Grubb & Ellis Company

THIRD EDITION

REAL ESTATE EDUCATION COMPANY
a division of Longman Financial Services Institute, Inc.

Contents

Preface   xiii

Introduction   xv

CHAPTER ONE   **Types of Transactions**   1
Leasing Existing Space • Subleasing Existing Space • Leasing New Projects • Build to Suit • Land Sale • Purchase or Ground Lease • Sale as an Investment

CHAPTER TWO   **Inventory System**   7
Area Assignment • Getting to Know the Area • Locating Retailers • Gathering Necessary Information • The Retail Inventory System • Property Files • Your Time Investment • Listing Agreements

CHAPTER THREE   **Marketing**   15
Locating the Information • Marketing Proposal

CHAPTER FOUR   **Qualifying Your Clients**   29
Overview of Tenant Needs • Building-to-Site Ratio • Space Needs and Transactions • Retail Tenant Requirement Form • Getting the Information from the Tenant • Visiting the Location • Financial Capability and Decision Making • Tenant Control • Short-term Control • Long-term Control

Contents

CHAPTER FIVE   **Forms and Legal Documents**   47
Tenant Representation Agreement • Commission Agreement • Presenting the Agreement • Schedule of Commissions • Leases • Gross • Percentage • Net • The Lease Document • Lease Clauses • Construction Exhibit • Offer to Lease • Exclusive Right to Sublease

CHAPTER SIX   **Ethical Questions**   77
Broker's Responsibility to the Seller • Broker's Responsibility to the Buyer • Cooperating with Outside Brokers

CHAPTER SEVEN   **Telephone Techniques**   83
Strategy For Telephone Cold Calls • Get to the Decision Maker • Identify Yourself • Explain Why You Are Calling • Describe a Benefit of Your Meeting • Ask for an Appointment • Counter Objections • Follow-up Calls • Effective Telephone Procedures • Practice is Important

CHAPTER EIGHT   **Basic Selling Skills**   97
The Task • Prospects' Needs • Features and Benefits • Selling You and Your Company • Drill Questions • Selling to the Right Person • Handling Objections • Closing the Transaction

CHAPTER NINE   **Time Management**   113
Planning • Long-term Goals • Short-term Objectives • Time Organization • Tickler System • Monthly Plan • Weekly Plan • Daily Plan • Organization • Pending Files • Tickler Files • Escrow Files • Skills for Effective Time Management

CHAPTER TEN   **The Use of Signs**   135
Contents of the Sign • Techniques for Persuading Owners • Property for Sale or Lease by Owner • One Broker's Sign • Sign Requisitions

CHAPTER ELEVEN   **Retail Promotion**   143
Types of Advertising • Classified Advertising • Display Advertising • Brochures • Letters • The Salesperson's Function

CHAPTER TWELVE   **Showing Retail Property**   155
Preparation • Plan Your Route—Then Drive It Yourself • Showing to Local Users • What about Owners? • The Presentation • Follow-up • Rent Schedules • Moving Toward a Close • Showing Vacant Property • A Final Word about Local Users

CHAPTER THIRTEEN   **Site Presentation**   165
Site Identification and Description • Assessor's Map • Zoning • Utilities and Improvements • Area Description • Sales Forecast • Accessibility • Competition • Terms of Site Availability

CHAPTER FOURTEEN   **Local Developers**   191
Types of Developers • Joint Venture • Implementing the Joint Venture • A 50–50 Partnership • Ground Lease Versus Joint Venture • Payment of Commission • Other Types of Joint Ventures • Development for a Fee • Get to Know the Developers • Working with Developers • Commission Agreements • Knowing the Market

CHAPTER FIFTEEN	**Leasing and Building to Suit**	**199**

Small-shop Leasing • Retail Space • Retail Tenants • Tenant Mix • Follow-up • National Chains • Multi-Market Tenants • Building to Suit • Tenant Qualification • Preliminary Meeting • Proposal Preparation and Presentation • The Salesperson's Role • The Tenant's Role • Supermarket Pro Forma (Build to Suit)

CHAPTER SIXTEEN	**Shopping Center Development**	**213**

Types of Centers • Rehabilitation • Strategy • During Rehabilitation • The Pro Forma • Capital Cost and Income Definitions • On- and Off-Site Costs • Direct and Indirect Costs • Calculating Income • Financing the Development • Permanent and Construction Loans • Analysis of a Sample Pro Forma • Land • Sales • Development Costs (Shops) • Annual Income and Net Operating Income • Loan, Debt Service and Cash Flow • Gross Sales Price • The Napkin Pro Forma • Napkin Pro Formas and Land Costs • Setting Up the Napkin Pro Forma

CHAPTER SEVENTEEN	**Development Financing**	**231**

Why Know about Development Financing? • Financing Defined • Types of Development Financing • Debt Financing Alternatives • Permanent Financing • Equity Financing • Partnerships • Syndications • Private Placements • Financing and the Development Process • Steps in Equity Development • Can the Project Be Debt-Financed? • Step 1 Result: Insufficient Debt Coverage • Step 2: The Land Option and Option Period • Step 3: The Construction Period

CHAPTER EIGHTEEN	**Tenant Representation**	**245**

Your Role • Using an Exclusive Representative-the Tenant's Perspective • The Landlord's Perspective • The Tenant Representation Agreement

CHAPTER NINETEEN	**Negotiation**	**249**

Your Role • Rules for Negotiation • Trust, Confidence and Control • Promises • When to Negotiate • Process • Planning • Preparation • Compromise • Agreement

CHAPTER TWENTY	**Safety and Environmental Issues**	**255**

Underground Tanks • Asbestos • Polychlorinated Biphenyls • Soil and Groundwater Contamination • Your Responsibilities • Physical Inspection • Owner Tenant Inquiry • Testing • Documentation

CHAPTER TWENTY-ONE	**Sale-Leasebacks**	**267**

Analysis of a Sale-Leaseback • The Process • Identifying a Start Date and Obtaining Information • Ownership Inflows and Outflows • Leasing Outflows • Discounting Ownership and Lease Cash Flows • Other Considerations • Types of Sale-Leaseback • When to Discuss the Sale-Leaseback Option

Glossary	**273**
Index	**285**

Preface

This program has been developed by Longman Financial Services Publishing as a result of several years of work with Grubb & Ellis Company.

Grubb & Ellis Company is one of the country's largest companies providing a full range of real estate services. With headquarters in San Francisco, California, the company has over 160 offices throughout the United States.

The association between Grubb & Ellis Company and Longman began with Grubb & Ellis Company's recognition of the need to be able to adequately train great numbers of new salespeople. The company had developed and proven many techniques and procedures for leasing and selling real property that contributed to its continued success. The challenge was to organize and convey the knowledge, skills and experience necessary to make the new people coming into the organization successful as quickly as possible.

Because of Grubb & Ellis Company's extensive commitment to the development of highly qualified salespeople, Longman was given the task of developing training programs and materials in many facets of the company's operations. The materials that have resulted represent the combined contributions of many highly successful Grubb & Ellis company salespeople, managers and training staff and professional educators and trainers from Longman.

Because of the proven effectiveness of these materials and the basic selling procedures and techniques they reflect, Grubb & Ellis Company agreed to make several of these programs available for general distribution to the industry. *Successful Leasing and Selling of Retail Property* has two companion programs dealing with specialized phases of the real estate industry: *Successful Leasing and Selling of Office Property* and *Successful Industrial Real Estate Brokerage*. They are also available from Longman Financial Services Publishing, Chicago, Illinois.

Introduction

Successful real estate salespeople are well-paid for their services. They should be—the profession requires a very special kind of person. Many attributes go into successful selling, but one stands out: real estate sales representatives are constantly making decisions. The typical office worker makes essentially one daily decision: whether to get up and go to work that day. When such a worker arrives at the office, the job itself takes over. Phones must be answered. Supervisors devise tasks. The worker's day is a series of reactions to outside stimuli.

Not so the days of real estate sales representatives! These salespeople work largely on their own, organizing their own tasks and assigning their own priorities, while coping with the unexpected and making quick adjustments to new situations.

As a specialist in office properties, you will deal with sophisticated business people. You will be working with very complicated, difficult transactions. This manual has been devised to help you not only recognize and meet the challenges involved but enjoy the process as well. You will get lots of help. Teamwork is an important component of office property brokerage. Furthermore, as your efforts and the efforts of other salespeople in your office help to increase your firm's dominance in the field, you will have an even greater opportunity to achieve the high degree of financial success that is so rare in almost every other profession. Simultaneously, you will enjoy the high measure of personal satisfaction that comes only with real accomplishment.

The program of instruction you are about to begin has been carefully structured. It begins with the nuts-and-bolts information you will need in order to understand your product thoroughly. Only after you know the general characteristics of office property, without which knowledge you could not hope to meet your prospects' needs, will you proceed to

Introduction

the marketing techniques and selling skills so necessary to your own personal and financial satisfaction.

You will be introduced first to the physical aspects of office buildings, and from that proceed to their economics. Here you will learn, among other things, why rents are priced as they are. After a look at the legal aspects of leasing and selling, you will find a detailed discussion of office leases. The chapter on marketing includes a description of a unique team method of area coverage and a consideration of your place in that picture. Selling skills will be outlined next, followed by a look at a case history. The manual ends with a Glossary, which you may want to refer to as you study the material.

This program has been developed to help you to become an effective, successful office-property salesperson. To accomplish this is not easy—it will come about only as the result of your own hard work. The manual attempts to ease that task as much as possible, but it represents only one of many types of experience that will mold you into a professional. To be fully effective, the program must be combined with your other real estate activities—weekly sales meetings, special training sessions, related books and audio cassettes, outside courses and seminars, your own independent reading, and, most important of all, the learning experiences you encounter in the actual practice of your profession.

To get the most benefit from the program, you must actively participate by answering questions, evaluating hypothetical situations and completing exercises. These tasks are designed to help you become thoroughly familiar with the material. Consider each question carefully, write your response and check your answer against the answer given in the manual. Many of the questions are broad-based and may have no one right answer.

Remember, this manual is only a starting point. Many of the subjects presented will merit further discussion with your managers and colleagues. Some chapters will provide the basis for special office training sessions.

All of the material in this program reflects practices and attitudes that have proved successful over the years for experienced office property salespeople. Yet it also offers maximum flexibility. If you discover a solution that works for you better than the one presented here, by all means use it. In some cases, too, practices will vary from one geographical area to another.

In today's fast-paced world of real estate brokerage, personal development is a never-ending process. For that reason, this program should be of value to the experienced salesperson as well as to the beginner.

Successful Leasing and Selling of Retail Property

1

Types of Transactions

INTRODUCTION

This chapter will give you a general picture of various types of transactions: leasing either existing or newly created space; building to suit a tenant; and selling land to an individual user or a developer. The material will touch briefly on the advantages and disadvantages of some transactions and discuss the economic motivations behind others.

The information presented in these first chapters will be discussed in more detail throughout the manual: Leasing will be treated both in the chapter on legal documents and in the discussion of small-shop leasing in the chapter *Shopping Center Development*. The complexities of the build-to-suit transaction will also be examined in the small-shop leasing module.

LEASING EXISTING SPACE

Leasing existing space can be approached from the viewpoint of either the prospective tenant or the owner. If your initial contact is with the tenant, you become that company's representative, hopefully its exclusive representative. Once you have qualified your tenant's needs, you will locate suitable space and set up lease negotiations with the property owner.

If you are working with a property owner, the task is somewhat more difficult. There are more variables involved in locating acceptable prospects and qualifying their requirements. If you try to find a suitable tenant by simply knocking on doors, it may be a long time, if ever, before the right retailer turns up. On the other hand, you might begin by contacting tenants in the area whose existing space size is already known to you and who might, because of increased business or an expiring lease, be looking for a location. Your job will be easier if you have already made extensive contacts with tenants as you work your trade area. An active search along with an intelligent use of leads will yield the best results in matching tenants to available space.

SUBLEASING EXISTING SPACE

Occasionally, tenants need to leave existing space before their lease terms expire. The original tenants use your services to locate new tenants to sublease all or part of the existing space. As with leasing existing space, it is important to establish contacts with potential tenants.

LEASING NEW PROJECTS

A developer must be able to lease the available space in a development in order to realize an operating profit. In general, not until nearly 80 percent of the space has been leased will the development begin to generate enough cash flow to give the developer a return on investment.

If you are working with a developer to lease newly created space, you will need to devise a marketing plan for the leasing assignment. Your goal is to have the shortest possible absorption rate for the center. Again, the issue is one of knowing where to look for the right tenants. It usually makes sense to begin in the immediate area and approach tenants who are already aware of the new development, then gradually extend your inquiries to cover a broader radius. Cold calls, referrals from other brokers and the *Retail Tenant Directory* are all viable means of locating prospects. Placing your company's sign on the property will greatly increase the number of calls from interested retailers.

You have a distinct advantage in leasing new space, since a newly constructed shopping center is itself a drawing card for businesses. If you have worked with the developer from the initial stages of the project, you can speak knowledgeably about the advantages of the center and you will have fresh statistics on demographics and market trends in the area.

Once you have an agreement with a developer to handle leasing space in a project, you can also try to list the property for sale. A clause can be added to the listing contract stating that you will receive a sales commission should the property be sold. Developers who have no intention of selling really have nothing to lose by this arrangement, and if an attractive offer happens to come along, they may well change their mind about holding the property.

BUILD TO SUIT

The two parties involved in a build-to-suit transaction are a landowner and a user. The owner could be someone who has held the property for many years or a developer who has recently purchased it. Initially, the user, usually a national or strong regional tenant such as a bank or restaurant, determines whether the location would benefit the business. If the landowner will not consider selling the property, or if the user does not want to purchase, but merely wants the advantages of the location, a build-to-suit arrangement may be the best solution.

If both parties are in agreement, the owner will offer to build to the user's specifications and lease the building. The owner's return is based on a percentage of development costs plus a return on the determined value of the land. Since the profit to the owner is through the leasing arrangement, the lease is ordinarily long-term, from 20 to 25 years. The tenant will have to demonstrate sufficient financial strength to maintain the terms of the lease.

A build to suit, because of the complexity of the transaction and the time involved to bring it to completion, is usually a last-resort for a broker. You will need to examine tenant needs carefully to determine whether a facility should be custom built. Of equal importance is the tenant's financial qualification, since long-range leasing requires that the company's stability be established beyond doubt. Even though time-consuming, a build-to-suit arrangement represents a substantial commission—a broker can receive anywhere from 45 to 55 percent of one year's rent.

LAND SALE

You will be selling land to users, who will put up their own facility on the property, or to developers, who will in turn create some type of retail development—a freestanding building, a build to suit for a user or a shopping center.

As with all real estate transactions, your first responsibility is to qualify the developer or user in terms of requirements. You will need to know size specifications, the number of square feet or the amount of acreage for the building area and parking facilities, and where the desired property should be located. Plat maps will give you the exact size, shape and location of the most interesting parcels. The city planning department will provide zoning information, while the appropriate municipal department will be able to tell you what utilities are available. These details should be recorded on the plats. Your next step is to contact the owners of the parcels and find out if they would be willing to sell, and under what conditions.

For a retail salesperson, the most important consideration is control of the property. A supermarket chain may communicate to a developer where it wants to build a new outlet. The developer, in turn, may pass that information on to you. Your job is to do the research for the developer, or for the real estate representative of a chain, and find the most suitable location. Once you have located a site the next questions are, can you control it with an exclusive listing and can the developer control it with an option?

PURCHASE OR GROUND LEASE

In a ground leasing transaction, a developer will lease a parcel of the retail center to a tenant on a long-term basis. The ground lease tenant owns the improvements to the land throughout the lease term, after which ownership of the improvements reverts to the landowner. The ground lease is primarily used to segregate ownership of land from ownership of the improvements during the lease period.

It may be assumed that the developer has already decided to purchase the land and has eliminated ground leasing as a possibility. However, the issue may come up after the choice has been narrowed to one or a few appropriate sites. The developer may want to know whether a purchase or ground-lease transaction would produce the greatest profit and have the greatest long-range potential for investment. The answer may depend on how much cash the developer has to invest. Ordinarily, the cash required to complete a development is less in ground leasing than for a land purchase.

The disadvantage to leasing land for a development is that problems invariably arise if the lessor is constantly checking to make sure all the leasing conditions are being met. You may have to renegotiate the terms to resolve disputes over land use. In addition, a ground lease can be difficult to finance if the lessor is not willing to subordinate his or her interest in the property to the need for interim or permanent financing.

Many developers have clearly outlined procedures for acquiring commercial property for development. If owning property is part of their program, they will want to purchase the land. However, some consideration should be given to ground leasing as well.

SALE AS AN INVESTMENT

Investment refers to an income-producing property that provides a return on the money invested in it. The person involved in such a transaction may be an investor who has earmarked a substantial amount of money to be put into retail property. As a retail specialist, you are in a unique position to offer investment services because you understand the retail approach. You might set a goal of selling one investment property a year.

One word of caution: Restrict your activity in investment sales to retail property, since this is the area you know best. There are separate divisions to handle industrial, office and residential sales. If someone comes to you looking for an apartment building, you would do well to refer them to a specialist.

Investors are interested in receiving the maximum return on their investments. In the chapter on developers, preferred return is discussed

CHAPTER 1 / Types of Transactions 5

in the context of a joint-venture transaction. This is one way of realizing a profit through a particular kind of investment arrangement.

A developer or investor in need of deductions might well be interested in income-producing properties that break even in terms of cash flow but show a significant operating loss that will offset other taxable income. Before any investment transaction is considered, a tax specialist should be consulted for the latest information on tax laws.

Exercise A

1. What are the most effective ways to locate the right tenants for a new development?
2. a. Define the term *build to suit*.
   b. Why is the financial qualification of the client so important?
   c. How is the owner's return calculated?
3. What might be one disadvantage in leasing land for a development?
4. What is the main advantage of leasing new space?

Answer A

1. *The most effective way to locate tenants for a new development is to begin canvassing in the immediate area and gradually extend the search to cover a broader radius.*
2. *A build to suit is an agreement between the landlord and tenant whereby the landlord assumes the obligation of modifying the space to the tenant's specifications. It is important to have a financially qualified tenant since the term of the lease is usually 20 to 25 years. The owner's return is calculated based on a percentage of development costs plus a return on the value of the land.*
3. *One disadvantage in leasing land for development is that it can be more difficult to finance.*
4. *The main advantage of leasing new space is that a newly constructed center is a drawing card for businesses.*

2

Inventory System

INTRODUCTION

All retail salespeople are property specialists. As such, it is your responsibility to keep up to date on all properties, land and existing space that are now or will be for sale, lease or development within your area. In other words, you must know the *inventory*. It is also critical to become familiar with tenants currently in your marketplace and those tenants not yet in your market who would be likely candidates for inclusion. The aim of this chapter is to give you an overview of retail property inventory and to familiarize you with methods and resources that will help you gather and organize property data. Keep in mind that basic principles and information are being presented here and that much of this information will be discussed in greater detail throughout the manual.

AREA ASSIGNMENT

As in other classifications of property, real estate activity in the retail area tends to be clustered around "hot spots" in a particular community. Hot spots are best defined as those areas of intense commercial activity where there are thriving developments, where highly competitive retail businesses are seeking space and where there is a steady flow of consumer traffic. If too many salespeople gravitate toward such areas, the company will not have adequate information about other locations.

8 Successful Leasing and Selling of Retail Property

This can be prevented if the company assigns each salesperson a geographic area for which he or she is responsible. Salespeople then become thoroughly familiar with their territory: its available inventory, land value, rental rates, retail trends, current developments and general market picture. Remember, the key to successful transactions lies in your ability to draw on a complete knowledge of the area in order to meet a variety of client needs.

Getting To Know the Area

The only way you can really know your market territory is to drive through the entire area. Observe locations carefully and take notes on population clusters, transportation facilities, traffic flow, schools, and the older and more recently developed sections.

Locating Retailers

As you become more familiar with the market, you will begin to notice the locations of vacant and developed land, single and multiple retail spaces, specialty shops, regional stores and national chains. An efficient way to keep track of these locations is by marking them on a sheet of clear acetate fixed over an area map. Plot all users within your area: department stores, markets, drugstores, financial institutions, discount stores, restaurants and the like. Use a different color dot to represent each type of retailer or developer, and put the key in the corner of the overlay. Since users tend to cluster, you can simply mark the intersections where they are located. These maps will help you to visualize the trade area in terms of potential users for a site.

Keep in mind that in canvassing and documenting your trade area you're making a market survey. You'll be presenting this information on the competition to prospective tenants and developers. For example, if a developer is considering moving into a new area, you'll be able to show him or her a map of the competition and their major tenants in all the neighborhood, community and regional shopping centers.

GATHERING NECESSARY INFORMATION

Knowing the composition of the area is the first step. The second step is to concentrate on specifics. As you work the area, ask yourself the following questions.

1. Is there any current vacant retail space in the area?
2. Where are any vacant parcels of land and how are they zoned?
3. What might be the best retail use for them?
4. What are the types of retailing areas in the territory? Blue collar? High income? Middle income?
5. What retailing categories are not in the area, and why not?
6. What kind of tenant mixes do existing centers have?

CHAPTER 2 / Inventory System 9

7. What are the building sizes within existing centers?
8. What major tenants are present in the area, and when do their leases expire?
9. What types of major tenants are *not* in the area that could or should be?
10. What are the areas of retail activity besides shopping centers, and what kinds of tenants rent space in them?

Being acquainted with the retailers in your area is an essential part of knowing the territory. Start calling on the tenants; you can obtain much valuable information from them.

THE RETAIL INVENTORY SYSTEM

As a retail salesperson, you are responsible for investigating all buildings and parcels of land for sale or lease in your area. It is your responsibility to keep inventory information current so that it will be accurate and available to all the salespeople in your division. For this purpose, you'll be researching information and recording it on forms such as the land worksheet and the commercial space worksheet. Study the copies of these forms on the following pages.

The land worksheet is used to describe the vacant land in your area with an eye to its possible development. Location information is important, as are zoning, taxes, traffic count and available improvements.

The commercial space worksheet is used in describing the property itself: its size, location and other significant features. If there is no sign on the property with the owner's name, you can obtain the information from three sources. First, the property ownership books in your office will provide you with a plat map and the owner's name and address. Or you can go through the customer service department of a title company. By furnishing a plat number or a street address, you can get the owner's name and address and any other information about the property that is on file. The third source for property data is the county assessor's office.

The commercial space worksheet contains information vital to retail users, such as traffic counts, demographics and the other major tenants in a center. Many offices have access to computerized demographic surveys and statistics that you can use in filling out the form.

The information on your worksheets should be typed on small file cards. Make enough copies of these cards so that you can file the information according to the area under "commercial land" or "retail space" in the master book, and you can retain a copy for your personal book and then file the cards:

1. by "commercial land" or "retail space"
2. within the above designations by area
3. by square footage in ascending order

Placing dividers between the designations and particular areas will make it easier for you to find the right property for a tenant.

FIGURE 2.1 Land Worksheet

_____ acres   Type: _____
Address _____   City _____
Cross Streets _____
Dim. _____ = _____ or = _____ acres   Assessors No. _____
Topography: Level Y☐ N☐   Rail: Y☐ N☐ Easements: Y☐ N☐   _____
Water: Y☐ N☐ _____"   Gas: Y☐ N☐ _" Sewers: Y☐ N☐ _"   Storm Drain: Y☐ N☐ _____
Zoning _____   Traffic Count _____   Left Turn: Y☐ N☐ _____
Corner: Y☐ N☐   Improvements _____   Income $_____
Taxes: $_____ (____/____ yr.) Assessed Valuation $_____ Rate $_____
Sale Price $_____   = $_____ Soil Test: Y☐ N☐   Available _____
Lease/BTS Price: $_____/mo. G☐ N☐ Rate: _____/mo. $_____/yr.
Remarks:

Lister _____   Signs _____   Date _____
Tenant _____   Contact _____   Phone _____
Ex. Broker _____   Contact _____   Phone _____
Owner _____   Phone _____
Owner Address _____   Key _____

PLEASE ASK YOUR CLIENT THE FOLLOWING QUESTIONS

A Sign?

B Exclusive?

C Market to buy other properties?

D Own other properties?
    1. Available for lease?
    2. Lease Expiration?

FIGURE 2.2 Commercial Space Worksheet

OFFICE ☐   RETAIL ☐   _____

Address _____ City _____

Cross Streets _____ Dim. _____

Building/Center Name _____ Stories _____ Suite _____

All Services: Y☐ N☐   A/C: Y☐ N☐   Utilities: Y☐ N☐   Janitorial: Y☐ N☐   Subdivisible: Y☐ N☐

Elevators _____ Parking _____ $_____/month

Traffice Count _____ Left Turn: Y☐ N☐   Corner: Y☐ N☐   Zoning _____

Taxes: $_____(_____/_____) yr.)   Assessed Valuation $_____   Rate $_____

Sale Price $_____ = $_____ Age _____ Available _____

Lease Price: $_____/mo. G☐ N☐   Rate: _____/mo. $_____/yr.   Usable ☐   Rentable ☐

Space Descr., Potential Uses, Remarks, etc.:

Lister _____ Signs _____ Date _____

Tenant _____ Contact _____ Phone _____

Ex. Broker _____ Contact _____ Phone _____

Owner _____ Phone _____

Owner Address _____ Key _____

Address _____ Size _____

PLEASE ASK YOUR CLIENT THE FOLLOWING QUESTIONS

A <u>Sign?</u>

B <u>Exclusive?</u>

C <u>Market to buy other properties?</u>

D <u>Own other properties?</u>
    1. <u>Available for lease?</u>
    2. <u>Lease Expiration?</u>

All salespeople in a retail division should have access to the master book so they can quickly determine what is available for a tenant in a given area. Your primary responsibility is to be thoroughly familiar with the listings in your market area. When a property is sold, leased, taken off the market or changes status in any way you must inform a secretary who will note the change on the master list and on the appropriate card in your file.

Remember, it is difficult for new salespeople to discriminate between good and bad property or among different parts of their area. Experienced salespeople can direct you to hot spots, and you should cover those thoroughly. Keep in mind, though, that the entire area is important, particularly for the future. Quiet spots can suddenly become hot, so don't neglect any part of your territory. Study the current listing on file, and make a note of others as you drive around the area. Drop in and chat with merchants during their slack times.

PROPERTY FILES

Property files is something of a catch-all phrase. In most offices it is a file system of records for all completed transactions. Some offices may work with a sale and lease record index of properties, which is composed of the completed files of all successful transactions. The property files may also contain information on any significant real estate parcels, even if no transaction was ever consummated. If, for example, you worked on a transaction involving a 100-acre parcel but it never closed, that file should still be indexed and available to your office for future reference. The file should contain such information as parcel maps and descriptions, copies of grant deeds, preliminary title reports, and other documents that pertain to the land, and it should be maintained by office managers and individual salespeople.

YOUR TIME INVESTMENT

As you become more skilled at drawing up your inventory, you will also learn how to make the most profitable use of your time. Leasing in neighborhood shopping centers is the bread and butter of the retail business, so you must know the existing centers in your market area. Organize your inventory by size; for example four to ten acres, ten acres and above, and so on. Establish a minimum size; working on deals of less than 1,000 square feet offers rather slim rewards, and such spaces take as much of your time as larger ones. As a general rule, it is more efficient to work on a larger inventory.

Salespeople should always attempt to maximize their credibility in the eyes of users and developers. When qualified people make an inquiry through you, your knowledge of different spaces should help you meet their requirements.

LISTING AGREEMENTS

New salespeople often ask, "Should I work with an exclusive listing, or go along with open listings?" The answer to that important question is to consult with your manager on which listing type is preferable for a given property. Ultimately the goal should be to obtain exclusive listings on properties that will move. For properties that are unlikely to move easily, or at all, neither an open listing nor an exclusive listing may prove to be worth your efforts. For the neophyte, it does take time and experience to learn which properties are movable and which ones are not. In the short term, it is safest to discuss properties, and how they should be listed, with your manager.

CONCLUSION

As you work your market area, ask yourself several key questions.

1. What is a given parcel's value?
2. What would you say the evaluation is or should be?
3. What would you say is the best use for a particular parcel?

Remember, you are not simply recording data as a passive observer. You are constantly assimilating, revising, and updating information in order to bring two parties together—tenant and landlord or developer and owner—in a successful real estate transaction.

Exercise A

1. Why is it important to inventory all the property for sale or lease in your area?
2. Why should new salespeople be cautious about taking an exclusive listing?
3. What key questions should you ask yourself as you work your territory?
4. Name three ways of obtaining an owner's name and address.
5. Describe the purpose and procedures of the retail inventory system.
6. Discuss the benefits of plotting the users in your territory on an area map.

Answer A

1. It is important to inventory all the property for sale or lease in your area because it insures that you are the expert on your market place.

2. New salespeople should be cautious about taking an exclusive listing because they may not have the knowledge to differentiate between a good and a bad listing.

3. As you work your territory ask yourself what retailing categories are not in the area, what retailers should be in the area, and what space is available.

4. Three ways to obtain an owner's name and address are: 1) the title company, 2) property ownership books in your office, and 3) the county assessor's office.

5. The purpose of the retail inventory system is to insure that accurate information on the marketplace is available to the salespeople. It is maintained using information gathered by the salespeople and recorded on worksheets.

6. By plotting the users in your territory on an area map, you can visualize each trade area in terms of potential users.

3

Marketing

INTRODUCTION

This chapter presents an outline of publications, directories, organizations and contacts that will be both excellent sources of detailed information on the retail business and potential sources of leads for you. Leads are precious in the real estate business. Where you find them depends on your persistence and ingenuity; if you work at developing leads consistently, they will more than repay your efforts. Become familiar with the resources listed here and refer to them regularly.

LOCATING THE INFORMATION

The *Retail Tenant Directory* is the most extensive of its kind and an important source of information. It is indexed according to a number code for each user as well as by an alphabetical listing by user. If you are putting together a competition profile, looking for specific users, or working on a tenant mix, and would like to make calls or contacts, simply get the page number for the appropriate user category from the index and refer to the listings.

The ICSC (International Council of Shopping Centers) is a nationwide organization that holds annual conventions and regional meetings for the purpose of bringing together developers and users from the national scene. If your goal is to build a relationship with national chains, you should make every effort to attend the ICSC regional meetings, known as idea exchanges. The panel presentations, which have covered topics such as "Tenant Mix" and "Rent Maximization in Shopping Centers," are highly informative; in addition, the contacts you'll make with developers and national chain representatives can be very helpful to you.

Restaurant News is a bimonthly magazine to which virtually every retail marketing office subscribes. Even if you are not involved in restaurant transactions, it is a valuable publication to read.

Shopping Center World tends to deal with the operations of regional shopping centers and contains good marketing articles on such topics as store merchandising and floor planning. This publication can help you understand all of the functions involved in putting a satellite store together.

Criss-Cross Directories is an index service that crosses a street to a phone number for any city or county that is indexed. You simply call a local service number, and the person who answers will give you a criss-cross listing for the area you want. For example, if you know a suite number at an office building address, you can obtain the firm's phone number from that information.

Your office's listing system contains a wealth of information. Take advantage of it. Go through the files, discover what retail space is available, examine lease survey forms that have expired and study the documents on business successfully transacted. From this source you will learn which people and which firms to contact about possible relocation or expansion needs.

You can obtain the names of firms and individuals from directories published by Dun & Bradstreet, chambers of commerce and associations of commerce and industry. These directories contain the names of companies' chief executives and other key decision makers. These are the individuals you want to reach when you are cold calling.

Chambers of commerce are also excellent sources of information. For example, they can provide you with taxable retail sales information that shows the tax collected by the state on a particular merchandise item. You can use this as a base for figuring dollar volume sales.

Keep up with the financial news each day. Be alert for the announcement of a company's plan to expand, develop a new shopping center or open a new outlet. You can also study the ads of different retailers, especially in the Sunday papers, and see if any have more than one location listed. You may find information in an article on a company's upward sales and profits for the year or for a quarter. Make notes from any such stories, and refer to them when you cold call.

A client whom you have served well can be a valuable source of leads. Never let a satisfied client go without inquiring about retail firms and decision makers he or she knows who might need space or a new location. Use other brokers, too. REALTORS® are happy to talk about the business, and some are not always as discreet about what they're doing as they should be. Your competitors can inadvertently give you leads that could bring valuable business your way.

Clubs and organizations can be extremely good sources of leads as well. When you join a particular group, avoid giving the impression that you're doing so purely for business purposes. Choose your organizations for personal reasons, and simply keep your eyes and ears open. Chances are you'll find several leads for retail real estate business.

Get acquainted with managers, salespeople and wholesalers of office machine, store equipment, restaurant equipment, moving and insurance companies. They are all out seeking business, and they can help you with names of retail firms that are planning moves or expansion.

Direct mailing programs, if done effectively, can turn up leads. This is especially true in the case of a shopping center in which your office has a particular interest or exclusives on space. However, brochures and other mailing pieces by themselves seldom bring in business. Mailings are entrees for cold calls—so follow up either by phone or in person, and use the mailing as a way to open the conversation.

Signs can be a source of leads. A sign on a building means that some business has moved. Find out why from that business's manager. Are other businesses in the area thinking of moving? Real estate company signs certainly furnish leads. A person who takes the trouble to record a phone number from a company sign and make a call must be highly motivated. If the location the person is calling about isn't suitable, another in your files might be. The callers themselves may lead you to companies looking for additional space or contemplating a move.

Referrals are extremely important and can bring you a considerable amount of business. Get to know the other salespeople in your office, and become acquainted for referral purposes with salespeople in other companies. Make sure they know that you want referrals and that you'll gladly pay a referral fee or split a commission. Referrals, of course, work both ways—you can also give them. In most real estate companies, each manager must acknowledge a referral from another office. Once a referral is acknowledged, the person making it is covered for his or her share of the commission. Always ask a user with whom you have done business, "Where else were you interested in locating?" A user can also be a source of referrals.

MARKETING PROPOSAL

The ability to create a quality marketing proposal is one of a retail salesperson's most critical skills. You can facilitate the presentation of these proposals by using a standard presentation format and content, which can be adapted to the needs of various projects. It is essential that you include the points covered in the marketing outline that follows without going beyond the scope of the commitments it suggests. If you model your proposals on this outline, you can save yourself a great deal of time and still develop consistently effective marketing proposals.

When preparing and presenting the proposal, remember the following elements:

1. *Folder.* Enclose the proposal and all other inserts in a standard legal-sized folder. The proposal can also be spiral or velobound.

2. *Proposal.* If a folder is used, the proposal should be bound and placed in the flap on the inside front cover. The proposal itself should resemble the sample outline that follows.

3. *Inserts.* The proposal should include a reference list, the salesperson's personal history, maps, brochures and the like.

Whenever possible, personalize the proposal by addressing the specific requirements of the project at hand. Under personal canvassing, describe the canvassing program for the project's immediate area. Include information on your sales staff and tenant information systems. When discussing the direct mail effort, describe what the mail piece should be and to whom it should be mailed. Also, be specific about who assumes the cost responsibility for this program. Comment on the brochure requirements, covering general content, quantity and overall quality needed for the project. If the project already has a brochure, evaluate its effectiveness. The brochure cost is almost always borne by the owner. A deviation from this policy requires management approval.

In the section on reporting (marketing administration), note the type and frequency of reports to the owner. Most brokerage firms submit written reports at least once a month. Weekly or biweekly reporting may be appropriate in some cases. These reports inform the owner of the number of prospects contacted, the results, the number of referrals from other offices, all efforts being made to promote the project and any trends affecting the project's marketability.

Once you have compiled the proposal, meet the developer or owner and make the presentation in person. Never mail a marketing proposal. If you take the time to hand-deliver it, the owner will be impressed by your professionalism and you will be able to respond to any questions or objections that the owner may raise.

Your office will have on file various proposals that have proved successful. Don't reinvent the wheel. With your manager's assistance, you can adapt existing proposals to satisfy your requirements. The following standard format is suggested for the proposal presentation.

FIGURE 3.1 Marketing Proposal

TABLE OF CONTENTS

I. INTRODUCTION

II. LEASING GOALS

III. SCOPE OF EMPLOYMENT

IV. MARKETING PROGRAM

  A. Direct Sales

   1. Personal Canvassing

   2. San Diego—Proximity of Project

   3. Southern California Smith and Jones Offices

   4. Other Smith and Jones Offices

   5. Other Markets

  B. Marketing Tools

   1. Demographic Studies

   2. Direct Mail

   3. Advertising and Public Relations

   4. Brochures

   5. Signs

   6. Lease Form

V. BROKER COOPERATION

  A. Communication

  B. Outside Broker Commission

VI. MARKETING ADMINISTRATION

  A. Securing Lessees

  B. Reporting

I. INTRODUCTION

Smith and Jones Commercial Brokerage Company is one of the largest real estate organizations in the United States, with offices throughout the country. Smith and Jones specializes in retail, office, industrial and investment marketing. See Exhibit 1 for our company brochure.

The San Diego office of Smith and Jones, established in 1970, consists of 35 full-time sales and marketing specialists and was responsible for generating over $200 million in sales/leasing transactions in 1988.

The following proposal outlines the goals, methods and procedures of Smith and Jones Commercial Brokerage Company in marketing your project.

II. LEASING GOALS

As a marketing organization, our primary goal is the maximum return on the developer's investment. This means directing our efforts to lease space as quickly as possible to qualified tenants at the highest attainable rents.

Our experience shows that the successful marketing of a major retail project is the result of a strong, leading effort on the part of the leasing agent, together with a team effort involving the lessor or owner, architect, contractor and space planner. The coordination of all of these parties is essential to attaining our goals.

This proposal is submitted with this goal in mind and the prospect that a coordinated team effort will be made.

III. SCOPE OF EMPLOYMENT

Smith and Jones Commercial Brokerage Company proposes to assume an overall responsibility for marketing of the project. This includes overseeing all direct sales efforts of Smith and Jones salespersons as well as coordinating the

FIGURE 3.1 Marketing Proposal (continued)

efforts of the brokerage community. It also includes the planning and executing successful advertising and public relations programs in conjunction with the people charged with that responsibility by the lessor or owner.

IV. MARKETING PROGRAM

A. Direct Sales

1. Personal Canvassing. The most important aspect of the entire campaign will be a direct sales effort through personal contact with all prospective tenants in the San Diego area. Our efforts will be concentrated in a direct marketing approach, not just a random door-to-door approach. That is, we will contact tenants with lease expirations, space and geographic requirements that are compatible with the project goal. We will document these efforts on a retail tenant requirement form set forth in Exhibit 2.

Our wide network of offices and the operating concept of area coverage insure this contact over the broadest possible area. Area coverage means that each salesperson is encouraged to cover one of the geographic areas into which the market is divided and to learn all aspects of the territory, including land values, ownerships, tenant needs and available inventory. Although each retail specialist has his or her own suggested area of responsibility (as shown in Exhibit 3), all must still be familiar with the entire county in order to satisfy the tenant's and owner's requirements. This team approach has allowed Smith and Jones to stay abreast of the current retail market in San Diego.

Canvassing and documenting the market conditions in this manner enables us to maintain a retail absorption survey (see Exhibit 4) showing both past and present inventory, rental rates and absorption figures. With these tools, we are better able to provide valuable input on market data to landlords, owners, developers and tenants. Decisions regarding the use and development of existing or future retail space can be made more effectively.

2. San Diego—Proximity of Project. The project coordinator, the leasing representative and the other retail specialists will contact all logical prospects for space in the project.

We have available on computer a retail tenant directory (national, regional, and local) that includes the names of all retail companies and decision makers, along with addresses, telephone numbers, areas of premises and types of transactions of prospects contacted by Smith and Jones Commercial Brokerage Company agents over the past ten years. Tenants meeting your specific requirements will be solicited on behalf of the project.

3. Southern California Smith and Jones Offices. In addition to the San Diego Office, Smith and Jones Commercial Brokerage Company maintains large commercial staffs in our other Southern California offices. All of these offices operate under a well-established system of personal canvassing and follow-up. It will be the responsibility of the project coordinator and leasing representative to inform each of these offices of the current disposition of the project. This will enable our project coordinator and leasing representative, to learn of—and to capitalize on—any space requirements, logical for your project, of tenants outside the area of intensive coverage.

4. Other Smith and Jones Offices. Smith and Jones Commercial Brokerage Company also has offices located throughout the United States. The specialists in these office have been detailing with prospects within their respective areas for a number of years. Our experience has shown that many of the tenants contacted through these other offices also have expansion or relocation requirements in Southern California.

It will be the responsibility of the project coordinator and leasing representative to disseminate complete information about your project to these offices and to coordinate the identification and solicitation of prospective tenants for the project.

5. Other Markets. Through the company's affiliation with various national professional organizations and because of our reputation, Smith and Jones Commercial Brokerage Company has developed strong relationships with real estate brokers throughout the United States. We can refer our valued clients to these brokers in markets in which we do not operate. In turn, we receive tenant referrals from these markets. This will be very helpful in marketing your project. We will solicit the assistance of our correspondent brokers in identifying potential tenants.

B. Marketing Tools

1. Demographic Studies. Smith and Jones maintains a computer data bank specifically designed for the needs of its marketing staff and clients. Key elements of the most recent census can be retrieved from the data bank for any specific site, geographic area or census tract (see Exhibit 4). These elements include population, family income, age and sex, rent, education, per capita income, marital status, home value and occupation.

2. Direct Mail. An integral part of the direct sales campaign will be mailings, at the expense of Smith and Jones Commercial Brokerage Company, to both tenants and the brokerage community. Initially, brochures and general information will be mailed to selected tenants. The project coordinator and leasing representative will follow up with personal calls. At periodic intervals, the project will be reexposed to those tenants who should logically be associated with the development.

3. Advertising and Public Relations. A carefully coordinated advertising and public relations campaign can contribute significantly to the successful marketing of a major project. Smith and Jones Commercial Brokerage Company

FIGURE 3.1 Marketing Proposal (continued)

has had extensive experience in planning and coordinating real estate campaigns, and retains the public relations firm of John Doe and Sons, which has been successful in servicing our developer clients and instrumental in publicizing our accomplishments in major publications (see Exhibit 5).

Smith and Jones Commercial Brokerage Company has been exclusively selected to furnish semiannual absorption studies on retail real estate conditions in San Diego for the *San Diego Union/Tribune* (see Exhibit 6).

4. Brochures. We will assist in the preparation and coordination of a quality brochure depicting the project, the cost of which will be borne by the lessor or owner. We will work with you to arrive at a basic concept and then arrange for a qualified designer to prepare a copy and layout. We propose to supervise all aspects of the origination of the brochure, thereby minimizing the overall cost and your involvement.

5. Signs. We propose to install at our expense project leasing signs at agreed-upon locations.

6. Lease Form. We propose to use the Smith and Jones Commercial Brokerage Company standard retail lease, which has been successfully utilized in the local market (see Exhibit 7).

V. BROKER COOPERATION

A. Communication

Smith and Jones Commercial Brokerage Company believes in cooperating with the relatively small segment of the brokerage community that, along with Smith and Jones, does 80 to 90 percent of the commercial brokerage business. It will be the responsibility of the project coordinator and leasing representative to keep the brokerage community informed of current leasing activities and of the project's status. They will meet with these brokers to promote the project, conduct monthly mailings and invite the active retail brokers on a personal tour to introduce them to the project.

B. Outside Broker Commission

When outside brokers are responsible for bringing tenants to the project, we will share all commissions on a fifty-fifty basis.

VI. MARKETING ADMINISTRATION

A. Securing Lessees

After prospects have been identified, the project coordinator and leasing representative will take the following steps:

1. qualifying the lessee financially
2. selling the lessee on your project versus the competition
3. determining the lessee's space requirements
4. assisting in any lease modifications or revisions requested by the lessee, the lessor or owner and their attorneys
5. preparing a package for presentation to the lessor or owner that includes:
    a. the lease executed by the lessee
    b. the first month's rent and security deposit
    c. financial statements
6. ensuring good liaison between the lessee, the lessor or owner and contractors

While the responsibility for total project coordination properly belongs in the hands of the lessor or owner, Smith and Jones Commercial Brokerage Company will be available to augment any and all endeavors. Our marketing staff is experienced in accomplishing these delicate steps.

B. Reporting

It is essential that the lessor or owner be available to the project coordinator and leasing representative on a periodic basis. Should the lessor or owner designate a representative as project manager, that person must have the authority to act solely on behalf of the lessor or owner.

The project coordinator and leasing representative will meet monthly with the lessor or owner or a representative to review the current status of the marketing program and to consider pending and potential transactions, market conditions and strategy. In addition, we will provide the lessor or owner or the representative with a monthly written report detailing our activities and the status of our negotiations with qualified prospective tenants.

The articles used as exhibits in this sample marketing proposal are:

Exhibit 1.	company fact sheet
	division brochure
	company organization chart
Exhibit 2.	retail tenant requirement form
Exhibit 3.	area coverage map
Exhibit 4.	demographic study
Exhibit 5.	WREN San Diego County special report
	National Real Estate Investor, San Diego market overview

FIGURE 3.1 Marketing Proposal (concluded)

Exhibit 6. *Union/Tribune* absorption articles
Exhibit 7. retail lease form

EXCLUSIVE MARKETING AGREEMENT

The exclusive marketing agreement shown in this chapter should be attached to the marketing proposal. The agreement, or market contract, is to be signed by both the owner of the property and the broker. The contract covers any possible transaction connected with the property: lease, sale, ground lease or build to suit. It outlines the obligations of the owner to provide project plans and to uphold the exclusive agreement with your office. It also states your obligations to provide marketing coverage adequate to fulfill the leasing or sales goal for the project.

The agreement incorporates a commission agreement, a schedule of commissions and an expiration clause. This clause states that if, within six months of the contract's expiration, any part of the project is leased or sold to a tenant whom the broker has registered with the owner within 30 days of the expiration, the owner is obligated to pay the broker a commission.

Reproductions of other documents follow the exclusive marketing agreement. They are a purchase agreement, an exclusive authorization of lease, a nonexclusive authorization of lease and an income and expense summary form.

FIGURE 3.2 Exclusive Marketing Agreement

This Agreement made this _____ day of _____, 19____, by and between _____ _____ hereinafter referred to as "Lessor/Owner" and SMITH AND JONES COMMERCIAL BROKERAGE COMPANY, a California corporation, hereinafter referred to as "Broker."

WITNESSETH:

WHEREAS, Lessor/Owner is the owner of record of that certain real property, more specifically identified in Exhibit "A," attached hereto, and hereinafter referred to as the "Project"; and

WHEREAS, Broker is a licensed real estate brokerage company experienced in handling the planning and execution of the marketing of the type of property constituting the Project;

NOW THEREFORE, in consideration of the mutual covenants herein contained, the parties hereto do hereby agree as follows:

1. APPOINTMENT AS AGENT:
Lessor/Owner retains Broker to act as its sole and exclusive agent hereunder to lease and/or sell those portions of the Project which are available for leasing and/or sale subject to the terms and conditions hereinafter set forth.

2. TERM OF AGREEMENT:
The term of this Agreement shall commence on the date of this Agreement as set forth above and, subject to the termination provisions set forth hereinafter in Section 6, shall terminate automatically at midnight on _____ 19_____; unless prior thereto the parties hereto agree in writing to an extension of the term. If during the term of this Agreement or any extension hereof an escrow is opened or negotiations involving the sale, transfer, conveyance, or leasing of the Project have commenced and are continuing, then the term of this Agreement shall be extended for a period through the closing of such escrow, the termination of such negotiations, or the consummation of such transactions, provided this Agreement would otherwise have expired during such period.

3. DUTIES OF BROKER:
3.1 Broker shall plan and administer all activities related to the marketing of the Project, subject to the direction and approval of Lessor/Owner. These activities shall include, among others, cooperating with all organizations and individuals performing functions for the Project so as to coordinate marketing requirements with all applicable planning considerations.
3.2 Broker shall consult with Lessor/Owner regarding all facets of the Project, including tenant categorization and orientation in the Project, tenant construction requirements, market rental conditions, and the overall decor and design of the Project.
3.3 Broker shall coordinate with Lessor/Owner in order that the advertising and public relations campaigns for the Project are planned and executed in a professional, effective manner. Any brochures that are specifically prepared in order to market the Project shall be prepared at the sole cost and expense of Lessor/Owner, provided that such costs and expenses have been previously approved.
3.4 Broker shall assist in the origination and preparation of a standard form of Proposal to Lease or Letter of Intent, and a standard form of tenant lease, including those provisions or exhibits governing landlord/tenant construction responsibilities. Broker shall also develop a package for presentation to Lessor/Owner, including any financial statements or operating projections which may be required by Lessor/Owner.
3.5 Broker shall use its best efforts in order to obtain and present to Lessor/Owner lease proposals from qualified prospective lessees. In performing this phase of the marketing program, Broker shall conduct a canvassing campaign and supervise a direct mailing campaign in order to solicit and follow through on any and all prospects.
3.6 Broker shall report periodically to Lessor/Owner and deliver monthly written reports regarding the status of its performance under this Agreement. Broker shall furnish whatever other reports of its activities on the Project that Lessor/Owner may from time to time reasonably request.
3.7 Broker shall solicit and encourage the cooperative support of other real estate organizations qualified in the field of commercial (retail) real estate in _____ County in order to maximize the number of potential leases that can be consummated with prospective tenants. Broker shall from time to time keep the other real estate firms informed regarding the status of said Project.
3.8 Broker shall designate one individual from its staff as Project Coordinator and another as the Leasing Representative:
A. The Project Coordinator shall be directly responsible for interfacing with Lessor/Owner. Duties shall include but not necessarily be limited to the following:
   I. Organization of overall leasing program
   II. Daily Consultation with individual leasing agents
   III. Coordination of leasing efforts with outside brokers

FIGURE 3.2 Exclusive Marketing Agreement (continued)

    IV. Scheduling periodic meetings with Lessor/Owner, the contractor, the architect and any third party agents of Lessor/Owner if appropriate
    V. Preparation and Presentation of the Monthly status report to Lessor/Owner
    VI. Submission of the financial operating statements and leasing documents to Lessor/Owner for its approval
    VII. Evaluation of Performance of Broker's personnel to achieve maximum leasing results

B. The Leasing Representative shall be responsible for day-to-day contact with tenants and their interfacing with the architect, the contractor, and the Project Coordinator as required, including activities such as:
1. Solicitation of tenants
2. Physical inspection of current tenant operations
3. Review of the financial operating statements and presentation of reports to the Project Coordinator
4. Submission of Proposals to Lease or Letters of Intent to the Project Coordinator
5. Participation in the review of the lease form with tenants and their attorneys
6. Assisting in the preparation of the final lease documents and exhibits and addenda thereto
7. Securing tenant's execution of the lease, and;
8. Presentation of the final package to the Project Coordinator

4. OBLIGATIONS OF LESSOR/OWNER:

4.1 Lessor/Owner agrees to provide at its expense the following material to Broker no later than sixty (60) days after the commencement of the term.
A. Leasing plans, plot plans, elevation and renderings
B. Leasing brochures
C. Tenant improvement schedules, including tenant construction allowances, if any
D. Estimates of "additional rent," such as property taxes, insurance premiums, common area expenses and merchants' association dues, etc.
E. Approval of the standard leasing documents and exhibits thereto
F. Rental schedules and acceptable parameters of terms and conditions of tenant leases, and
G. Project sign(s) designating Broker as the exclusive marketing agent, if other than Broker's standard sign(s) are required.

5. COMPENSATION OF BROKER:

5.1 Lessor/Owner shall pay a commission to Broker if:
A. During the term of this Agreement or any extension hereof, Lessor/Owner and any lessee execute a lease covering any part of the Project, whether said lease is procured by Broker, by Lessor/Owner, or by any other party; or
B. During the term of this Agreement or any extension hereof, a lease is executed by a ready, willing, and able lessee covering any part of the Project, whether said lease is procured by Broker, by Lessor/Owner, or by any other party, on terms acceptable to Lessor/Owner and any contingencies regarding the lessee's or lessor's obligations under such lease are not removed or waived (and such lease does not become fully effective) due to the default of Lessor/Owner; or
C. During the term of this Agreement or any extension hereof, Lessor/Owner sells or agrees to sell all or any portion of the Project or executes an Agreement to construct a building on the Project for the use of a long-term lessee (a "build to suit") or executes a ground lease covering any part of the Project, whether any of the above is procured by Broker, by Lessor/Owner, or by any other party; or
D. During the term of this Agreement or any extension hereof, an Agreement of sale, build to suit or ground lease is executed by a ready, willing, and able purchaser or lessee covering any part of the Project whether said lease is procured by Broker, by Lessor/Owner, or by any other party on terms reasonably acceptable to Lessor/Owner and any contingencies regarding the lessee's or lessor's obligations under such sale or lease are not removed or waived (and such sale or lease does not become fully effective or finally consummated) due to the default of Lessor/Owner; or

Within six (6) months after the expiration of this Agreement or any extension hereof, all or any portion of the Project is leased or sold to any person or entity with whom Broker has negotiated or to whom the Project has been submitted by Broker prior to the expiration of this Agreement or any extension hereof and whose name appears on any list of such persons or entities which Broker shall have delivered to Lessor/Owner no later than thirty (30) days after such expiration.

FIGURE 3.2 Exclusive Marketing Agreement (continued)

5.2 Commission rates payable to Broker and the time of payment are as follows:
A. (Rates from your company's schedule of commissions will be listed here)
B. Time of Payment:
One-half (½) of each commission shall be due Broker at the time the lease is executed and the remaining one-half (½) upon the occupancy of the lessee in the Project and in each instance such to be paid within ten (10) days after submission of invoice provided that:
1. Any leasing commission earned by Broker pursuant to Subparagraphs 5.1B or 5.1D above shall be paid to Broker in its entirety at the time of the default of Lessor/Owner, and
2. In the event a lessee does not take occupancy of its premises in the Project, then the remaining one-half (½) of Broker's commission shall be paid to Broker when the notice of completion is filed on the Project or six (6) months following the execution of the lease, whichever first occurs, and
3. If a lessee does not take occupancy of its premises in the Project or vacates such premises (for any reason except for the default by Lessor/Owner under its lease) within three (3) months after taking occupancy, then Broker will use its best efforts to secure a replacement lessee, and if secured then no additional commission shall be payable to Broker except only to the extent that there may be an increase in the minimum rental payable under the replacement lease, in which case, Lessor/Owner shall pay to Broker a sum equal to the difference by which the commission payable under the replacement lease exceeds that which was paid to Broker under the prior lease.
4. Broker is hereby authorized to deduct its commission pursuant to the preceding schedule from funds held in its trust account.
C. Should the term of any lease for which a commission is payable hereunder be extended or the lessee under such lease occupy any additional space, then Lessor/Owner shall pay a commission to Broker at such time as said term is extended or such additional space is occupied computed in accordance with the provisions of this Section 5 as if the initial term of the subject lease had included said extension period or the premises initially demised had included such additional space.
D. In the event Lessor/Owner sells the Project, Broker shall be paid a sales commission at close of escrow, provided that any sales commission earned by Broker pursuant to Subparagraphs 5.1C or 5.1D above shall be paid to Broker in its entirety at the time of the default of Lessor/Owner.
5.3 In the event a prospective lessee or purchaser fails to consummate a lease or sale and Lessor/Owner thus receives a defaulted deposit from said lessee or purchaser, then Lessor/Owner shall first deduct from such defaulted deposit its out-of-pocket costs (limited to legal fees, title fees, escrow fees, and expenses of collection) incurred in connection with such transaction, and Broker shall receive one-half (½) of the remainder of such defaulted deposit not to exceed the amount of any commission payable to Broker under this Agreement.

6. TERMINATION:
6.1 Either party hereto shall have the right to terminate this Agreement in the event of any material default by the other party hereto in the performance of any covenant, condition, or other provision of this Agreement to be performed by such other party by giving at least sixty (60) days' prior written notice of such termination to the other party.
6.2 Each of the parties hereto shall perform all of its respective obligations under this Agreement to the date of termination, and thereafter Lessor/Owner shall continue to make payments on earned commissions on the schedule set forth in Section 5 above. No termination of this Agreement shall relieve either of the parties hereto of the responsibility for obligations incurred prior to termination.

7. INDEMNIFICATION:
7.1 Provided that Lessor/Owner complies with all of the provisions of this Agreement, Broker shall indemnify, defend, and hold Lessor/Owner harmless from any liability arising out of the claim of any broker, agent, or finder for a commission pursuant to a lease allegedly procured by any such third party, except only as to any party with whom Lessor/Owner has dealt without the knowledge and consent of Broker. Lessor/Owner agrees to advise any broker, agent, or finder who contacts Lessor/Owner of the fact that Broker has exclusive right to lease the Project and that all negotiations must be conducted through Broker.
7.2 Lessor/Owner agrees to indemnify, defend, and hold Broker harmless, except in instances where Broker has acted in a grossly negligent or willfully fraudulent manner, from all claims, lawsuits, and causes of action which may arise, directly or indirectly, from the execution of or performance under this Agreement by either party hereto or in any way related to or connected therewith. For the purposes of this Subparagraph, the term Broker shall include all of Broker's affiliates and successor and all officers, directors, agents and employees of each.

FIGURE 3.2   Exclusive Marketing Agreement (concluded)

8. NOTICES:
   Any and all notices provided for herein shall be in writing and shall be delivered personally or deposited as certified United States mail, return receipt requested, in an envelope with postage prepaid, addressed to Lessor/Owner or to Broker with a copy to Broker's general counsel.

9. MISCELLANEOUS:
   9.1 In the event either party hereto institutes legal action to enforce the provisions of this Agreement, the prevailing party therein shall receive reasonable attorney's fee incurred in said action and all costs and expenses of such action.
   9.2 Neither party to this Agreement shall assign its right or delegate its duties hereunder without the prior written consent of the other party.
   9.3 Whenever possible, each provision of this Agreement shall be interpreted so as to be effective and valid under applicable law, but if any provision of this Agreement shall be prohibited or invalid under applicable law, the remainder of such provision and the remaining provisions of this Agreement shall continue in full force and effect. This Agreement shall be construed under the laws of the State of California.
   9.4 The provisions of this Agreement constitute the entire Agreement of the parties hereto. No terms, conditions, warranties, promises, or understandings of any nature whatsoever, expressed or implied, exist between the parties except as herein expressly set forth. This Agreement cannot be amended or modified except by instrument in writing signed by both parties to the Agreement.

IN WITNESS WHEREOF, the parties hereto have executed this Agreement as of the date first above written.

SMITH AND JONES COMMERCIAL BROKERAGE COMPANY

By _____

By _____

By _____

By _____

CHAPTER 3 / Marketing   27

CONCLUSION

As you grow more experienced you will develop "retail awareness." Instead of a vacant space in a shopping center, you'll imagine a particular store for which the space is ideal. Above all, you must know your territory and the various facets of the retail business. You must know your customers, both those you have already satisfied and those who may become clients.

The sources of leads are many and varied, but you must follow up on them and determine whether or not you can capture a potential client's business. When you get a lead, act on it immediately.

Exercise A

1. Name three productive sources of leads.
2. In what way might reading newspapers help you to obtain leads?
3. Name possible sources of referrals.
4. Why can employees of companies that deal with retailers be an important source of leads?
5. Is a mailing alone sufficient to generate client interest? What else must you do?

Answer A

1. *Clubs and organizations, your office's listing system, and signs are among the important sources of leads available to you.*
2. *From the financial news, you can learn which companies are planning to expand or open a new outlet.*
3. *Salespeople in your own office or in other offices may provide you with referrals.*
4. *Managers and salespeople of companies specializing in office and store equipment usually have information about retail companies' plans to move or expand.*
5. *No. Mailings must be followed up either by phone or in person. The mailing itself is only an entree to further contact.*

4

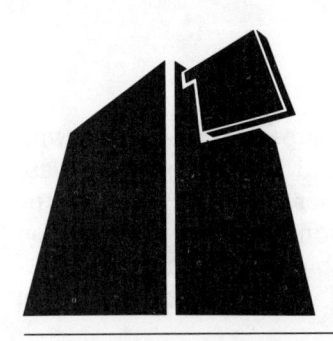

Qualifying Tenants

INTRODUCTION

Tenant qualification means determining whether a tenant is seriously interested in leasing or buying space. There are three vital areas of qualification:

1. What are the company's real estate needs and motivations?
2. What is the company's financial capacity?
3. Who in the company has authority to make the decision to purchase or lease real estate and what is the process for reaching that decision?

All three subjects are significant aspects of a single goal: completing a successful transaction with a tenant. Qualification is important because in the real estate business, time is money. Qualify your tenant before starting to look at property and taking the time to gather all the necessary information.

OVERVIEW OF TENANT NEEDS

The user is the retailer, the person who will occupy whatever space is created. You will need to learn how various retailers operate and what their real estate needs are. For example, what are the needs of clothing stores, hardware chains, or fast food and supermarket chains with respect to property and building size, preferred transactions (purchase or lease), location, necessary volume and other factors involved in the retail business? You'll become familiar with some of these needs as you talk with the tenants in your area. You can also turn to many good reference sources on retail marketing, a number of which will be described in the marketing chapter.

Even though you will probably specialize in some aspect of the retail area, such as banking or restaurants, you must have an overview of a broad range of users and be familiar with their particular requirements. You should know such basic facts as the typical space requirements of a retail business and the type of transactions you are likely to be involved in with different users. Most of the terms used in describing the transactions here are also listed in the glossary.

BUILDING-TO-SITE RATIO

In computing space size for shopping centers and newer developments, a distinction is made between the size of the building and the size of the total site. This relationship of building to total site is usually computed on a 3-to-1 ratio: three square feet of the site for every square foot of building space. You can compute the site area requirements for the various buildings a user needs by simply multiplying the building square footage by four. This is sometimes referred to as 25 percent coverage. It's generally a reliable estimate of total space need, but may vary somewhat according to the user and various government regulations.

SPACE NEEDS AND TRANSACTIONS

Financial Institutions. The average size of a bank is from 5,000 to 10,000 square feet. A savings and loan will usually require approximately 5,000 square feet. Because banks and savings and loans will have money available to them at considerably better rates than will the average landowner, they traditionally pay the highest prices on land and the highest rents of any user. In most cases, financial institutions prefer to purchase the property and put up their own building. Their second and third preferences, respectively, are ground leases (the company leases the land and constructs its own building) and build-to-suit arrangements (the landowner retains ownership of the land and agrees to build to the specifications of the tenant who leases the property).

Theaters. The space range will be from 2,500 to 10,000 square feet and in some cases as high as 20,000 square feet depending on the number of screens. Theatres will typically situate on a rental basis and pay relatively low rent per square foot. However, they attract other users, particularly restaurants, who will pay higher rents.

Restaurants. Space can be in the range of 1,200 to 3,500 square feet for a fast-food chain, while a dinner house may average 5,000 to 10,000 square feet. Some even go as high as 15,000. A 24-hour family-style restaurant is usually 5,000 to 6,000 square feet. The capital cost of acquiring real estate, putting up a building and furnishing it generally makes it too expensive for most restaurant owners to build on their own. For this reason, they often enter into a sale-leaseback transaction. Restaurant owners purchase the land and build to meet their specifications. They then sell the property and simultaneously become the lessee of the new owner.

Service Stations. The average size is 2,500 square feet. Ordinarily these users will either be involved in a ground lease transaction or will purchase the property and build.

Discount Stores. Discount stores usually average 50,000 to 100,000 square feet and can be freestanding or part of a community shopping center. Because they are anchor tenants (major tenants that attract considerable consumer traffic to a shopping center) they usually pay low rent.

Supermarkets. The size may range from 25,000 to 50,000 square feet. Supermarkets will either purchase the pad in the shopping center and build or want a build-to-suit transaction. A supermarket may act as an anchor tenant.

Chain Tenants. The space averages between 5,000 and 10,000 square feet. These are active tenants—carrying such items as stereo equipment, records, shoes, clothing or sporting goods—and will be expanding and adding new locations. The transaction is typically a lease, but on occasion can be a purchase, build-to-suit, ground lease or sale/leaseback transaction.

Drugstores. If the drugstore is an independent retail outlet, the average size is 4,000 square feet. A location for a drugstore chain, however, can be as big as 25,000 square feet, with build to suit and leasing as first and second choices.

RETAIL TENANT REQUIREMENT FORM

Study the retail tenant requirement form in this chapter. You will be using this form to record the needed information on space size, acquisition requirements and the like. Fill it out as completely as possible on your initial contact with a tenant.

Location. Placement in a shopping center is important to retailers. A drugstore, for example, frequently goes alongside a supermarket in a neighborhood center. In a regional center, a supermarket might be located on the periphery, where close-in parking is available. It may not matter what shops are next door. A bank may also want a periphery location for easy access by its customers, particularly if it has a drive-through window.

Tenant mix (desired cotenants). Where would tenants prefer to be placed? The most efficient means of learning tenant mix for a multiple space listing is to notice how stores are grouped in successful shopping centers. After a while you'll discover various patterns. These patterns can serve as guidelines when you begin to establish what kinds of tenants you should have in the center. You'll want to create a good mix of regional, national and local tenants that merchandise such items as fabrics, clothing, candy, food and records. You'll also be looking for local tenants for such specialty shops as gourmet foods, tobacco or wine. Remember that tenant mix should be designed so that the businesses in a shopping center draw customers for each other.

Demographics. Retailers are concerned with demographics, that is, the population distribution and the per capita income within a given radius of the trading area. This information is in census reports and can be retrieved from computer data banks, which many offices subscribe to, for any specific site or geographic area.

GETTING THE INFORMATION FROM THE TENANT

Ask your tenant direct questions and bring up items that may have been overlooked or that may seem too obvious for the tenant to mention. Under "other pertinent data" you might include such items as electrical equipment that needs special wiring, heavy machinery that requires a reconsideration of floor-load capacity or special parking requirements.

If your tenant is well-informed and you write down the answers to your questions, your first contact should produce all the necessary information. This will be especially true when you work with regional and national chains that usually have their own checklist of specifications.

Frequently, when medium-sized or small companies feel they need to expand, they have no clear idea of how or in what direction, or of exactly what kinds of property they should be seeking. Many times you will have to help these tenants be more specific about their needs.

VISITING THE LOCATION

Whether tenants are based locally or are part of a regional or national chain, visit the location. Observe what is going on. Do tenants seem to like shopping centers or downtown locations? Do they prefer freestanding buildings? What kind of access do they have? What is the parking situation? What can you learn about traffic flow at the location? What kind of cotenants do they seem to prefer? What can you learn from talking to the store manager? Observing a company's present location will tell you much about its needs.

CHAPTER 4 / Qualifying Your Tenants   33

FIGURE 4.1   Retail-Client Requirements

DATE: _____

COMPANY: _____   ADDRESS: _____

CONTACT: _____   POSITION: _____ PHONE: _____

TYPE OF BUSINESS: _____

LAND REQUIREMENTS

   Maximum Price Per Square Foot $ _____
   Minimum Square Feet Required _____
   Dimensions _____ By _____
   Corner Location _____ Yes _____ No
   Desired Parking Ratio _____ To _____

BUILDING REQUIREMENTS

   Typical Building Size (Square Feet) _____
   Dimensions _____ By _____
   Typical Building Costs ($/Sq. Ft.) _____

ACQUISITION REQUIREMENTS

Buy   Yes ☐   No ☐
Ground Lease   Yes ☐   No ☐
   Minimum _____ Years
   Percent to Investor _____ %
   Subordination   Yes ☐   No ☐
Build-To-Suit   Yes ☐   No ☐
   Maximum Lease Term _____ Years
   Annual Rent $ _____ Gross ☐   Net ☐
   Financial Strength of Lease Signature $ _____
Preferred Developers _____

SHOPPING CENTER LOCATION   Yes ☐   No ☐

   Neighborhood ☐   Community ☐   Regional ☐   Freestanding ☐
   Desired Co-Tenants _____

EXISTING OPERATION DATA

   Area Presently Operating In _____

   Number of Units _____ Attach List of Addresses of Existing Units

DEMOGRAPHICS REQUIRED

   Trading Area Radius _____ Miles
   Distance Between Units _____
   Population In Trading Area _____
   Average Household Income ($/Yr.) _____

EXPANSION PLANS

   Primary Areas _____ Quota _____

ACTION TO TAKE & ACTION TAKEN

   _____
   _____
   _____
   _____

SALESMAN   DISTRIBUTION
_____   Name _____
                                                      Office _____

OTHER PERTINENT DATA

As a broker, you must analyze a company before you can fully understand and meet its needs. You must know something about the company's history, the product it sells and the promotion and marketing methods it uses. While essential to success, getting to know a company well can also be a time-consuming process. There are no fixed rules about choosing which company to pursue. You will have to rely on experience, and to some extent intuition, when determining which tenant will be worth the time and effort you invest. As a rule, it is unwise to spend a great deal of time with a company that requires only a small space at each outlet. However, in many instances, the choice is not clear-cut. You will have to decide each case on an individual basis.

Exercise A

1. What is the significance of the 3-to-1 ratio? How else is it referred to?
2. What is meant by an anchor tenant?
3. What is meant by acquisition requirements?
4. Why is tenant mix an important consideration in a shopping center? How might you learn about it?
5. What might you learn from observing a tenant's present location?

Answer A

1. *The 3-to-1 ratio establishes the relationship of total site to building: three square feet of site for every square foot of building. It is computed by multiplying the square footage of the building by four, and is also referred to as 25 percent coverage.*
2. *An anchor tenant is usually a nationally known chain tenant that draws a great deal of traffic to a shopping center and ensures a profitable operation for all the other tenants.*
3. *Acquisition requirements refer to a user's needs in terms of location, space and operation requirements specific to a particular use, and preferred transactions, such as a ground lease or a build to suit.*
4. *With a properly planned tenant mix, the businesses in a shopping center should attract customers for each other. The best way to learn about tenant mix is to visit shopping centers and observe the groupings of different types of users.*
5. *By observing a tenant's present site, you can learn much about a company's needs and preferences regarding location, type of building, access, traffic flow, parking needs and the like.*

FINANCIAL CAPABILITY AND DECISION MAKING

You, the broker, represent the owner of a building seeking a buyer or lessee. The owner is being asked to turn over a property for a period of time or to surrender to a buyer something of considerable value. Can the lessee or buyer carry through financially on the transaction? The owner has the right to know. Ask the buyer or lessee for a financial statement. If you encounter resistance, educate the tenant on why the owner needs this information.

As part of your analysis you will want to talk with the tenant about inventory costs in a new outlet, how long the company expects to operate at the new location before being in the black and how the operation will be financed until that time. In other words, does the tenant have staying power?

You must have financial information on every company for every transaction. The difficulty in obtaining information varies from company to company. Large companies are listed in Dun & Bradstreet and can be checked easily. (Although you should keep in mind that much of the information Dun & Bradstreet has is self-volunteered.) Most medium-sized companies are also in Dun & Bradstreet and other well-known references. If a smaller or less well-known company is growing, its officers are usually willing to discuss their capability and disclose financial statements.

A salesperson sometimes runs into a problem with small, privately owned companies because the officers are reluctant to disclose the financial details of their operations. In this case you must stress the right of the property owner to be sure of the buyer or lessee's ability to pay. You yourself are not asking for the statement. You can arrange for the tenant and property owner to meet in a neutral setting, such as a bank.

Wholly owned subsidiaries can also present problems. Such companies often do not possess strong financial statements. Their representatives typically quote the net worth of the parent corporation, which can be irrelevant because the corporation will not sign or guarantee the lease. The corporation might furnish a letter saying that it will back up a financial transaction, but this is no guarantee. Consequently, the important consideration is who signs the lease. If it is to be the subsidiary, then you must be absolutely certain of its financial capability. The same criterion applies to franchises, which frequently do not have sufficient net worth to follow through on a purchase or lease transaction.

Many people at one time or another think about starting a small business. Your first question in this case should be, "How have you prepared financially to start and maintain a business of your own?" People often act on an emotional rather than a practical basis. However, treat each case individually and try not to prejudge.

If the tenant refuses to furnish financial information, there is only one answer: Break off the transaction. Such refusal usually means the company is reaching farther than its financial arm will allow. It may also indicate a poor credit rating. You would be wasting your time to continue negotiating with this tenant.

Small companies generally want to own their buildings. Large companies will usually lease. Sometimes a company cannot afford to buy the space it needs. Here is where the salesperson becomes important. Much time can be wasted looking at properties for sale before the tenant finally realizes that he or she simply cannot afford to buy. Find out early in the game if a lease is best for a tenant. Then, if necessary, educate the tenant on this fact. Otherwise, you may spend a great deal of time showing sale properties, only to have the tenant end up at another broker's office with a lease agreement.

Make sure in the beginning that tenants know and accept the amount of rent they will be paying, particularly if they are from out of the area or this is their first business. Here your knowledge of your territory becomes very important. You will know what locations will be within your tenant's range based on the company's expected volume of business.

Tenant motivation should also be explored early in the qualifying procedure. Ask your tenants how many stores they intend to open in the current year. If the number is substantial, it is usually an indication that the company is highly motivated. Also, explore when and how the tenant might be able to open an operation if you could provide the right site. If you're dealing with a local tenant, try to discover the motivating factor behind his or her interest in a particular location.

Finding out who has the power to make decisions can save time in completing a transaction. In dealing with a larger company, your initial contact will probably be a real estate representative, some other officer, or a regional or area manager. The person's main job will be to search for locations and to start the transaction process. The information will then be passed on to two or three others in the company until it finally reaches the decision maker who actually signs the agreement. This person might come to your territory, but only when the transaction is ready to be completed. If you proceed on the belief that the local people have authority to sign a lease or an agreement, you may waste your time selling the wrong person. Find out who the decision maker is in the company. At the same time, be careful not to circumvent the real estate representative's authority. Remember, local representatives may not be able to say yes, but they can say no.

When working with a company that has a real estate specialist, you probably won't be able to avoid dealing with several people. In large companies, two or three people will normally be involved in gathering information and making real estate recommendations and decisions. Should the company be acquiring or leasing space for a division already in existence, the local manager will have an important role in the decision. Should the division be new, you'll probably spend most of your time with someone from the company headquarters. That person will make recommendations and some other officer at headquarters will sign the lease or agreement.

When you must deal through channels, problems with interpersonal relations may arise. Almost as a hard and fast rule, don't bypass the representative in the field. Feelings are easily hurt, and you can lose a tenant before you really get started. The best approach in a transaction in which you suspect you are not working with the decision maker is tactful probing. You might try this question: "What is the process for making a decision like this within your organization?" Or, "When it gets to the point of putting something in writing, I'll send the information to you. To whom should I send the copy?" If the person you ask has the authority to sign, he or she will let you know. If that person can't sign, find out who can. Also, keep in mind that even if the person is the final decision maker, there may be others within the organization who will heavily influence that decision.

There are rare occasions when you'll want to bypass the field representative. If the person you're dealing with doesn't have the authority to make decisions; if it seems that the deal is not progressing; if the representative seems to be overshopping the market and you feel that he or she really doesn't know what's going on; and if you might lose the tenant to another broker anyway—then perhaps you'll want to take a chance and go over the representative's head to a superior. Consider this option only if you are convinced that you have the best real estate package for the company. You must judge each situation and decide whether to take the risk.

In most cases, relatively little paperwork is involved in qualifying tenants and following through on transactions. You will not need to write many letters or circulate memos when dealing with a small company. Information gathering and negotiations are usually handled face-to-face or on the phone. However, you should always make written notes to document all conversations that you have. The final agreement is, of course, put in writing.

In dealing with a company contact who is not the decision maker, put all information in writing. When you transmit information orally to your contact, who relays it orally to his or her superior, the message will inevitably become somewhat distorted. To retain control of the situation, give the company contact written information to pass along to the person in charge.

The time needed to complete a transaction will depend in part upon the size of the company and its location. In a small company, the president or another officer who has decision making power will usually make the decision unilaterally. Ordinarily the officers of a small company, especially a local one, have been thinking of moving or expanding for some time. They have studied the market and learned for themselves what property is available. When they decide to move, a transaction usually goes through fairly quickly.

When dealing with a larger company, you will usually have to work with more than one layer of authority, especially if the company has its headquarters outside your area. As a rule, there will be a field representative who looks for property and passes information back to headquarters. There, one person or a group of people will evaluate the information and make recommendations. Finally, another office will sign the lease or the purchase agreement. All this can take quite a while. The situation is balanced to some extent by the fact that a large company usually knows what it wants. It has worked out careful and detailed specifications for its outlets. It approaches the real estate market in a businesslike manner. If you have shown the company real estate that looks good to its officers, you will have sped up the transaction. Once a location has been selected, signing the lease or agreement generally takes little time.

Someday you may find yourself simply unable to work with a particular tenant because of a personality conflict. This is especially likely to happen with middle-management people, who may resent the fact that they do not have final authority.

If the situation deteriorates beyond a certain point, the tenant will simply find another broker without saying anything to the salesperson. Your first clue will be when the tenant is suddenly unavailable for phone calls. When this happens, it's too late to remedy the problem.

Don't let an awkward situation deteriorate that far. If you sense that a personality problem is developing, act while you can still salvage something from the situation. Quickly try to substitute someone else from your office, someone whose personality will fit the tenant's better. This will mean a split commission if your colleague closes the deal, but a portion of a commission is infinitely better than none.

Within a few months you will probably have developed a list of two dozen or more companies you consider prospects. Analyze that list, and you're likely to find that no more than five or six are really prospects. These are the companies that you have thoroughly qualified, the ones that might complete a transaction. If prospects do not look good, quickly but tactfully refer them to someone else, or simply let the matter rest. Don't waste your time and talent.

Qualify owners as well as tenants. Be sure that the property is priced in accord with the market. If it is overpriced, try to find out why. Perhaps the owner doesn't know the current market and will accept your judgment about lowering the price. On the other hand, the owner might not have a real incentive to sell or lease. He or she may not need the income, or may simply be speculating and can afford to wait until someone meets the high price. This much is certain: If the property is not priced right, your chances of moving it are very slim.

If the owner is selling, you will want to find out why. This will have a bearing on the price and terms and the owner's eagerness to make a sale. Perhaps the person needs money, or wants to recover an investment or make other investments. Examine the owner's tax bill and any leases or easements on the property. Get some idea from the owner about the age and condition of the building, and double-check the information. Take a look at the title and ask for a copy of the abstract or a relatively recent title policy. Don't be afraid to ask questions, and make no assumptions. The owner is in the best position—or should be—to know the most about the property in question.

In a leasing situation, find out what lease stipulations the owner has in mind. Will the rent be on a square-footage basis or a percentage of sales? If a percentage, will it be on net or gross? What about a tax increase clause? Will it be a straight lease or have a cost-of-living index? Get answers to these questions early in the game. They will save you time later and help you avoid blind alleys.

Most owners have certain criteria regarding the type and quality of retailer they will rent to. Be sure to ask about these preferences.

If the transaction concerns vacant property, you need to find out if the owners will build to suit. Can they obtain the necessary financing? Here you'll need a financial statement and perhaps additional information from their bank. If they seriously want to make a sale, they'll provide the information you need.

Questions may arise concerning title validity. Real estate brokers are not lawyers. They're not equipped to handle legal matters. If you have any questions or reservations about title, discuss them with your manager or supervisor. If they can't clear up the situation, the matter should go to counsel.

Situations occur where a property just won't move even at the right price. There is really no such thing as a bad piece of real estate. The question is one of timing and need. Perhaps a building lost money for everyone who owned it, or no lessee ever made money at a particular location. Yet even that building or location has a value to someone, and will eventually be sold or leased. The same is true with vacant land; perhaps it's not ripe for development today, but it will be in the future. You simply have to convince a tenant that now is the time to buy or lease.

Earning commissions requires an expenditure of time, and no one has an unlimited supply. Qualify your tenants to determine which ones are most likely to bring in a commission. Buyers and lessees should be qualified on the basis of the company's real estate needs, its financial capability and the availability of a decision maker with authority to sign a lease or purchase agreement. Qualify owners on the basis of price, their incentive to sell or lease and their financial capability if they intend to build to suit. All of these factors are vital to your success.

Exercise B

Answer the following questions.

1. What are the three areas of tenant qualification discussed in this chapter?
2. What is the importance of each of these areas?
3. What must you watch for when dealing with a company's field representative who is seeking a location? Why?
4. When might you choose to go around a field representative to his or her superior?
5. How do small and large companies differ with respect to: (a) knowing real estate needs; (b) financial capability; and (c) the number of people to be dealt with and the speed of decision making?
6. What financial points should you discuss with tenants?
7. How can you test the seriousness of individuals who would like to start a small business?
8. What is the best procedure to follow should you and the tenant not get along?
9. In what ways should you qualify owners?

Answer B

1. The tenant company must be qualified in terms of: (a) its need for new space; (b) its financial capability to enter into a transaction; and (c) its decision making process.

2. These areas of qualification are vital for the following reasons. (a) You must ascertain that the company is serious about moving and that its space needs have been perceived accurately before you devote your energy to locating new space for it. (b) You must have financial information on all tenants. If you are representing an owner, your responsiblity is to make certain that the buyer or lessee can carry through financially on any agreement. If the tenant company cannot fulfill its obligations, both the owner's time and your time will be wasted, and you will lose credibility. (c) The company must provide you with a contact who has the authority to close the deal.

3. The person in the field may give you the impression that he or she has the authority to sign a lease or an agreement. You may proceed on that basis only to discover that someone else has that power and that you have wasted time selling the wrong person.

4. You may wish to bypass the person in the field if negotiations seem to be going nowhere, if the person you're dealing with has no authority to make decisions, or if it appears that you may lose the transaction to another broker. You must decide whether to accept the risk.

5. *(a) A large company usually knows what it wants and has worked out detailed specifications for its outlets. The same is generally true of a small company where the officers have contemplated a move for some time. They will usually have studied the market and learned what property is available. (b) Small, privately owned companies may not want to disclose their financial information or put anything in writing. Most large companies, and many medium-sized firms, are listed in Dun & Bradstreet and are easily checked for financial capability. (c) In a small company, the owner usually makes the final decision. The deal is consummated faster when you work with the owner directly or with officers of a small company. In a large company, two or more people are involved in the process. Typically, the real estate representative must pass on the information to one or more persons until it reaches the officer who has the authority to sign the agreement. This procedure can be time-consuming, but once a location has been selected, the lease or agreement usually is signed fairly quickly.*

6. *You will want to know what their inventory will cost in a new outlet, how long they expect to operate at the location before being in the black and how they expect to finance the operation until that time and still pay the rent.*

7. *While you should try not to prejudge the situation, begin by determining their financial capability. If they will not furnish this information, either refer them to another salesperson or tactfully discourage them.*

8. *Handle the situation at the first sign of difficulty. If your relationship with the tenant is too strained, you might introduce someone else from your office who would be more compatible with the tenant. This will mean a shared commission, but it is preferable to losing control of the transaction altogether.*

9. *Owners should be qualified in three areas: (a) their motivation in selling—their eagerness to make a sale can affect the price and terms; (b) the lease stipulations they want; and (c) their financial capability if a build-to-suit arrangement is involved.*

TENANT CONTROL

Tenant control is one of the mainstays of the real estate business. Every time a tenant completes a transaction through your office, you can be sure there was effective tenant control. Each time a series of transactions is completed with a chain operation, tenant control is again behind the scene. In real estate, the phrase "tenant control" applies in two ways. One type of control is short-term, focused on leading the tenant successfully through a specific transaction. The second type is more far-reaching. It is the acquisition of repeat business from a particular tenant who is regularly concerned with finding new retail outlets.

Short-term Control

Short-term tenant control could be called transaction control. Here, your goal is to structure a situation so that a transaction is completed in the most economical and effective manner for all concerned.

Your approach to each transaction will be smoother if you keep these ideas in mind:

Educate your tenants. Let them know what is involved in your work. Explain the time and effort taken to compile your listing so that they'll understand how you can help them. Let them know that by using your services they are not giving up other brokers' listings. Let them know how you're going to help them. Explain that your services usually involve no direct cost to them because the owner generally pays the commission.

Be firm. Now that they have an idea of what you will do for them, explain that for this service you would simply like to be their exclusive broker.

Build rapport. After assessing your tenants' needs and qualifying them, a good presentation of your property and your knowledge about their requirements will go a long way toward building broker-tenant rapport. Tenants will know that you will do everything possible to find what they need.

Get feedback. Find out what the tenants like or dislike about the property that you're showing. Use this information for future property selections.

Register your tenants. When you feel it is necessary, particularly if you don't have a written tenant representation agreement, protect your commission by sending a registration letter to tenants, owners or other brokers.

Close the transaction. If you have done your groundwork well, this step should not be difficult.

Long-term Control

You can do a great deal of business with a regional or national user who must periodically open new outlets. If you do a good job of fulfilling this user's needs the first few times, the firm will tend to come back to you again and again as the need to open additional outlets develops.

Your aim is to become the user's exclusive agent. You want him or her to call you whenever a real estate problem arises. You can imagine what this can mean in terms of commissions over the long term. You may not need to service this tenant more than once or twice a year, or you may have to find several locations within a few months. The point is, as real estate needs arise, you are the one who will help fulfill them. To reach this point, you must build a sound relationship, and make yourself indispensable. The important elements of long-range tenant control are as follows:

Qualify Your Tenants Carefully. In the real estate business, and especially in a retail division, the whole is not necessarily the sum of its parts. In many cases, a number of small transactions will not add up to as much as one large transaction. Yet several small arrangements might require as much or even more of your time as one large one.

Suppose a representative of a dry-cleaning chain comes to you looking for one or more locations. You qualify the tenant with respect to financial capability, track record, intentions and so on. The tenant is entirely satisfied with your work and keeps returning as the business grows. Well and good. You're involved in numerous transactions, and you're doing fine in terms of volume. But how much time are you spending on this account, and what are you getting in return?

A dry-cleaning outlet normally requires only 600 to 800 square feet, just enough to take in clothing and laundry and store it for pickup. In locating and securing such space, you could be spending a great deal of time in return for very small commissions. If you worked with a user of 20,000 to 25,000 square feet, you would be involved in fewer transactions but receive a higher commission. This would result in more money for the same expenditure of time.

Qualify your tenants with respect to the size of recurring real estate needs. It is unwise to spend most of your time on small transactions when you could be working on large ones.

However, it is extremely important that as a new retail salesperson you start out on a smaller scale, for several reasons. First, you will be working on many different types of transactions, and will be learning many new ways to structure agreements, overcome objections and close deals. Second, if you lose a tenant, it is much better to lose a smaller one from a financial standpoint. Third, you need the small transactions as a base to support yourself while you are working for larger tenants. The salesperson who tries to work only on larger arrangements from the start rarely succeeds in real estate. Larger transactions come from working on smaller ones.

Concentrate on More Than One Tenant. There is a real danger in being too closely tied to one company. We have emphasized that achieving an exclusive position with a multiple-location company requires an investment of time. In some cases a salesperson may be involved in as many as three transactions for one company at one time, transactions that have moved nearly to completion. Then, at the last moment, the company pulls back on expansion or is acquired, the broker has nothing to show for the effort but lost time unless he or she has provided for that contingency.

One way, at least, to avoid being bruised if a transaction falls through is to have backup tenants whom the locations might suit. In this way you can still complete a transaction even if the original tenants change their mind.

Consider Being The Exclusive Agent. With a few exceptions, it is not necessary to be an exclusive agent, nor will a company ordinarily be willing to write an exclusive contract with you. Most companies want to be in a position to do business with other brokers. Remember, their objective is to find suitable locations.

Besides, an exclusive contract can be dangerous to you for two reasons. Suppose you fail to come up with the number of locations a company representative needs in order to fill an outlet quota? The representative may blame you, and you can lose the good relationship you have built up. The other danger of a written contract is that you will naturally feel obligated to spend time fulfilling it. In the process, you might neglect other business that could benefit you more.

An exclusive arrangement usually develops on the basis of service you have rendered. If you have done well in arranging the first few transactions, the company representative in charge of real estate will turn to you when further needs arise. He or she will channel communications from other brokers to you and inform them that you are the company's agent. A long-term tenant relationship will develop naturally, because you have become indispensable to the company.

If the exclusive relationship does not develop naturally, you might initiate it, although not necessarily with the aim of putting it in writing. If you decide to initiate the relationship, arm yourself with your record, your knowledge of the territory, your knowledge of the company in question and its needs, and your firm's reputation. Then make your proposition to the appropriate officer, either the real estate manager or the president of the company.

There are occasions when an exclusive arrangement specified in writing might be appropriate. One instance might be with a national company whose headquarters are in another city. A developer or owner might not be convinced that you represent that company exclusively. The question can be settled by a letter from the company president on the company letterhead. You should naturally be very selective when signing an exclusive agreement with a tenant, but if it is a qualified firm that is growing, the arrangement could prove to be very profitable for you. Other brokers would have to submit all their transactions for the tenant through you.

One caveat: If you know that a company with an exclusive broker arrangement is looking for a location and you have one that might suit it, you have a choice. You can take the location to that company's broker and perhaps receive a split commission, or you can keep the location and try to work with another chain, earning the entire fee. The choice in such cases will be clearer as you gain more experience.

Naturally, in dealing with tenants, you will want to promote your own listing as fully as possible. But remember, a broker is obligated to show a tenant all available locations. Be willing to work with other brokers. The aim, after all, is service and satisfaction. By failing to make all listings known, you would work against the tenant control you wish to establish and maintain.

Keep in mind a tenant to whom you can turn if the original transaction does not work out. This will protect you against losing the investment of your time, one of a broker's most valuable commodities.

Protect Your Tenants. The next step might be to register your tenants, primarily for your own protection. The word "might" is emphasized here, for under certain circumstances registration will not be necessary.

Registration means three things:

1. Registering a letter or memo with the tenant stating that you have shown them certain properties. You should include a list of addresses and the dates on which the properties were shown.

2. Registering the tenant with the owner or developer of the property.

3. Registering the tenant with other brokers.

Of course, you do not want to spend all your time writing registration letters for each tenant. Probably the best rule of thumb is that if you have reason to believe that you might lose a transaction or a commission by not registering a tenant, then register him or her.

In most cases, commissions are paid by owner, not by tenants seeking space. In effect, you are rendering a service to tenants at no direct cost to them. For a further discussion of the agency issues this raises, refer to the chapter on Ethical Questions. Some tenants believe that making a deal directly with an owner will save them money simply because there will be no commission. This may or may not be true, but to you it is immaterial. If a tenant deals directly with an owner, you are out. Consequently, letters to tenants registering the properties you have shown them confirm your participation and ensure that you will receive a fee if a deal is consummated.

If you immediately register a tenant with an owner or developer, giving the tenant's name, you may be tipping your hand to your own disadvantage. The best procedure is first to approach owners and mention that you have an interested tenant. Then tell them that you want a commission agreement before proceeding further. Regardless of an owner's attitude, you must get that agreement to avoid possible trouble. If you go ahead without it, you may lose the fee. While most owners are ethical and realize the value of the brokerage community, a few will try to avoid paying a fair commission. So protect yourself by getting a commission agreement and registering your tenant with the owner.

Word travels quickly regarding real estate transactions, particularly large ones. Other brokers naturally will try to capture some of the business for themselves. To protect yourself, register your tenant with other brokers. Again, this can be done in the form of a letter.

It should be stressed that registration is a matter of judgment. You will not use it in every case.

Work with other brokers. More than half of your transactions in the retail division will probably be on a split-commission basis with other brokers. This is true regardless of how many transactions you complete for a company. Working with other brokers saves you time and enables you to do more business.

Company real estate representatives might fear that by putting all their business in your hands they will miss good opportunities other brokers might bring them. This objection is easily overcome. Simply tell the tenant that you will consider any location any broker brings to you. If the location suits the tenant, you will make the arrangements, and the other broker will get 50 percent of the commission.

Conversely, the fact that a company has another exclusive broker does not mean you have lost the firm's business. Take locations to that broker, a move he or she will ordinarily welcome, and the broker will do the rest. If a deal goes through, you will have earned 50 percent of the commission. In general, cooperate with other brokers and encourage them to cooperate with you.

Companies that deal in multiple locations are more profitably handled on an exclusive basis. Such a broker-tenant relationship takes time to develop and must be built with care. The tenant must be carefully selected. But an exclusive arrangement can be extremely profitable for you.

This chapter has offered a number of guidelines for developing tenant control. The essential principle is full and complete service to a tenant.

CHAPTER 4 / Qualifying Your Tenants 45

The art of developing and maintaining tenant control begins with such service.

Exercise C

1. Why must you be discriminating in choosing tenants with whom to develop an exclusive relationship?
2. What are two initial elements leading to tenant control?
3. Why is an exclusive arrangement in writing not always necessary and sometimes not even a good idea?
4. How should you respond to tenants who think an exclusive relationship will mean the loss of other brokers' listings?
5. Why should you cooperate with other brokers and encourage them to cooperate with you?
6. What danger lies in an exclusive relationship with a tenant?
7. What is tenant registration and under what circumstances might it be necessary?
8. What is the key to developing a sound relationship and exclusive arrangement with a tenant?

Answer C

1. You must be discriminating to insure that your transactions will be a worthwhile investment of your time and energy.

2. Two initial elements leading to tenant control are educating your tenants and successfully fulfilling their needs.

3. An exclusive arrangement in writing is not always a good idea because you may feel obligated to spend time fulfilling it and neglect other, more profitable, business.

4. If a tenant believes that an exclusive relationship will mean the loss of other brokers' listings, explain that you will still consider any location that any broker brings to you.

5. You should cooperate with other brokers because it saves you time, helps you to service your tenants better, and enables you to earn more money.

6. The danger of an exclusive relationship with a tenant is that you will be at the mercy of the plans of one company and may overlook other, more profitable, transactions.

7. Tenant registration is the method by which you let the landlord/developer know that you are responsible for bringing the tenant to a site. A tenant should be registered if you have any reason to believe that your commission might be in jeopardy.

8. The key to developing a sound relationship with a tenant is to become indispensible by servicing their needs professionally.

5

Forms and Legal Documents

INTRODUCTION

This section contains forms and legal documents that you will be using to control tenants and property and to finalize transactions. Each form or document will be discussed in detail, with special features highlighted. Since your signature will be on many of these forms, it is vital that you understand the scope and the limitations of each agreement.

As a salesperson, you are not authorized to originate or modify legal documents; you may only fill out standard forms. However, under various circumstances, you will find it necessary to alter contracts. Because of legal difficulties inherent in making such changes, always be sure you have your manager's approval for every alteration. Also, do not allow your company's approved forms to pass from your control. If you give a blank contract to a potential client who modifies it or uses it for another transaction, your office may be liable for any problems that arise from the wording, even though the company is not otherwise involved in the transaction.

TENANT REPRESENTATION AGREEMENT

The *tenant representation agreement* protects your right to a commission when you are doing site location work for a tenant. The agreement gives you an exclusive arrangement with the tenant while allowing you to contact other brokers and inform them of your tenant's requirements. A copy of the agreement follows.

FIGURE 5.1 Tenant Representation Agreement

TENANT REPRESENTATION AGREEMENT

TENANT hereby appoints GRUBB & ELLIS COMPANY ("Broker") as its exclusive agent with the exclusive right to select property and negotiate for its lease on behalf of Tenant, subject to the following provisions:

1. *Time.* The period of this agency shall commence on _____, 19_____, and terminate at midnight on _____, 19_____.

2. *Property and Authority.* Broker is authorized only: (a) to select properties that substantially meet the requirements set forth below, as modified from time to time in writing by Tenant; (b) to present those properties to Tenant; and (c) on Tenant's approval to negotiate for their lease, but not to commit Tenant to the lease of any premises or to sign any instruments on behalf of Tenant without Tenant's express written consent.

3. The requirements for the property are:
   A. Type of Property: _____
   _____
   _____

   B. Rent; Other Charges: _____
   _____
   _____

   C. Location: _____
   _____
   _____

4. *Compensation.* The Owner of the property shall pay Broker's commissions in accordance with the attached Schedule of Lease Commissions. If the Owner does not agree to pay a commission which is acceptable to Broker, but a lease of the property is consummated, then Tenant shall pay a commission in accordance with said Schedule of Lease Commissions, payment to be made upon execution of the lease by both parties. Broker shall also be entitled to receive the aforesaid commission from Tenant in the event of Tenant's default on an executed lease. Tenant agrees that in the event of a purchase of the property presented to Tenant during the term of this agency or any extension thereof, or during the one hundred fifty (150) day period referred to in Section 5 hereof, Broker shall be entitled to be paid a commission based upon _____% of the sales price to be paid through escrow.

5. If within one hundred fifty (150) days after the expiration of the period of the agency described above or any extension of it, Buyer shall enter into an agreement to lease property from any person with whom Broker has communicated in pursuit of the objectives of the agency before its expiration, Buyer shall pay compensation as though the transaction were procured during the agency period provided Broker notifies Buyer of the communication in writing during the agency period or within ten (10) days after the expiration thereof, identifying the Owner and the property.

6. In consideration of this Agreement, Broker agrees to utilize reasonable effort and diligence to achieve the purpose of this Agreement.

7. Tenant acknowledges receipt of a copy of this Agreement.

DATED: _____, 19_____   TENANT: _____

GRUBB & ELLIS COMPANY   By _____

By _____   By _____

Address: _____   Address: _____

City _____ State _____   City _____ State _____

Telephone: _____   Telephone: _____

CHAPTER 5 / Forms and Legal Documents

The tenant company hires your firm as "its exclusive agent with the exclusive right to select property and negotiate for its lease on behalf of the tenant." You can also negotiate for other types of transactions the tenant may wish to make. If something other than a lease is indicated, you should add to the agreement, "negotiate for its lease, purchase or ground lease."

All exclusive agreements must have a commencement and a termination date. Make sure you have a reasonable amount of time in which to accomplish the transaction—at least six months, although this will depend on the tenant's requirements. If the tenant is already in contact with other brokers and reluctantly enters into an exclusive agreement, you can shorten the time to 60 to 90 days, provided the term can be extended if you present the sites to them as agreed.

"Property and Authority" refers to qualifying tenants on the basis of their requirements. This you will have already carried out according to the procedures described in the chapter on tenant qualification. The reference in the agreement simply indicates that you have a clear understanding of the type of space needed and that you will not present unsuitable locations. It is also agreed that you will not pursue any negotiations without the tenant's written consent. In filling out the requirements for the property, be as specific as possible about the square footage range and the desired location—for example, an urban area or a neighborhood shopping center.

The notation for the rent, however, should be restricted to the type of lease, such as "triple-net lease at current market rates." Avoid filling in a specific amount. If you specify $.50 per square foot and the site you ultimately submit leases at $.60, the exclusive agreement is technically void. Instead, fill in a rent range of "$.50 to $.60 per square foot, each site to be considered individually by the tenant."

The paragraph on "Compensation" states that you will be paid by the property owner if a lease agreement is executed with your tenant. However, if you do not have a separate agreement with the owner, he or she is not obligated to pay your commission. The tenant representation agreement states that if you are not paid by the property owner, the tenant will pay you. But always try to use the owner as the source of the commission in both lease and sale situations. The manner in which you are compensated has both legal and ethical ramifications. For further discussion on this area refer to Chapter 6 in this manual and *Agency Relationships in Real Estate* by John Reilly.

If within 150 days after the expiration of the agreement the tenant executes a lease on property that you have shown during the agreement's stipulated term, you are to be paid a commission. However you must have registered this property with the tenant within 10 days after the agreement's expiration. The registration letter can be very simple: "Pursuant to paragraph 5 of the tenant representation agreement, the following is a list of properties that we have contacted on your behalf."

The agreement is not signed by your office until the tenant has returned a signed copy to you. This is very important. If you sign before the tenant receives the document for signing, the tenant may feel free to change the agreement with respect to commission or certain properties. You should also be aware that you are not authorized to enter into a contractual agreement on behalf of your office. Only your manager can do this. Technically, you do not have an agreement with the tenant until the document has been initialed by a manager. You should hand-deliver the copy with your manager's initials over your signature.

COMMISSION AGREEMENT

The *commission agreement,* shown in this chapter can be used for either the purchase or leasing of a piece of property. It simply states that if a transaction agreeable to both parties is consummated, you will be paid a commission for services rendered. Because it is not an employment contract, there is no time stipulation. If you already have an exclusive agreement, this detail is covered in that document.

If the transaction is a lease, it is important that you attach the schedule of commissions to the commission agreement. The two documents together state that the signer has agreed to pay you a commission and that he or she agrees to pay you per the attached schedule. The landlord or the tenant must sign the commission agreement and also sign and date the schedule. You cannot fill in a dollar amount for the commission because the lease term and the exact rental rate are not yet known. It is sufficient to place an asterisk in the blank. At the bottom of the agreement, write "*Per attached schedule of commissions."

In the case of a land sale, you would write in the percentage of the total sale price that you stipulate as your commission. Again, until the transaction is completed, the exact sum you will receive is not known. Since the percentage of the final purchase price can be written into the commission agreement, this document is a complete contract and guarantees that you will be paid a fee based on that percentage figure.

One word of caution: Any specific figure mentioned in the execution of a contract must be adhered to or the contract is considered void. For example, assume that you have a contract with a commission amount based on a sales price of $1.5 million but the total acreage is less than you thought it was. If you lower the sales price to $1 million, you will no longer have a viable contract. A detail such as this can cost you a commission.

Presenting the Agreement

Before you contact a landowner or developer on behalf of your tenant, you must arrive at an understanding about your commission. The essence of your communication to the owner or developer is that you have a user who would be a likely prospect to lease space or purchase a piece of property. In order to guarantee payment for your services, you want to have a commission agreement signed before you bring the two parties together to negotiate a lease or sale.

You may not always know in advance whether a developer has a good reputation regarding payment of broker commissions. Some developers with excellent records may be insulted if you ask them to sign an agreement. However, to be on the safe side with property owners and developers who may not be so sophisticated in their dealings, make every effort to secure their signatures. If you are not familiar with a developer's reputation, ask a more experienced broker about the firm's record before deciding whether it would be appropriate to draw up a commission agreement.

FIGURE 5.2 Commission Agreement

COMMISSION AGREEMENT

For and in consideration of the efforts and services rendered by Grubb and Ellis Commercial Brokerage Company in connection with the lease of that certain property described as:

_____

_____

_____

_____

from _____

_____

_____ as Landlord

to _____

_____

_____ as Tenant, the undersigned

agrees hereby to pay to Grubb and Ellis Commercial Brokerage Company the sum of $_____ in lawful money of the United States to be payable when both parties have signed an appropriate lease agreement, and all contingencies set forth in said lease agreement have been satisfied or waived by the party for whose benefit such contingency has been included. Grubb and Ellis Commercial Brokerage Company is hereby authorized to deduct the foregoing sums from funds held in its trust account, if any, and the undersigned agrees to pay any difference in cash in accordance herewith.

In the event an action is commenced to enforce the right of Grubb and Ellis Commercial Brokerage Company to payment, the undersigned hereby agrees to pay to Grubb and Ellis Commercial Brokerage Company reasonable attorney's fees and expenses, whether said action is prosecuted to judgment or not.

Receipt of a copy of this Agreement is hereby acknowledged.

DATED:_____, 19_____

GRUBB AND ELLIS COMMERCIAL BROKERAGE COMPANY

By_____

Address:_____

City_____, State_____

Telephone:_____

LANDLORD_____

By_____

By_____

Address:_____

City_____, State_____

Telephone:_____

Schedule of Commissions

Keep in mind that the schedule is not a commitment to pay you a commission. Even when it has been signed by an owner or a tenant, it cannot by itself be used to enforce payment.

Each brokerage firm has its own fee schedule, but most have certain things in common. Yours probably states that you are to be paid by the owner upon execution of the lease. Ideally, you would like to receive 100 percent of the commission at that time. In reality, it is difficult to collect from the owner before the tenant has taken possession. Typically, you are paid 50 percent upon execution and 50 percent upon occupancy by the tenant.

In transactions other than a lease, payment may be made at different points in the negotiations. The commission for a joint venture transaction is usually paid through escrow at the time the partnership is formed. Like a lease, a build-to-suit transaction is usually paid half upon execution and half upon occupancy.

If you are trying to exercise tenant control, the schedule should be attached to an exclusive representation agreement. If you have an exclusive agreement to lease space for a developer, the form should accompany the listing agreement. Always make certain that, in addition to obtaining a signature on the representation or listing agreement, you obtain a dated signature on the schedule of commissions. This is particularly important when the schedule is attached to a commission agreement.

LEASES

Three basic types of leases are used for commercial property: gross, percentage and net. Each describes a different method for calculating the rent base and paying expenses associated with property ownership.

Gross

According to the terms of a *gross lease,* the landlord agrees to pay the real estate taxes, insurance for the building and maintenance for the roof and exterior walls. In turn, the tenant is responsible for any increase in real estate taxes, liability insurance and maintenance other than the exterior walls and roof.

You will seldom encounter a gross lease on retail property. Office and industrial leasing still use this form, but most retail property is now based on a net basis.

Percentage

With *percentage rental,* the space is leased at a flat rate against a percentage of the tenant's gross volume of business. If this percentage exceeds the minimum guaranteed rental, the additional rent accrues on a monthly or annual basis. The minimum rental remains constant even if the determined percentage of gross sales falls below that base rent. In a shopping center, stores that do the largest volume of business, such as supermarkets or department stores, usually pay the lowest percentage rate. Small shops with a lower volume of sales will pay the highest percentage factor against minimum rent.

Net

There are three types of *net leases,* defined by how many of the expense items—taxes, maintenance of the common area and insurance—are paid by the tenant:

1. *Net-net-net:* The tenant pays taxes, maintenance of the common area and insurance.

2. *Net-net:* The tenant pays taxes and maintenance of the common area. (The landlord is responsible for insurance.)

3. *Net:* The tenant pays only taxes. (The landlord is responsible for maintenance of the common area and insurance.)

The words "net and "net-net-net" are used interchangeably, because it is generally assumed that a net lease is a triple net lease. In fact, it is unlikely that developers or owners will accept any lease that is not triple net, since they are eager to minimize expenses. This means the tenant will pay rent per square foot on the space, plus a monthly charge for his or her share of the property taxes, insurance and maintenance of the common area.

Usually you will find a combination percentage and triple net lease. This type of lease guarantees not only that tenants will meet tax, maintenance and insurance costs, but also that percentage factors will increase the landlord's income as the sales volume grows or as the rate of inflation increases.

THE LEASE DOCUMENT

Whenever possible, use the lease form the owner suggests. As a second choice, use your office's standard form. This will help you avoid liability. For simple changes, each office should have a book of standard legal clauses that can be inserted in the standard lease forms. When you are using a lease that is not your office's standard form, it is to your advantage to insert the words "other than Smith and Jones," in the section under "Brokers" (see section 23.19 of the lease form included in this chapter).

A lease is a binding legal document with which you must be thoroughly familiar. You should be able to locate any clause a tenant wishes to have explained. Not all leases have subject headings and unless you know the outline and contents of a lease, it will be hard to find a particular section or clause. Never simply hand a tenant a lease and tell him or her to read it. Part of tenant control is letting tenants know you are available to answer questions and supply information.

Lease Clauses

Some of the important lease clauses are examined in the following section. In some cases, these clauses may be the subject of discussion or negotiation between a landlord and tenant.

1. *Rent:* If the space is in a shopping center that already exists or in one newly completed and ready for occupancy, the lease is in effect from the day that is negotiated. If the space is not ready for occupancy, the tenant has up to 30 days from the time the landlord completes construction before the lease takes effect. If the premises are ready for occupancy before the 30 days are up, the lease is in effect on the day the store opens.

2. *Security Deposit:* Generally, the security deposit is equal to two months' rent. However, it may be calculated on the basis of one dollar per square foot of occupied space. It is not to be construed by the tenant as prepaid or advance rent, but is rather a good-faith deposit for the fulfillment of the terms and conditions of the lease.

3. *Rental Adjustments:* This section contains a definition of what is meant by a tenant's *pro rata share* of the common property: "That percentage of the total cost...tenant's total floor area bears to the total floor area of the shopping center." In some leases, this may also be phrased: "As tenant's total floor area bears to the total floor area occupied." If the tenant pays no taxes directly, or carries his or her own insurance, then the square footage of the store is deemed part of the total floor area of the center and is taxed accordingly. A tenant who leases 1,500 square feet of a total 100,000 square feet in the shopping center is responsible for a pro rata share of 1.5 percent of taxes, maintenance for common areas and insurance.

4. *Use:* It is very important to specify a tenant's exact purpose in leasing a specific space. For example, a tenant in the fur coat business may also sell related items such as shoes or purses; however, sales from these items must be less than 50 percent of the store's business. The primary reason behind this restriction is to protect the value of the property by ensuring that a nuisance is not created on the premises. The type of business should be fully described, and the lease should state that the designated space can be used for no other purpose without the landlord's written consent.

   Developers in smaller centers will not put in a use that is in direct competition with another tenant. Ordinarily, they want to maximize their ability to get percentage, or overage, rents and will thus work parallel with the tenants' interests. Competition and compatibility with the other tenants is an important consideration.

5. *Waiver of Subrogation:* The tenant and the landlord both agree to waive their rights of recovery against each other in the event that there is joint damage, loss or destruction to the property. In the lease shown here, the waiver is mutual; most leases, however, are written by the landlord and state that the tenant agrees to waive his or her rights against the landlord.

FIGURE 5.3 Shopping Center Lease

SHOPPING CENTER LEASE

On _____, THIS LEASE is entered into by and between _____ (hereinafter "Landlord") and _____ (hereinafter "Tenant"), for the term, at the rental and subject to and upon all of the terms, covenants and agreements hereinafter set forth.

1. PREMISES

1.1 Premises. Landlord hereby leases to Tenant and Tenant hereby rents from Landlord those certain Premises situated in the City of _____, County of _____, State of California as shown on Exhibit A hereto. The Premises are approximately _____ feet in frontage by _____ feet in depth, containing approximately _____ square feet of floor area. The Premises, together with and including other property opwned by Landlord, comprise a Shopping Center Development (hereinafter "Shopping Center") and are now devoted to or are being developed for the purpose of a shopping center. Tenant acknowledges that the site plan for the Shopping Center is tentative and that Landlord may change the shape, size, location, number and extent of the improvements or tenancies now existing or presently contemplated and eliminate or add any improvements to any portion of the Shopping Center, provided Landlord shall not change the size or location of the Premises without Tenant's consent.

1.2 Work of Improvement. The obligations of Landlord and Tenant to perform the work and supply material and labor to prepare the Premises for occupancy are set forth in detail in Exhibit B hereto. Landlord and Tenant shall expend all funds and do all acts required of them in Exhibit B and shall have the work performed promptly and diligently in a first-class workmanlike manner.

2. TERM

The lease term shall be _____ full calendar years, plus the partial year in which the rental commences. The parties hereto acknowledge that certain obligations under various provisions hereof may commence prior to the lease term (for example, construction, indemnity, liability insurance, and others), and the parties agree to be bound by such provisions prior to the commencement of the lease term.

3. RENT

3.1 Minimum Rent. Tenant agrees to pay to Landlord as Minimum Rent, without notice or demand, the monthly sum of _____ _____ ($ _____), in advance, on or before the first day of each and every month during the term hereof, except that the first month's rent shall be paid upon the execution of this Lease. The rental shall commence (check applicable box):

☐ On _____, if the Premises are being leased in their "as is" condition or subject to such incidental work as is to be performed by Landlord prior to said date (this work, if any, to be set forth in the attached Exhibit B and in this latter event, the rental shall commence on said date only if Landlord shall have completed said work).

☐ 30 days after substantial completion of Landlord's Work as set forth in the attached Exhibit B or when the Tenant opens for business, whichever is sooner. Landlord agrees that it will, at its sole cost and expense and as soon as is reasonably possible, commence and pursue to completion the improvements to be erected by Landlord as shown on the attached Exhibit B. The term "substantial completion of the Premises" shall mean the date on which Landlord notifies Tenant in writing that the Premises are substantially complete to the extent of Landlord's Work specified in Exhibit B, with the exception of the work that Landlord cannot complete until Tenant performs necessary portions of its work or notifies Landlord of the selection of certain of its choices, if applicable. Tenant shall commence the installation of its fixtures and equipment and any of Tenant's Work as set forth in Exhibit B, promptly upon substantial completion of Landlord's Work in the Premises and shall diligently prosecute such installation to completion and shall open the Premises for business not later than the expiration of said 30-day period.

Rent for any period which is for less than one (1) month shall be a prorated portion of the monthly installment herein based upon a thirty (30)-day month. Said rental shall be paid to Landlord, without deduction or offset, in lawful money of the United States of America and at such place as Landlord may from time to time designate in writing.

3.2 Percentage Rent. Tenant shall also pay to Landlord additional rent in an amount equal to _____% of the amount of Tenant's gross sales made in, upon or from the Premises during each calendar year of the Lease term, less the aggregate amount of the Minimum Rent previously paid by Tenant for said calendar year.

A. Payment. Within thirty (30) days after the end of each calendar month following the commencement of the obligation to pay Minimum Rent, Tenant shall furnish to Landlord a written statement, certified by Tenant to be correct, showing the total gross sales made in, upon, or from the Premises during the preceding calendar month, and shall accompany each such statement with a payment to Landlord equal to the above stated percentage of the total monthly gross sales made in, upon, or from the Premises during each such month, less the Minimum Rent for such month if previously paid. Said statement and payment shall be made with the succeeding month's regular rental payment. Within thirty (30) days after the end of each calendar year of the term hereof, Tenant shall furnish to Landlord a written statement, certified to be correct, showing the total gross sales by months made in, upon, or from the Premises during the preceding calendar year, at which time an adjustment shall be made between Landlord and Tenant to the end that the total percentage rent paid for each such calendar year shall be a sum equal to the above stated percentage of the total gross sales made in, upon, or from the Premises during each such year of the term hereof, less the Minimum Rent for such year if previously paid, so that the percentage rent, although payable monthly, shall be computed and adjusted on an annual basis.

B. Gross Sales. The term "gross sales" as used in this Lease shall include the gross sales prices of every kind and nature from sales and services made in, upon, or from the Premises, whether upon credit or for cash, whether operated by Tenant or by subtenants, concessionaires or licensees of Tenant, excepting any rebates and/or refunds to customers and the amount of all sales tax receipts for which Tenant must account to any governmental agency. Sales upon credit shall be deemed cash sales and shall be included in the gross sales for the period during which the merchandise is delivered to the customer, whether or not title to the merchandise passes with delivery. All sales originating at the Premises shall be considered as made and completed there, though bookkeeping and payment of the account may be transferred to another place for collection and though actual filing of the sale or service order and actual delivery of the merchandise may be made from a place other than the Premises.

C. Bookkeeping and Inspection. Tenant shall keep full, complete and proper books, records and accounts of its daily gross sales, both for cash and on credit, whether by Tenant or by subtenants, concessionaires or licensees of Tenant, made in, upon or from the Premises. Such books, records and accounts shall be kept at the Premises or at such other place as Landlord may approve in writing. Landlord and its agents and employees shall have the right at any and all times, during regular business hours, to examine, inspect and copy all such books, records and accounts, including any sales or use tax reports or returns pertaining to the business of Tenant conducted in, upon or from the Premises for the purpose of investigating and verifying the accuracy of any statement of gross sales. Landlord may once in any calendar year cause an audit of the business of Tenant to be made by an accountant of Landlord's selection, and if the statement of gross sales previously made to Landlord shall be found to be inaccurate, then there shall be an adjustment and one party shall pay to the other on demand such sums as may be necessary to settle in full the accurate amount of said percentage rent that should have been paid for the period or periods covered by such inaccurate statement or statements. Tenant shall keep all said records for three (3) years. If said audit shall disclose an inaccuracy in favor of Tenant of greater than a two (2%) percent error with respect to the amount of gross sales reported by Tenant for the period of said report, then Tenant shall immediately pay to Landlord the cost of such audit; otherwise, the cost of such audit shall be paid by Landlord. If such audit shall disclose any willful or substantial inaccuracies this Lease may thereupon be cancelled and terminated at the option of Landlord.

FIGURE 5.3 Shopping Center Lease (Continued)

4. SECURITY DEPOSIT

Concurrently with Tenant's execution of this Lease, Tenant shall deposit with Landlord the sum of _____ ($_____).
Said sum shall be held by Landlord as a Security Deposit for the faithful performance by Tenant of all of the terms, covenants, and conditions of this Lease to be kept and performed by Tenant during the term hereof. If Tenant defaults with respect to any provision of this Lease, including but not limited to the provisions relating to payment of rent or any monetary sums due hereunder, Landlord may (but shall not be required to) use, apply or retain all or any part of this Security Deposit for the payment of any rent or any such monetary sum in default or any other amount which Landlord may spend or become obligated to spend by reason of Tenant's default or to compensate Landlord for any other loss or damage which Landlord may suffer by reason of Tenant's default. If any portion of said Deposit is so used or applied, Tenant shall, within ten (10) days after written demand therefor, deposit cash with Landlord in an amount sufficient to restore the Security Deposit to its original amount; Tenant's failure to do so shall be a material breach of this Lease. Landlord shall not be required to keep this Security Deposit separate from its general funds, and Tenant shall not be entitled to interest on such Deposit. If Tenant shall fully and faithfully perform every provision of this Lease to be performed by it, the Security Deposit or any balance thereof shall be returned to Tenant (or, at Landlord's option, to the last assignee of Tenant's interest hereunder) at the expiration of the Lease term and after Tenant has vacated the Premises. In the event of termination of Landlord's interest in this Lease, Landlord shall transfer said Deposit to Landlord's successor in interest, whereupon Tenant agrees to release Landlord from all liability for the return of such Deposit or the accounting therefor.

5. RENTAL ADJUSTMENTS

5.1 Tax and Other Charges. In addition to the rental otherwise provided in this Lease, and as of the commencement of the obligation to pay Minimum Rent, Tenant shall pay to Landlord the following items, herein called Adjustments:

A. All real estate taxes and insurance premiums on the Premises, including land, building, and improvements thereon. Said real estate taxes shall include all real estate taxes and assessments that are levied upon or assessed against the Premises, including any gross income taxes or excise taxes or any taxes which may be levied on rents, possession, leasing, operation or management or which are based on this transaction or any document to which Tenant is a party creating or transferring any interest in the Premises or in this Lease. Said insurance shall include all insurance premiums for fire, extended coverage, public liability, and any other insurance that Landlord deems necessary on the Premises. Said taxes and insurance premiums for purpose of this provision shall be reasonably apportioned in accordance with the total floor area of the Premises as it relates to the total floor area of the Shopping Center which is from time to time leased as of the first day of each calendar quarter (provided that if any tenants in said building or buildings pay taxes directly to any taxing authority or carry their own insurance, as may be provided in their leases, their square footage shall not be deemed a part of the total floor area of the Shopping Center).

B. That percentage of the total cost of the following items as Tenant's total floor area bears to the total floor area of the Shopping Center which is from time to time completed as of the first day of each calendar quarter:

(i) All real estate taxes and assessments and all insurance costs both as above defined, and all costs to maintain, repair, and replace the parking lots, sidewalks, driveways and other areas used in common by the tenants or occupants of the Shopping Center.

(ii) All costs to supervise and administer said parking lots, sidewalks, driveways and other areas used in common by the tenants or occupants of the Shopping Center. Said costs shall include such fees as may be paid to a third party and shall in any event include a fee to Landlord for supervision and administration in an amount equal to ten percent (10%) of the total costs of (i) above.

(iii) Any parking charges, utilities surcharges, or any other costs levied, assessed or imposed by or at the direction of or resulting from statutes or regulations or interpretations thereof, promulgated by any governmental authority in connection with the use or occupancy of the Premises or the parking facilities serving the Premises.

5.2 Payments. Upon commencement of rental Landlord shall submit to Tenant a statement of the anticipated, monthly adjustments for the period between such commencement and the following December 31st, and Tenant shall pay these Adjustments on a monthly basis concurrently with the payment of rental. Tenant shall continue to make said monthly payments until notified by Landlord of a change thereof. By March 1st of each year Landlord shall endeavor to give Tenant a statement showing the total Adjustments for the Shopping Center for the prior calendar year and Tenant's allocable share thereof, prorated from the commencement of rental. In the event the total of the monthly payments which Tenant has made for the prior calendar year is less than Tenant's actual share of such Adjustments, then Tenant shall pay the difference in one lump sum within ten (10) days after receipt of such statement from Landlord and shall concurrently pay the difference in monthly payments made in the then calendar year and the amount of monthly payments which are then calculated as monthly Adjustments based on the prior year's experience. Any overpayment by Tenant shall be credited towards the monthly Adjustments next coming due. The actual Adjustments for the prior year shall be used for purposes of calculating the anticipated monthly Adjustments for the then current year with actual determination of such Adjustments after each calendar year as above provided, except that in any year in which resurfacing is contemplated Landlord shall be permitted to include the anticipated cost of same as part of the estimated monthly Adjustments. Though the term has expired and Tenant has vacated the Premises, when the final determination is made of Tenant's share of said Adjustments for the year in which this Lease terminates, Tenant shall immediately pay any increase due over the estimated Adjustments previously paid and, conversely, any overpayment made shall be immediately rebated by Landlord to Tenant. Failure of Landlord to submit statements as called for herein shall not be deemed to be a waiver of Tenant's requirement to pay sums as herein provided.

5.3 Cost of Living Adjustment. Upon each fifth (5th) anniversary date of the commencement of the term of this Lease, the Minimum Rent shall be changed to an amount that bears the same relationship to the Minimum Rent in effect immediately preceding such adjustment which the consumer price index for the month in which said adjustment occurs bears to the index for the month five (5) years preceding the month in which such adjustment occurs. However, in no event shall the rent be reduced below the Minimum Rent in effect immediately preceding such adjustment. The consumer price index to be used is the <u>Consumer Price Index – All Items</u>, for the United States, published monthly by the United States Department of Labor, in which 1967 equals 100. If said Consumer Price Index is discontinued, the parties shall select another similar index which reflects consumer price levels and if the parties cannot agree on another index it shall be determined by binding arbitration.

6. PERSONAL PROPERTY TAXES

Tenant shall pay before delinquency all taxes, assessments, license fees and public charges levied, assessed or imposed upon or measured by the value of its business operation or its furniture, fixtures, leasehold improvements, equipment and other property of Tenant at any time situated on or installed in the Premises by Tenant. If at any time during the term of this Lease any of the foregoing are assessed as a part of the real property of which the Premises are a part, Tenant shall pay to Landlord upon demand the amount of such additional taxes as may be levied against said real property by reason thereof as reasonably apportioned by Landlord.

7. USE

7.1 Use. Tenant shall use the Premises for _____
and under the trade name, if any, specified in Section 1.1 hereof and for no other purpose and under no other trade name without the prior written consent of Landlord.

7.2 Suitability. Tenant acknowledges that neither Landlord nor any agent of Landlord has made any representation or warranty with respect to the Premises or the suitability of the Premises or the Shopping Center for the conduct of Tenant's business, nor has Landlord agreed to undertake any modification, alteration or improvement to the Premises except as provided in this Lease. The taking of possession of the Premises by Tenant shall conclusively establish that the Premises were at such time in satisfactory condition unless within fifteen (15) days after such date Tenant shall give Landlord written notice specifying in reasonable detail the respects in which the Premises or the building were not in satisfactory condition.

7.3 Uses Prohibited.

A. Tenant agrees that it will not use or permit any person to use the Premises for a second-hand store, auction, distress or fire sale or bankruptcy or going-out-of-business sale (whether or not pursuant to any insolvency proceedings), or for any use or purpose in violation of any governmental law or authority and that Tenant shall at its sole cost and expense promptly comply with all laws, statutes, ordinances and governmental rules, regulations and requirements now in force or which may hereafter be in force and with the requirements of any board of fire underwriters or other similar body now or hereafter constituted relating to or affecting the condition, use or

FIGURE 5.3 Shopping Center Lease (Continued)

occupancy of the Premises, excluding structural changes not relating to or affecting the condition, use of occupancy of the Premises, or not related or afforded by Tenant's improvements or acts. The judgment of any court of competent jurisdiction or the admission of Tenant in any action against Tenant, whether Landlord be a party thereto or not, that Tenant has violated any law, statute, ordinance or governmental rule, regulation or requirement, shall be conclusive of that fact as between Landlord and Tenant.

B. Tenant may not display or sell merchandise or allow carts, portable signs, devices or any other objects to be stored or to remain outside the defined exterior walls and permanent doorways of the Premises. Tenant further agrees not to install any exterior lighting, amplifiers or similar devices or use in or about the Premises any advertising medium which may be heard or seen outside the Premises, such as flashing lights, searchlights, loudspeakers, phonographs or radio broadcasts.

C. Tenant shall not do or permit anything to be done in or about the Premises nor bring or keep anything therein which will in any way increase the existing rate or affect any fire or other insurance upon the Premises or any building of which the Premises may be a part or any of its contents (unless Tenant shall pay any increased premium as a result of such use or acts), or cause a cancellation of any insurance policy covering the Premises or any building of which the Premises may be a part or any of its contents, nor shall Tenant sell or permit to be kept, used or sold in or about the Premises any articles which may be prohibited by a standard form policy of fire insurance.

D. Tenant shall not do or permit anything to be done in or about the Premises which will in any way obstruct or interfere with the rights of other tenants or occupants of the building of which the Premises may be a part or any other building in the Shopping Center, or injure or annoy them, or use or allow the Premises to be used for any unlawful or objectionable purpose, nor shall Tenant cause, maintain or permit any nuisance in, on or about the Premises. Tenant shall not commit or allow to be committed any waste in or upon the Premises. Tenant shall keep the Premises in a clean and wholesome condition, free of any objectionable noises, odors or nuisances.

7.4 Covenants to Operate; Radius Clause

A. Tenant agrees, continuously and uninterruptedly during the term of this Lease, it will operate and conduct Tenant's business in the Premises and be open for business and continuously remain open for business at least those days and hours as is customary for businesses of like character in the city in which the Premises are situated, except while the Premises are untenantable by reason of fire or other casualty or if Tenant's business is temporarily interrupted by strikes, lockouts or similar causes beyond the reasonable control of Tenant. Tenant agrees that it will at all times keep and maintain within and upon the Premises an adequate stock of merchandise and trade fixtures to service and supply the usual and ordinary demands and requirements of its customers and that it will keep its Premises in a neat, clean and orderly condition. Tenant agrees that all trash and rubbish of Tenant shall be deposited within receptacles and that there shall be no trash receptacles permitted to remain outside of the building. Tenant further agrees to cause such receptacles to be emptied and trash removed at its own cost and expense.

B. Tenant agrees that it will not directly or indirectly operate or own any similar type of business within a radius of three (3) miles from the location of the Premises. Without limiting Landlord's remedies, in the event Tenant should violate this covenant, Landlord may at its option include the gross sales of such other business as a part of the gross sales transacted from the Premises for the purpose of computing the percentage rent due hereunder.

8. UTILITIES

Tenant agrees to pay for all water, gas, power and electric current and all other utilities supplied to the Premises. If any utilities are furnished by Landlord, then the rates charged to Tenant shall not exceed those of the local public utility company if its services were furnished directly to Tenant, and shall not be less than its pro rata share of any jointly metered service as reasonably determined by Landlord. Landlord shall not be liable in damages or otherwise for any failure or interruption of any utility service being furnished to the Premises, and as such failure or interruption shall entitle Tenant to terminate this Lease.

9. MAINTENANCE AND REPAIRS; ALTERATIONS AND ADDITIONS; FIXTURES

9.1 Maintenance and Repairs

A. Repairs by Landlord. Landlord shall repair and maintain the structural portion of the Premises, including exterior walls and roof but excluding windows, plate glass and doors, unless such maintenance or repair is caused in whole or in part by the neglect, fault or omission of Tenant, its agents, employees or invitees, or by unauthorized breaking and entering, in which event Tenant shall pay to Landlord the cost of such maintenance and repair. Landlord shall have no obligation to repair until a reasonable time after the receipt by Landlord of written notice of the need for repairs. Unless otherwise specifically provided in this Lease, there shall be no abatement of rent and no liability of Landlord by reason of any injury to or interference with Tenant's business arising from the making of any repairs, alterations or improvements in or to any portion of the Premises, the building or the Shopping Center. Tenant waives the provisions of any law permitting Tenant to make repairs at Landlord's expense.

B. Repairs by Tenant. Tenant shall maintain in good order, condition and repair the interior of the Premises, including all heating and electrical equipment, any air conditioning equipment (and if there is an air conditioning system, Tenant shall secure and pay for a service contract for repairs and maintenance of said system to conform to the terms or requirements of any warranty which may be in effect) and plumbing and sprinkler systems installed therein, and the improvements and equipment installed by Tenant in the Premises, and shall replace all broken glass, including plate glass and exterior show windows, and repair any broken doors. Tenant shall make all other repairs, whether of a like or different nature, except those which Landlord is specifically obligated to make under the provisions of Section 9.1A above.

C. Tenant's Failure to Maintain. In the event Tenant fails to maintain the Premises in good order, condition and repair, Landlord shall give Tenant notice to do such acts as are reasonably required so to maintain the Premises. In the event Tenant fails promptly to commence such work or diligently prosecute the same to completion, Landlord may but is not obligated to do such acts and expend such funds at the expense of Tenant as are reasonably required to perform such work. Any amount so expended by Landlord shall be paid by Tenant promptly after demand with interest at ten percent (10%) per annum from the date of such work. Landlord shall have no liability to Tenant for any damage, inconvenience or interference with the use of the Premises by Tenant as a result of performing any such work or by reason of undertaking the repairs required by Section 9.1A above.

D. Condition Upon Expiration of Term. Upon the expiration or earlier termination of this Lease, Tenant shall surrender the Premises in good condition, ordinary wear and tear and damage by causes beyond the reasonable control of Tenant only excepted. Tenant shall indemnify Landlord against any loss or liability resulting from delay by Tenant in so surrendering the Premises, including without limitation any claims made by any succeeding tenant founded on such delay.

9.2 Alterations and Additions

A. Tenant shall not make any alterations or additions to the Premises without Landlord's prior written consent. All alterations, additions, and improvements made by Tenant to or upon the Premises, except counters or other removable trade fixtures, shall at once when made or installed be deemed to have attached to the freehold and to have become the property of Landlord; provided, however, if prior to termination of this Lease, or within fifteen (15) days thereafter, Landlord so directs by written notice to Tenant, Tenant shall promptly remove the additions, improvements, fixtures, trade fixtures and installations which were placed in the Premises by Tenant and which are designated in said notice and shall repair any damage occasioned by such removal and in default thereof Landlord may effect said removal and repairs at Tenant's expense.

B. Before commencing any such work or construction in or about the Premises, Tenant shall notify Landlord in writing of the expected date of commencement thereof. Landlord shall have the right at any time and from time to time to post and maintain on the Premises such notices as Landlord deems necessary to protect the Premises and Landlord from mechanics' liens, materialmen's liens, or any other liens.

9.3 Installation of Fixtures.
It is mutually agreed that in order to expedite the commencement of Tenant's business in the Premises, Tenant may enter upon the Premises for the purpose of installing trade fixtures and furnishings during the construction period, provided that such activity on the part of Tenant shall be done only in such manner as not to interfere with construction and that Landlord shall not be liable to Tenant for damage to or loss of such fixtures, equipment or furnishings, Tenant accepting the full risk for such damage or loss, if any. Tenant shall pay for all utilities consumed by Tenant or its contractors in preparing the Premises for the opening of Tenant's business.

FIGURE 5.3 Shopping Center Lease (Continued)

10. ENTRY BY LANDLORD

Landlord, its agents and employees, may enter the Premises at all reasonable times for the purpose of exhibiting the same to prospective purchasers or tenants.

Tenant hereby grants to Landlord such licenses or easements in and over the Premises or any portion thereof as shall be reasonably required for the installation or maintenance of mains, conduits, pipes or other facilities to serve the Shopping Center or any part thereof.

Landlord, its agents and employees, shall have free access to the Premises during all reasonable hours for the purpose of examining the same to ascertain if they are in good repair and to make reasonable repairs which Landlord may be required or permitted to make hereunder.

11. LIENS

Tenant shall keep the Premises and the property in which the Premises are situated free from any liens arising out of any work performed, materials furnished or obligations incurred by or on behalf of Tenant. Landlord may require, at Landlord's sole option, that Tenant provide to Landlord, at Tenant's sole cost and expense, a lien and completion bond in an amount equal to one and one-half (1½) times the estimated cost of any improvements, additions, or alterations in the Premises which Tenant desires to make, to insure Landlord against any liability for mechanics' or materialmen's liens and to insure completion of the work.

12. INDEMNITY

12.1 Indemnity. Tenant shall indemnify and hold harmless Landlord from and against any and all claims arising from Tenant+s use of the Premises or the conduct of its business or from any activity, work, or thing done, permitted or suffered by Tenant in or about the Premises, and shall further indemnify and hold Landlord harmless from and against any and all claims arising from any breach or default in the performance of any obligation on Tenant's part to be performed under the terms of this Lease, or arising from any act or negligence of Tenant or any of its agents, employees, guests or invitees, and from and against all costs, attorney's fees, expenses and liabilities incurred in or about any such claim or any action or proceeding brought thereon; and in case any action or proceeding be brought against Landlord by reason of any such claim, Tenant upon notice from Landlord shall defend the same at Tenant's expense by counsel reasonably satisfactory to Landlord. Tenant, as a material part of the consideration to Landlord, hereby assumes all risk of damage to property or injury to persons in, upon or about the Premises from any cause other than Landlord's gross negligence or willful misconduct, and Tenant hereby waives all claims in respect thereof against Landlord.

12.2 Exemption of Landlord from Liability. Except for the gross negligence or willful misconduct of Landlord, Landlord shall not be liable for injury or damage which may be sustained by the person, goods, wares, merchandise or property of Tenant, its employees, invitees or customers, or any other person in or about the Premises, caused by or resulting from fire, steam, electricity, gas, water or rain, which may leak or flow from or into any part of the Premises, or from the breakage, leakage, obstruction or other defects of the pipes, sprinklers, wires, appliances, plumbing, air conditioning or lighting fixtures, whether the damage or injury results from conditions arising upon the Premises or upon other portions of the building of which the Premises are a part, or from any other source. Landlord shall not be liable for any damage arising from any act or neglect of any other tenant of the Shopping Center.

13. LIABILITY INSURANCE

Tenant shall, at Tenant's expense, obtain and keep in force during the term of this Lease a policy or comprehensive public liability insurance insuring Landlord and Tenant against any liability arising out of the ownership, use, occupancy or maintenance of the Premises and all areas appurtenant thereto in a combined single limit of not less than $1,000,000 for bodily injury and/or property damage. The limits of such insurance shall not limit the liability of Tenant hereunder. Tenant may provide this insurance under a blanket policy, provided that said insurance shall have a Landlord's protective liability endorsement attached thereto. If Tenant shall fail to procure and maintain said insurance, Landlord may, but shall not be required to, procure and maintain same, but at the expense of Tenant. Insurance required hereunder shall be in companies rated A+AAA or better in "Best Insurance Guide." Tenant shall deliver to Landlord, prior to right of entry, copies of policies of liability insurance required herein or certificates evidencing the existence and amounts of such insurance with loss payable clauses satisfactory to Landlord. No policy shall be cancellable or subject to reduction of coverage. All such policies shall be written as primary policies not contributing with and not in excess of coverage which Landlord may carry.

14. DAMAGE OR DESTRUCTION

In the event the Premises are damaged by fire or other perils covered by extended coverage insurance, Landlord agrees forthwith to repair them, and this Lease shall remain in full force and effect, except that Tenant shall be entitled to a proportionate reduction of the Minimum Rent from the date of damage and while such repairs are being made, such proportionate reduction to be based upon the extent to which the damage and making of such repairs shall reasonably interfere with the business carried on by Tenant in the Premises. If the damage is due to the fault or neglect of Tenant, its agents or employees, there shall be no abatement of rent. In no event shall percentage rent be abated.

In the event the Premises are damaged as a result of any cause other than the perils covered by fire and extended coverage insurance, then Landlord shall forthwith repair them provided the extent of the destruction is less than ten percent (10%) of the then full replacement cost of the Premises. In the event destruction of the Premises is to an extent of ten percent (10%) or more of the then full replacement cost, Landlord shall have the option either (1) to repair or restore such damage, this Lease continuing in full force and effect but the Minimum Rent to be proportionately reduced as above stated, or (2) to give notice to Tenant at any time within sixty (60) days after such damage, terminating this Lease as of the date specified in such notice, which date shall be no more than thirty (30) days after the giving of such notice. In the event of giving such notice, this Lease shall expire and all interest of Tenant in the Premises shall terminate on the date so specified in such notice and the Minimum Rent, reduced by a proportionate reduction as above stated, shall be paid to the date of such termination.

Notwithstanding anything to the contrary contained in this Article, Landlord shall have no obligation to repair, reconstruct or restore the Premises when the damage resulting from any casualty covered under this Article occurs during the last twenty-four (24) months of the term of this Lease or any extension thereof. If fifty percent (50%) or more of the Shopping Center is damaged by any cause even though the Premises may not be affected, Landlord may give notice to Tenant at any time within sixty (60) days after such damage, terminating this Lease as of the date specified in such notice, which date shall be no more than thirty (30) days after the giving of such notice.

Landlord shall not be required to repair any injury or damage by fire or other cause, or to make any repairs or replacements of any leasehold improvements, fixtures, or other personal property of Tenant.

15. CONDEMNATION

If twenty-five percent (25%) or more of the Premises shall be taken or appropriated by any public or quasi-public authority under the power of eminent domain, either party hereto shall have the right, at its option, within sixty (60) days after such taking or appropriation, to terminate this Lease upon thirty (30) days' written notice to the other. If any part of the Premises are so taken (and neither party elects to terminate as herein provided), the Minimum Rent thereafter to be paid shall be equitably reduced. If any part of the Shopping Center other than the Premises is so taken, Landlord shall have the right, at its option, within sixty (60) days of said taking, to terminate this Lease upon written notice to Tenant. In the event of any taking or appropriation whatsoever, Landlord shall be entitled to any and all awards and/or settlements which may be given and Tenant shall have to claim against Landlord for the value of any unexpired term of this Lease. Nothing contained herein, however, shall be deemed to preclude Tenant from obtaining, or to give Landlord any interest in, any award to Tenant for loss of or damage to Tenant's trade fixtures and removable personal property or for damage for cessation or interruption of Tenant's business.

16. ASSIGNMENT AND SUBLEASE

Tenant shall not voluntarily or by operation of law assign, transfer, mortgage or otherwise encumber all or any part of Tenant's interest in this Lease or in the Premises, and shall not sublet or license all or any part of the Premises, without the prior written consent of Landlord in each instance, and any attempted assignment, transfer, mortgage, encumbrance, subletting or license without such consent shall be wholly void. Without in any way limiting Landlord's right to refuse to give such consent for any other reason or reasons, Landlord reserves the right to refuse to give such consent if in Landlord's sole discretion and opinion the quality of merchandising operation is or

FIGURE 5.3 Shopping Center Lease (Continued)

may be in any way adversely affected during the term of this Lease or the financial worth of the proposed new tenant is less than that of the Tenant executing this Lease at the time of such execution.

No subletting or assignment, even with the consent of Landlord, shall relieve Tenant of its obligation to pay the rent and to perform all of the other obligations to be performed by Tenant hereunder. The acceptance of rent by Landlord from any other person shall not be deemed to be a waiver by Landlord of any provision of this Lease or to be a consent to any assignment, subletting or other transfer. Consent to one assignment, subletting or other transfer shall not be deemed to constitute consent to any subsequent assignment, subletting or other transfer.

The covenants and conditions herein contained shall apply to and bind the heirs, successors, executors, administrators and assigns of Tenant.

17. WAIVER OF SUBROGATION

Landlord and Tenant hereby mutually waive their respective rights of recovery against each other for any loss insured by fire, extended coverage and other property insurance policies existing for the benefit of the respective parties. Each party shall apply to its insurer to obtain said waivers and shall secure any special endorsements if required by its insurer to comply with this provision.

18. SUBORDINATION; ATTORNMENT; QUIET ENJOYMENT

18.1 Subordination. This Lease at Landlord's option shall be subordinate to all ground or underlying leases which now exist or may hereafter be executed affecting the Premises or the land upon which the Premises are situated or both, and to the lien of any mortgages or deeds of trust in any amount or amounts whatsoever now or hereafter placed on or against the land or improvements or either thereof, of which the Premises are a part, or on or against Landlord's interest or estate therein, or on or against any ground or underlying leases. Tenant agrees to execute any further instruments which may be requested or required to evidence such subordination. If any mortgage, trustee or ground lessor shall elect to have this Lease prior to the lien of its mortgage, deed of trust or ground lease, and shall give written notice thereof to Tenant, this Lease shall be deemed prior to such mortgage, deed of trust or ground lease, whether this Lease is dated prior or subsequent to the date of said mortgage, deed of trust or ground lease or the date of the recording thereof.

18.2 Attornment. In the event any proceedings are brought for default under any ground or underlying lease or in the event of foreclosure or the exercise of the power of sale under any mortgage or deed of trust covering the Premises, Tenant shall attorn to the purchaser upon any such foreclosure or sale and recognize such purchaser as the Landlord under this Lease, provided said purchaser expressly agrees in writing to be bound by the terms of this Lease.

18.3 Quiet Enjoyment. Upon Tenant paying the rent reserved herein and observing and performing all of the provisions on Tenant's part to be observed and performed hereunder, including compliance with any Covenants, Conditions or Restrictions affecting the Premises or the Shopping Center, Tenant shall have quiet possession of the Premises during the entire term of this Lease, subject to all provisions hereof and of any such Covenants, Conditions or Restrictions, and to the terms of any said ground or underlying lease, mortgage or deed of trust.

19. DEFAULT; REMEDIES

19.1 Default. The occurrence of any of the following shall constitute a default and breach of this Lease by Tenant:

A. Any failure by Tenant to pay the rent or any other monetary sums required to be paid hereunder (where such failure continues for five (5) days after written notice by Landlord to Tenant);

B. The abandonment or vacating of the Premises by Tenant;

C. A failure by Tenant to observe or perform any other provision of this Lease to be observed or performed by Tenant, where such failure continues for thirty (30) days after written notice thereof by Landlord to Tenant; provided, however, that if the nature of the default is such that the same cannot reasonably be cured within said thirty (30) day period, Tenant shall not be deemed to be in default if Tenant shall within such period commence such cure and thereafter diligently prosecute the same to completion.

D. The making by Tenant of any general assignment or general arrangement for the benefit of creditors; the filing by or against Tenant of a petition to have Tenant adjudged a bankrupt or of a petition for reorganization or arrangement under any law relating to bankruptcy (unless, in the case of a petition filed against Tenant, the same is dismissed within sixty (60) days); the appointment of a trustee or receiver to take possession of substantially all of Tenant's assets located at the Premises or of Tenant's interest in this Lease, where possession is not restored to Tenant within thirty (30) days; or the attachment, execution or other judicial seizure of substantially all of Tenant's assets located at the Premises or Tenant's interest in this Lease, where such seizure is not discharged within thirty (30) days.

19.2 Remedies. In the event of any such default or breach by Tenant, Landlord may at any time thereafter, without limiting Landlord in the exercise of any right or remedy at law or in equity which Landlord may have by reason of such default or breach:

A. Maintain this Lease in full force and effect and recover the rent and other monetary charges as they become due, without terminating Tenant's right to possession, irrespective of whether Tenant shall have abandoned the Premises. In the event Landlord elects not to terminate this Lease, Landlord shall have the right to attempt to re-let the Premises at such rent and upon such conditions and for such a term, and to do all acts necessary to maintain or preserve the Premises, as Landlord deems reasonable and necessary, without being deemed to have elected to terminate this Lease, including removal of all persons and property from the Premises; such property may be removed and stored in a public warehouse or elsewhere at the cost of and for the account of Tenant. In the event any such re-letting occurs, this Lease shall terminate automatically upon the new tenant taking possession of the Premises. Notwithstanding that Landlord fails to elect to terminate this Lease initially, Landlord at any time during the term of this Lease may elect to terminate this Lease by virtue of such previous default of Tenant.

B. Terminate Tenant's right to possession by any lawful means, in which case this Lease shall terminate and Tenant shall immediately surrender possession of the Premises to Landlord. In such event Landlord shall be entitled to recover from Tenant all damages incurred by Landlord by reason of Tenant's default, including without limitation the following; (i) The worth at the time of award of any unpaid rent which had been earned at the time of such termination; plus (ii) the worth at the time of award of the amount by which the unpaid rent which would have been earned after termination until the time of award exceeds the amount of such rental loss that is proved could have been reasonably avoided; plus (iii) the worth at the time of award of the amount by which the unpaid rent for the balance of the term after the time of award exceeds the amount of such rental loss that is proved could be reasonably avoided; plus (iv) any other amount necessary to compensate Landlord for all the detriment proximately caused by Tenant's failure to perform his obligations under this Lease or which in the ordinary course of events would be likely to result therefrom; plus (v) at Landlord's election, such other amounts in addition to or in lieu of the foregoing as may be permitted from time to time by applicable State law. Upon any such re-entry Landlord shall have the right to make any reasonable repairs, alterations or modifications to the Premises which Landlord in its sole discretion deems reasonable and necessary. As used in (i) above, the "worth at the time of award" is computed by allowing interest at the rate of ten percent (10%) per annum from the date of default. As used in (ii) and (iii) above, the "worth at the time of award" is computed by discounting such amount at the discount rate of the U.S. Federal Reserve Bank at the time of award plus one percent (1%). The term "rent," as used in this Section 19, shall be deemed to be the rent to be paid pursuant to Section 3 and all other monetary sums required to be paid by Tenant pursuant to the terms of this Lease.

19.3 Late Charges. Tenant hereby acknowledges that late payment by Tenant to Landlord of rent or other sums due hereunder will cause Landlord to incur costs not contemplated by this Lease, the exact amount of which will be extremely difficult to ascertain. Such costs include, but are not limited to, processing and accounting expenses and late charges which may be imposed on Landlord by the terms of any mortgage or deed of trust covering the Premises. Accordingly, if any installment of rent or any other sum due from Tenant shall not be received by Landlord or Landlord's designee within ten (10) days after such amount shall be due, Tenant shall pay to Landlord a late charge equal to ten percent (10%) of such overdue amount. The parties hereby agree that such late charge represents a fair and reasonable estimate of the costs that Landlord would incur by reason of late payment by Tenant. Acceptance of such late charge by Landlord shall in no event constitute a waiver of Tenant's default with respect to such overdue amount, nor prevent Landlord from exercising any of the other rights and remedies granted hereunder.

FIGURE 5.3 Shopping Center Lease (Continued)

19.4 Default by Landlord. Landlord shall not be in default unless Landlord fails to perform obligations required of it within a reasonable time, but in no event later than thirty (30) days after written notice by Tenant to Landlord and to the holder of any first mortgage or deed of trust covering the Premises whose name and address shall have theretofore been furnished to Tenant in writing, specifying wherein Landlord has failed to perform such obligations; provided that if the nature of Landlord's obligation is such that more than thirty (30) days are required for performance, then Landlord shall not be in default if Landlord commences performance within such thirty (30)-day period and thereafter diligently prosecutes the same to completion.

20. PARKING AND COMMON AREAS

Landlord covenants that upon completion of the Shopping Center certain common and parking areas shall lbe at all times available for the non-exclusive use of Tenant during the full term of this Lease, provided that the condemnation or other taking by any public authority, or sale in lieu of condemnation, of any or all of such common and parking areas shall not constitute a violation of this covenant, and Landlord reserves the right to close, if necessary, all or any portion of such common or parking areas to such extent as may in the opinion of Landlord's counsel be legally necessary to prevent a dedication thereof or the accrual of any rights of any person or of the public therein; to close temporarily all or any portion of the common areas to discourage non-customer use; to use portions of the common areas while engaged in making additional improvements or repairs or alterations to the Shopping Center; and to do and perform such other acts in, to, and with respect to the common areas as Landlord shall reasonably determine to be appropriate for the Shopping Center. Landlord further reserves the right to increase or reduce the common areas and to change the entrances, exits, traffic lanes and the boundaries and locations of such common and parking areas, provided that no such modifications or changes shall materially reduce the total amount of the common or parking areas available under this Section.

20.1 Prior to the date of Tenant's opening for business in the Premises, Landlord shall cause said common and parking area or areas to be graded, surfaced, marked and landscaped at no expense to Tenant.

20.2 Landlord shall keep said parking and common areas in a neat, clean and orderly condition and shall repair any damage to the facilities thereof, but all expenses in connection with said parking and common areas shall be charged and pro rated in the manner as set forth in Section 5 above.

20.3 Tenant, for the use and benefit of Tenant, its agents, employees, customers, licensees and sub-tenants, shall have the non-exclusive right in common with Landlord, and other present and future owners and tenants and their agents, employees, customers, licensees and sub-tenants, to use said common and parking areas during the entire term of this Lease.

20.4 Tenant, in the use of said common and parking areas, agrees to comply with such reasonable rules and regulations and charges for parking as Landlord may adopt from time to time for the orderly and proper operation of said common and parking areas. Such rules may include but shall not be limited to the following: (1) Restriction of employee parking to a limited, designated area or areas; and (2) Regulation of the removal, storage and disposal of Tenant's refuse and other rubbish at the sole cost and expense of Tenant.

21. MERCHANTS ASSOCIATION

Tenant will become a member of and participate fully and remain in good standing in the Merchants Association (as soon as it has been formed), organized for tenants occupying space in the Shopping Center, and Tenant will abide by the regulations of such Association. Each member tenant shall have one (1) vote, and Landlord shall also have one (1) vote, in the operation of said Association. The objects of such Association shall be to encourage its members to deal fairly and courteously with their customers, to encourage ethical business practices, and to assist the business of the tenants by sales promotion and centerwide advertising. Tenant agrees to pay the dues established by and to the Merchants Association, provided that in no event shall the dues paid by Tenant in any fiscal year of said Association exceed twenty cents (20¢) per square foot of the Premises leased to Tenant. Default in payment of dues shall be treated in similar manner to default in rent with like rights of Landlord at its option to the collection thereof on behalf of the Merchants Association.

22. SIGNS

Tenants may affix and maintain upon the glass panes and supports of the show windows and within twelve (12) inches of any window and upon the exterior walls of the Premises only such signs, advertising placards, names, insignia, trademarks and descriptive material as shall have first received the written approval of Landlord as to type, size, color, location, copy nature and display qualities. Anything to the contrary in this Lease notwithstanding, Tenant shall not affix any sign to the roof. Tenant shall, however, erect one sign on the front of the Premises not later than the date Tenant opens for business, in accordance with a design to be prepared by Tenant and approved in writing by Landlord.

23. MISCELLANEOUS

23.1 Rules and Regulations. Tenant shall faithfully observe and comply with the rules and regulations that Landlord shall from time to time promulgate and/or modify. Landlord shall not be responsible to Tenant for the non-performance of any of said rules and regulations by any other tenants or occupants.

23.2 Estoppel Certificate. Tenant shall at any time and from time to time, upon not less than three (3) days' prior written notice from Landlord, execute, acknowledge and deliver to Landlord a statement in writing (a) certifying that this Lease is unmodified and in full force and effect (or, if modified, stating the nature of such modification and certifying that this Lease as so modified is in full force and effect), and the date to which the rental and other charges are paid in advance, if any, and (b) acknowledging that there are not, to Tenant's knowledge, any uncured defaults on the part of Landlord hereunder, or specifying such defaults if any are claimed, and (c) setting forth the date of commencement of rents and expiration of the term hereof. Any such statement may be relied upon by any prospective purchaser or encumbrancer of all or any portion of the real property of which the Premises are a part.

23.3 Transfer of Landlord's Interest. In the event of a sale or conveyance by Landlord of Landlord's interest in the Premises or the Shopping Center, other than a transfer for security purposes only, Landlord shall be relieved of all obligations and liabilities accruing thereafter on the part of Landlord provided that any funds in the hands of Landlord at the time of transfer in which Tenant has an interest shall be delivered to Landlord's successor.

23.4 Captions; Attachments; Defined Terms.

A. The captions of the paragraphs of this Lease are for convenience only and shall not be deemed to be relevant in resolving any question of interpretation or construction of any section of this Lease.

B. Exhibits and addenda attached or affixed hereto are deemed a part of this Lease and are incorporated herein by reference.

C. If there be more than one Tenant, the obligations hereunder imposed shall be joint and several; as to a Tenant which consists of husband and wife, the obligations shall extend individually to their sole and separate property as well as community property. The term "Landlord" shall mean only the owner or owners at the time in question of the fee title or a tenant's interest in a ground lease of the Premises or the Shopping Center. The obligations contained in this Lease to be performed by Landlord shall be binding on Landlord's successors and assigns only during their respective periods of ownership.

23.5 Entire Agreement. This Lease constitutes the entire agreement between Landlord and Tenant relative to the Premises and supersedes any prior agreements, brochures or representations, whether written or oral. This Lease may be altered, amended or revoked only by an instrument in writing signed by both Landlord and Tenant. This Lease shall not be effective or binding on any party until fully executed by both parties hereto.

23.6 Severability. If any provision of this Lease shall be determined by a court of competent jurisdiction to be invalid or unenforceable, the remainder of this Lease shall not be affected thereby, and each term and provision of this Lease shall be valid and enforceable to the fullest extent permitted by law.

23.7 Costs of Suit. If Tenant or Landlord shall bring any action for any relief against the other, declaratory or otherwise, arising out of this Lease, including any suit by Landlord for the recovery of rent or possession of the Premises, the losing party shall pay the successful party a reasonable sum for attorneys' fees which shall be deemed to have accrued on the commencement of such action and shall be paid whether or not such action is prosecuted to judgment.

FIGURE 5.3   Shopping Center Lease (Concluded)

23.8 Time. Time is of the essence of this Lease and each and every provision hereof, except as to the conditions relating to the delivery of possession of the Premises to Tenant.

23.9 Binding Effect; Choice of Law. The parties hereto agree that all the provisions hereof are to be construed as both covenants and conditions as though the words importing such covenants and conditions were used in each separate paragraph hereof, and all rights and remedies of the parties shall be cumulative and non-exclusive of any other remedy at law or in equity. This Lease shall be governed by the laws of the state where the Shopping Center is situated.

23.10 Waiver. No covenant, term or condition or the breach thereof shall be deemed waived, except by written consent of the party against whom the waiver is claimed, and any waiver or the breach of any covenant, term or condition shall not be deemed to be a waiver of any covenant, term or condition. Acceptance by Landlord of any performance by Tenant after the time the same shall have become due shall not constitute a waiver by Landlord of the breach or default of any covenant, term or condition unless otherwise expressly agreed to by Landlord in writing.

23.11 Surrender of Premises. The voluntary or other surrender of this Lease by Tenant, or a mutual cancellation thereof, shall not work a merger, and shall at the option of Landlord terminate all or any existing subleases or may at the option of Landlord operate as an assignment to it of any or all such subleases.

23.12 Holding Over. If Tenant remains in possession of the Premises after the expiration of the term hereof with the written consent of Landlord, such occupancy shall be from month to month only, and not a renewal hereof or an extension for any further term, and in such case rent and other monetary sums due hereunder shall be payable in the amount and at the time specified in this Lease, and such month to month tenancy shall be subject to every other term, covenant and agreement contained herein.

23.13 Inability to Perform. If either party hereto shall be delayed or prevented from the performance of any act required hereunder by reason of strike, labor trouble, acts of God or any other cause beyond the reasonable control of such party (financial inability excepted), and such party is otherwise without fault, then performance of such act shall be excused for the period of the delay, provided that the foregoing shall not excuse Tenant from the prompt payment of any rental or other charge required of Tenant hereunder unless otherwise specifically so stated in this Lease.

23.14 Reasonable Consent. Wherever in this Lease Landlord or Tenant is required to give its consent or approval to any action on the part of the other, such consent or approval shall not be unreasonably withheld.

23.15 Interest on Past Due Obligation. Except as expressly herein provided, any amount not paid to Landlord when due shall bear interest at ten percent (10%) per annum from the due date. Payment of such interest shall not excuse or cure any default by Tenant under this Lease.

23.16 Notices. All notices or demands of any kind required or desired to be given by Landlord or Tenant hereunder shall be in writing and shall be deemed delivered forty-eight (48) hours after depositing the notice or demand in the United States mail, certified or registered, postage prepaid, addressed to Landlord or Tenant respectively at the addresses set forth after their signatures at the end of this Lease.

23.17 Corporate Authority. If Tenant is a corporation, each individual executing this Lease on behalf of said corporation represents and warrants that he is duly authorized to execute and deliver this Lease on behalf of said corporation in accordance with the By-Laws of said corporation, and that this Lease is binding upon said corporation in accordance with its terms.

23.18 Recordation. Neither Landlord nor Tenant shall record this Lease. If Landlord so elects, it may record a short form hereof, in which case Tenant agrees to execute and deliver to Landlord a notarized copy of the memorandum of such short form.

23.19 Brokers. Tenant warrants that it has had no dealings with any real estate broker or agents in connection with the negotiation of this Lease excepting only Grubb & Ellis Company and it knows of no other real estate broker or agent who is entitled to a commission in connection with this Lease.

IN WITNESS WHEREOF, Landlord and Tenant have executed this Lease the date and year first above written.

(If Landlord or Tenant is a corporation, the corporate seal must be affixed and the authorized officers must sign on behalf of the corporation. The Lease must be executed by the President or a Vice President and the Secretary or Assistant Secretary unless the By-Laws or a Resolution of the Board of Directors shall otherwise provide, in which event the By-Laws or a certified copy of the Resolution, as the case may be, must be furnished.)

Landlord:	Tenant:
By: _____	By: _____
By: _____	By: _____
Address:	Address:
_____	_____
_____	_____
_____	_____

THIS LEASE HAS BEEN PREPARED FOR SUBMISSION TO YOUR ATTORNEY WHO WILL REVIEW THE DOCUMENT AND ASSIST YOU TO DETERMINE WHETHER YOUR LEGAL RIGHTS ARE ADEQUATELY PROTECTED. GRUBB & ELLIS COMPANY IS NOT AUTHORIZED TO GIVE LEGAL OR TAX ADVICE; NO REPRESENTATION OR RECOMMENDATION IS MADE BY GRUBB & ELLIS COMPANY OR ITS AGENTS OR EMPLOYEES AS TO THE LEGAL SUFFICIENCY, LEGAL EFFECT OR TAX CONSEQUENCES OF THIS DOCUMENT OR ANY TRANSACTION RELATING THERETO. THESE ARE QUESTIONS FOR YOUR ATTORNEY WITH WHOM YOU SHOULD CONSULT BEFORE SIGNING THIS DOCUMENT.

6. *Subordination:* This provision states that the tenant, if not in default, will continue to enjoy the premises in the event of foreclosure or refinancing of the property. The lease will be subordinate to a mortgage in case of foreclosure, provided that the mortgage company agrees to recognize the tenant's lease and that the tenant is not in default. A financial institution will generally approve such a nondisturbance provision, particularly if it is part of a lease with a financially responsible chain tenant.

7. *Recapture:* A recapture clause is incorporated to enable the landlord to take back the store and terminate the lease should the tenant fail to do a minimum volume of business in a prescribed period of time. The clause is usually written to minimize a landlord's risk when dealing with unproven or financially weak tenants. If the owner wishes to rent to a new tenant who has limited capital but a promising future, it is often mutually advantageous to establish a low minimum rent. Such tenants can then use their funds to operate the store, enhancing their chances of success. The recapture provision limits the time factor of the risk. It is not uncommon to write a lease calling for no minimum rent, relying solely on the percentage. In both cases, the landlord is able to negotiate a higher than average percentage in lieu of the low minimum requirement. Most recapture clauses give the tenant the option to stay and pay a minimum rent based on recapture volume.

CONSTRUCTION EXHIBIT

This exhibit, which would accompany the lease, can be referred to as the *landlord's construction exhibit,* landlord's schedule of work to be performed or simply as Exhibit B or C. The document must be signed by both the owner and the tenant; it describes what the owner will furnish and what is expected from the tenant. A copy of this exhibit is shown in this chapter.

Within 10 days of the execution of the lease, the tenant is to provide the owner with a tenant improvement drawing—simple scaled construction plans for the space. A landlord will not permit work to be done that is inconsistent with the general plan of the shopping center. The tenant has to comply with a code that will ensure, for example, uniformity in the electrical wiring. The landlord reserves the right to approve all work performed by the tenant. If you have any difficulty reading a construction plan, consult with the landlord's architect or go directly to the landlord.

OFFER TO LEASE

When preparing an *offer to lease* for a landlord, attach a site or leasing plan to the form with the space for the prospective tenant outlined in

FIGURE 5.4 Construction Exhibit

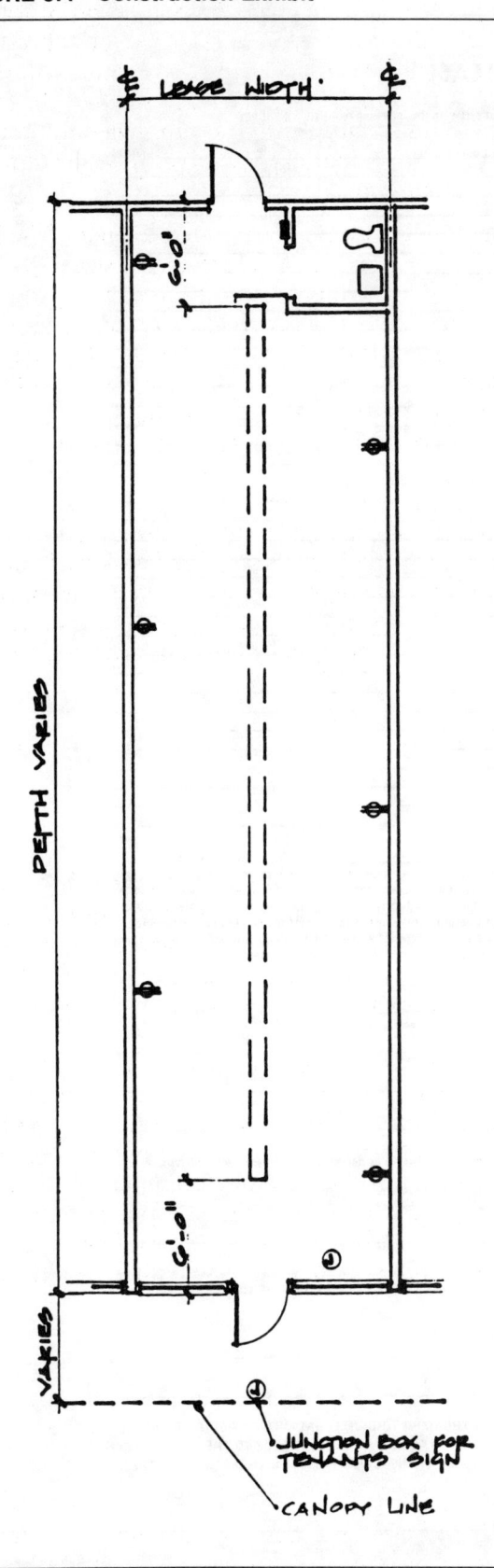

Owner agrees to furnish said store premises in the following manner:

- Rear door, if applicable.
- Electrical panel board and switches, not to exceed 100 AMP.
- Toilet including one water closet, one cold water lavatory, vent, one light bracket, outlet, partition and door to be located at rear wall in area to be designated by Owner.
- Concrete floors.
- 100 V duplex receptacles, three per party wall.
- One row, two tube fluorescent light fixtures provided and installed with one junction box. No lamps will be provided. Two rows light fixtures and two junction boxes provided and installed for stores wider than 16'.
- Heating and air conditioning for average retail use as provided by Owner's architect.
- Finished ceiling. Walls taped and spackled only. No paint.
- Sign outlets (sign by Tenant as per specifications provided by Owner's architect).
- Store front as designated by Owner's architect.

Tenant agrees:

Within 10 days from date hereof, to deliver to Owner fully dimensioned drawings with respect to requirements of Tenant, which drawings shall conform in all respects with the agreements of the Owner as above stated and shall be prepared by Owner's architect at Tenant's expense. Any work in addition to any of the items agreed to be performed by the Owner hereinbefore or any additional expenses, architectural or otherwise, accruing to Owner as a result of Tenant's use of demised premises or subsequent changes in drawings submitted by Tenant shall be at Tenant's own expense and cost, and shall be paid within 10 days after billing. Nonpayment of any of the above amounts shall be deemed a default under this lease.

To fixturize said store in a manner comparable to stores of a similar nature.

To provide signs, approved by Owner, partitions if required and all other requirements necessary to prepare and open said premises for the business herein authorized.

ACCEPTED BY:

TENANT _____

_____

OWNER _____

_____

FIGURE 5.5 Offer to Lease

OFFER TO LEASE

The undersigned (hereinafter "Tenant") hereby offers to lease the Premises described below on the following terms and conditions:

1. Premises. Located in the City of _____, County of _____, State of _____, described as follows: _____

2. Monthly Rent. _____

3. Term of Lease and Commencement Date. _____

4. Use of Premises. _____

5. Security Deposit; Prepaid Rent. _____

6. Taxes. _____

7. Insurance. _____

8. Utilities. _____

9. Improvements to Premises. _____

10. Other Terms and Conditions. _____

If this Offer to Lease is not accepted by the Landlord on or before _____, 19___ the Offer shall terminate, and all sums deposited herewith shall be promptly returned to Tenant upon receipt of a written request therefor. Upon acceptance of this Offer to Lease, Landlord is to proceed with the preparation of a Lease, it being expressly understood that this proposal is not binding on either of the parties and that the Lease, when executed by the parties, shall contain their full agreement. In the event the Landlord accepts this Offer to Lease and the parties are for any reason unable to consummate a Lease, all sums deposited herewith shall be promptly returned to Tenant upon receipt of a written request therefor. In consideration of Grubb & Ellis Company presenting this porposal to Landlord, Tenant agrees to conduct all negotiations through Grubb & Ellis Company in the event Tenant commences negotiation to lease or purchase the Premises during the one-year period following the date hereof.

Tenant acknowledges receipt of a copy hereof.

Date _____   Tenant _____

_____, _____   By _____
      City   State

Receipt is hereby acknowledged of cash ☐ check ☐ in the sum of _____

_____ dollars, to be delivered in accordance with the terms hereof.

Date: _____   Grubb & Ellis Company
                                            COMMERCIAL BROKERAGE SERVICES

_____, _____   By _____
      City   State

Landlord hereby accepts the foregoing Offer to Lease and appoints Grubb & Ellis Company its agent in connection with the lease of the Premises. Landlord agrees to pay a commission to Grubb & Ellis Company in accordance with the attached Schedule of Commissions. Landlord acknowledges receipt of a copy hereof.

Date: _____   Landlord _____

_____, _____   By _____
      City   State

NOTICE TO LANDLORD AND TENANT: GRUBB & ELLIS COMPANY IS NOT AUTHORIZED TO GIVE LEGAL OR TAX ADVICE; NO REPRESENTATION OR RECOMMENDATION IS MADE BY GRUBB & ELLIS COMPANY OR ITS AGENTS OR EMPLOYEES AS TO THE LEGAL SUFFICIENCY, LEGAL EFFECT OR TAX CONSEQUENCES OF THIS DOCUMENT OR ANY TRANSACTION RELATING THERETO, SINCE THESE ARE MATTERS WHICH SHOULD BE DISCUSSED WITH YOUR ATTORNEY.

red. An example of this form is shown later in this chapter. The location and description of the premises should be stated briefly but exactly. Indicate the per square footage foot as well as monthly and annual rental rates so the owner or developer can integrate the information into the overall financial plan of the center.

Note the specific type of lease that will be negotiated, for example, $.65 per square foot per month, net-net-net. The commencement date for the rental is usually 30 days from the time the landlord delivers the premises to the tenant or the day the store is opened to the public; if a tenant is able to open in three weeks, the rent starts at that time.

From a landlord's point of view, the statement concerning the use of premises should be as specific as possible; the tenant will usually want some leeway in this description to allow for the sale of related items.

Note that the security deposit is not to be interpreted by the tenant as rent paid in advance. Most landlords are sensitive about this point.

For taxes, insurance and utilities, write in "Paid by tenant."

Before you present any offer to lease, make certain that you have covered all major points in qualifying the tenant's financial capability.

EXCLUSIVE RIGHT TO SUBLEASE

As a retail salesperson, you handle both original leasing and subleasing. Market your services in basically the same fashion, but for a subleasing arrangement use a different document, the *exclusive right to sublease,* which follows.

FIGURE 5.6 Exclusive Right to Sublease

In consideration of the following agreements and of the efforts of GRUBB & ELLIS ("G&E") to secure sublet tenants for the property and improvements described below ("Property"), the undersigned ("Sublessor") hereby grants G&E the Exclusive Right to Sublease the Property for a period beginning on _____ and ending on _____ upon the following terms:

Address and/or legal description of Property:
_____
_____
_____

Rental Rates: _____
_____, or such lesser amount Sublessor may agree to accept.

Possession Date: _____

AGENCY TERMS

I. *SUBLESSOR WARRANTS:* That Sublessor leases the Property and has authority to execute this Agreement and grant to G&E the exclusive right to sublease the Property for the period provided herein.

II. *SUBLESSOR AGREES:* To cooperate fully with G&E and refer all inquiries to it, to conduct all negotiations through G&E, to pay G&E a real estate brokerage commission in the amount stipulated on and in accordance with the Schedule of Commissions included herein if (1) should a sublease agreement be consummated between the Sublessor and another party during the term of this Agreement of its extensions for all or a portion of the space described herein; (2) G&E or Sublessor or any other persons during the term of this appointment, produces a sublet tenant ready, willing and able to sublease the Property on the terms herein provided, or (3) a sublease is executed within six months after termination hereof to a prospect submitted by G&E during the term hereof, or to anyone on behalf thereof, whose name was disclosed to Sublessor. (4) Sublessor is relieved of their obligations under the original lease by the Landlord of the building or any other party through recapture, direct lease, etc. Sublessor also agrees to pay the cost of advertising the Property.

Sublessor also agrees, only in the event that G&E does not receive any commission(s) pursuant to or in connection with the terms of this Brokerage Agreement, that it will pay the cost of advertising the Property; provided, further, however, in such event, the costs of advertising shall not exceed _____ without the prior written authorization of the Sublessor.

III. *G&E AGREES:* To perform marketing efforts for the Property, take prospective tenants through the property at convenient times; to make a continued effort to sublease the property; and to direct the advertising for the property under the approval of the Sublessor. G&E is not charged hereunder with the custody of the Property, nor its management, upkeep or repair.

G&E shall enlist the services of other real estate brokers and agents ("Cooperating Brokers") in connection with the subleasing of the Property, and G&E agrees to act as coordinator of such Cooperating Brokers. Sublessor agrees to deliver to G&E a standard form of cooperating broker letter agreement to be used in connection with Co-operating Brokers.

IV. *ARBITRATION OF DISPUTES:* Any controversy or claim arising of or relating to this Agreement or the breach thereof, shall be settled by arbitration in Chicago, Illinois, in accordance with the rules of the American Arbitration Association, and judgement upon the award rendered by the arbitrators may be entered in any court having jurisdiction thereof.

V. *NON-DISCRIMINATION:* The parties hereto acknowledge that it is illegal for either Sublessor or G&E to refuse to display or to sell the Property to any person because of race, color, religion, national origin, sex or physical disability.

FIGURE 5.6 Exclusive Right to Sublease (Continued)

VI. *MISCELLANEOUS:* No amendment or alterations in the terms hereof with respect to the amount of commission or to the time of payment of commission shall be valid or binding unless made in writing and agreed to by Sublessor and G&E. Notices shall be given in writing by United States Registered Mail to the address indicated under the signature lines of this Agreement or as directed by either party from time to time. Notices are deemed to be given on the date deposited at an authorized United States mail receptacle. Sublessor agrees to indemnify and save harmless G&E, its officers and agents, against any and all actions, claims, damages and liabilities relating to damage or injury to person or property resulting from or occurring on or about the Property. If more than one Sublessor or sublet tenant is involved, the pronouns and grammatical structure shall be understood to conform. This Agreement shall be binding upon and inure to the benefit of their heirs, personal representatives, successors and assigns of the parties hereto.

COMMISSION

SUBLEASE COMMISSION

A. ON GROSS LEASES (subleases wherein the Sublessor is responsible for paying all or a major portion of the costs of maintaining and operating the Property).

Commission is 7% of the average annual rent, plus 2% of the remaining term rental. For gross leases less than one year, commissions shall be calculated as 8% of the total rental reserved in the sublease.

B. On NET LEASES (leases wherein the sublet tenant is responsible for paying all or a major portion of the costs of maintaining and operating the Property other than by way of tax and operating expense stops).

Initial commissions are calculated as 8% of the average annual rent, plus 3% of the remaining term rental reserved in the sublease. For subleases one year or less in term, commissions shall be calculated as 10% of the total rent reserved in the lease.

Notes: Average annual rental in A and B above is defined as the aggregate rental reserved in the sublease divided by the number of months defined by the term of that sublease multiplied by twelve (12).

Remaining term rental is the total rent reserved under the sublease less the amount of average annual rental. Rental shall exclude the rent reserved for any period which is subject to a Subtenant's option to cancel, unless cancellation fees are included in a sublet tenant's cancellation fee.

If a Cooperating Broker procures the subject tenant, G&E will receive a commission equal to one and one-half (1.5) times the amounts of the commissions, as defined herein, with the outside broker receiving one full commission distributed by G&E and G&E retaining one-half of a full commission as its compensation.

RENEWAL OPTION

If a sublease or separate instrument or agreement gives the sublet tenant an option of renewal or extension, the commission is due for the term of the sublease exclusive of the period covered by the renewal or extension period. In the event the sublet tenant exercises the option of renewal or extension, an additional commission will be due on the extended or additional period. In the event the sublet tenant remains in the premises under a new sublease or an amendment to the original lease, a commission shall be due equal to 2% of the rent for the entire renewal term. Any such commissions shall be due and payable at the time of the renewal or extension of the new sublease or amendment to the original lease.

ADDITIONAL SPACE OPTION

If a sublease or separate instrument or agreement gives the sublet tenant an option to lease additional space and the sublet tenant exercises such option, or at any time during the original term, whether or not the sublease or agreement for said additional space shall be upon the same terms and conditions as set forth in the original lease, then an additional commission is due equal to the amounts defined under A and B of this Commission Schedule shall apply. The additional commission shall be due and payable at the time the option is exercised or the new sublease is consummated.

FIGURE 5.6 Exclusive Right to Sublease (Concluded)

PAYMENT

Initial commissions are payable in full upon the consummation of the sublease. Nothing herein, however, shall preclude the broker from pursuing claims for a commission where the legal right to collect such commissions exists. Time is of the essence with respect to payment of all commissions.

By: G&E

Title: _____

Grubb & Ellis Company

By: Sublessor

Title: _____

_____

_____

_____

_____

Dated: _____

Dated: _____

FIGURE 5.7 Purchase Agreement

PURCHASE AGREEMENT
THIS DOCUMENT IS MORE THAN A RECEIPT FOR MONEY OR PRELIMINARY MEMORANDUM. IT WILL AFFECT YOUR LEGAL RIGHTS. READ IT CAREFULLY.

_____, STATE _____, 19_____
Received from _____
(hereinafter "Buyer") the sum of _____
dollars ($_____), by check ☐ note ☐ cash ☐ draft ☐ as a deposit on account of the purchase price of _____ dollars
($_____), for that certain property situated in the city of _____,
County of _____, State of _____, and described as follows: _____

TERMS OF SALE

1. The aforementioned deposit shall be placed in the trust account of Grubb & Ellis Company, Commercial Brokerage Services ("Broker") promptly upon acceptance of this Agreement by Seller. Upon opening of Escrow, Broker shall place the deposit in Escrow for the account of Buyer. The remainder of the purchase price shall be deposited in Escrow by Buyer as follows:

2. Within _____ days after Seller's acceptance of this Agreement, an Escrow shall be opened at _____ to consummate this transaction, which Escrow shall have a time limit of _____ days from the date of opening thereof.

3. As soon as reasonably possible following the opening of Escrow, Seller shall pay for and furnish to Buyer a Preliminary Title Report on the subject property, together with full copies of all Exceptions set forth therein, including but not limited to covenants, conditions, restrictions, reservations, easements, rights and rights of way of record, liens, leases and other matters of record. Buyer shall have _____ days after receipt of said Preliminary Title Report within which to notify Seller and Escrow in writing of Buyer's disapproval of any such Exceptions. In the event of such disapproval, Seller shall have until the time limit for closing of Escrow within which to attempt to eliminate any disapproved Exceptions from the Policy of Title Insurance to be issued in favor of Buyer. Failure of Buyer to disapprove any Exceptions within the above time limit shall be deemed an approval of said Preliminary Title Report. The Policy of Title Insurance shall be a California Land Title Association Standard Coverage Policy with a liability not exceeding the total purchase price and shall be paid for by _____.

4. Taxes, rentals, insurance premiums, interest on encumbrances and operating expenses, if any, shall be prorated as of the date of recordation of the deed to Buyer. Seller shall pay the costs of revenue stamps; Buyer and Seller shall each pay one-half of the Escrow fees.

5. Buyer acknowledges that the subject property has been examined to Buyer's satisfaction and agrees to purchase it in the condition disclosed by such examination and further acknowledges that Buyer is not making the purchase in reliance upon any statements or representations as to the condition of the subject property made by Seller or Broker other than as set forth in this Agreement.

6. By acceptance of this Agreement, Seller warrants that all appliances and mechanical equipment located on the subject property are and shall be in good working order, condition and repair as of the close of Escrow, except as follows:

By acceptance of this Agreement, Seller warrants that Seller has not received nor is Seller aware of any notification from any governmental authority requiring work to be done on the subject property. Seller further warrants that if such notice is received by Seller during the Escrow, and if Seller elects not to perform such work at its sole cost and expense, then Seller shall give notice of such requirement to Buyer and the Escrow. Buyer shall have five (5) days after receipt of said notice within which to elect not to consummate this transaction subject to said requirement; failure to so elect within the above time limit shall be deemed an approval of said requirement.

FIGURE 5.7 Purchase Agreement (Continued)

7. In the event any contingency to this offer has not been eliminated or satisfied within the time limits and pursuant to the provisions of this offer, the contract resulting from Seller's acceptance hereof shall be deemed null and void; the deposit, less Escrow expenses, shall be returned immediately to the Buyer, and the Escrow shall cancel automatically without further instructions to Escrow.

8. Without being relieved of any liability under the contract resulting from Seller's acceptance of this offer, Buyer reserves the right to take title to the subject property in a name other than as shown above.

9. This instrument along with any exhibits or addenda attached hereto shall constitute the entire Agreement between Seller and Buyer and supersedes any and all prior written or oral agreements between and among the parties and their agents, all of which are merged into or revoked by this Agreement.

10. In the event this offer is not accepted by Seller in writing on or before _____, 19_____, this offer shall become null and void and the deposit made herewith shall be returned to Buyer.

11. If Buyer fails to complete said purchase as herein provided by reason of any default of Buyer, Seller shall be released from his obligation to sell the subject property to Buyer and may proceed against Buyer upon any claim or remedy which he may have in law or equity; provided, however, that by placing their initials here, Buyer: (_____) and Seller: (_____) agree that Seller shall retain the above-mentioned deposit as his liquidated damages. If the subject property is a dwelling with no more than four units, one of which Buyer intends to occupy as his residence, Seller shall retain as liquidated damages the deposit actually paid, or an amount therefrom, not in excess of 3% of the purchase price, and promptly return any excess to Buyer. Each subsequent payment to be included hereunder as liquidated damages requires initialing of an additional like statement.

12. If the only controversy or claim between the parties arises out of or relates to the disposition of the deposit made by Buyer, such controversy or claim shall be decided by arbitration in accordance with the Rules of the American Arbitration Association, and judgment upon the award rendered by the arbitrator(s) may be entered in any court having jurisdiction thereof. The provisions of California Code of Civil Procedure Section 1283.05 shall be applicable to such arbitration.

13. In any action or proceeding arising out of this Agreement, the prevailing party shall be entitled to reasonable attorney's fees and costs.

14. Time is of the essence of this Agreement and every provision hereof. All modifications or extensions shall be in writing signed by both Buyer and Seller.

15. For additional terms of sale, see attached Addendum. ☐ (check here if applicable)

GRUBB & ELLIS COMPANY, COMMERCIAL
BROKERAGE SERVICES

By _____

Address _____

_____

_____

Telephone _____

I agree to purchase the property described above on the terms and conditions herein set forth and hereby acknowledge receipt of a copy of this Agreement.

BUYER

By _____

By _____

Address _____

_____

Telephone _____

Grubb & Ellis Company and its agents do not give legal or tax advice. This document should be submitted to an attorney and tax consultant for approval of the legal sufficiency and tax consequences.

FIGURE 5.7 Purchase Agreement (Concluded)

_____, _____   _____ 19____
                            STATE

The undersigned Seller acknowledges receipt of the foregoing Purchase Agreement and accepts same; Seller agrees to sell said property on the terms and conditions set forth in said Purchase Agreement.

A real estate commission for services rendered in the amount of _____ (_____ %) percent of the accepted sales price shall be paid to Grubb & Ellis Company in lawful money of the United States through escrow. The undersigned agrees to pay said commission at the time of closing of the transaction and to defend and hold harmless Grubb & Ellis Company, its agents and employees from and against any and all costs and expenses, including attorney's fees, resulting from the rights or demands of the parties under said Purchase Agreement, unless Grubb & Ellis Company is determined by a court of competent jurisdiction to be at fault in connection with said claim.

SELLER _____

By _____

By _____

Address _____

_____

Telephone _____

Grubb & Ellis Company and its agents do not give legal or tax advice. This document should be submitted to an attorney and tax consultant for approval of the legal sufficiency and tax consequences.

FIGURE 5.8 Exclusive Authorization of Lease

EXCLUSIVE AUTHORIZATION OF LEASE

OWNER hereby grants to GRUBB AND ELLIS COMMERCIAL BROKERAGE COMPANY ("Broker") the exclusive right to negotiate a lease or leases on the subject property (the "Property") for a period commencing on _____, 19___, and ending at midnight on _____, 19___. The Property is located in the City of _____, County of _____, State of _____, located at _____ and further described as _____,

_____.

The price and terms of the lease(s) shall be as follows: _____

In consideration of this Authorization and Broker's agreement diligently to pursue the procurement of a tenant or tenants for the Property, Owner agrees to pay Broker a commission or commissions as set forth in the attached SCHEDULE OF COMMISSIONS.

Owner shall pay said commission(s) to Broker if: (a) the Property is leased to tenant(s) by or through Broker, Owner or any other party prior to the expiration of this Authorization or any extension hereof; or (b) a tenant is procured by or through Broker, Owner or any other party who is ready, willing and able to lease the Property on the terms above stated or other terms reasonably acceptable to Owner prior to the expiration of this Authorization or any extension hereof; or (c) any contract for the lease of the Property is made directly or indirectly by Owner prior to the expiration of this Authorization or any extension hereof; or (d) the Property is withdrawn from lease without the written consent of Broker or made unmarketable by Owner's voluntary act during the term of this Authorization or any extension hereof; or (e) within one hundred eighty (180) days after the expiration of this Authorization or any extension hereof, the Property is leased to any person or entity with whom Broker has negotiated or to whom Broker has submitted the Property prior to such expiration in an effort to effect a transaction and whose name appears on any list of such persons or entities which Broker shall have mailed to Owner at the address below stated within thirty (30) days following such expiration, provided that if Broker has submitted a written offer to lease or purchase, it shall not be necessary to include the offeror's name on such list.

If a sale or other transfer or conveyance is made by Broker, Owner or any other party prior to the expiration of this Authorization or any extension hereof, or during the one hundred eighty (180)-day period thereafter, Owner shall pay Broker a commission as set forth in the attached SCHEDULE OF COMMISSIONS.

If during the term of this Authorization or any extension hereof an escrow is opened or negotiations involving the sale, transfer, conveyance or leasing of the Property have commenced and are continuing, then the term of this Authorization shall be extended for a period through the closing of such escrow, the termination of such negotiations or the consummation of such transaction, provided this Authorization would otherwise have expired during such period.

Owner agrees to cooperate with Broker in effecting a lease or leases of the Property and immediately to refer to Broker all inquiries of any party interested in the Property. All negotiations are to be through Broker. Broker is authorized to accept a deposit from any prospective tenant. Broker is further authorized to advertise the Property and shall have the exclusive right to place a sign or signs on the Property if, in Broker's opinion, such would facilitate the leasing thereof.

It is understood that it is illegal for either Owner or Broker to refuse to present, lease or sell to any person because of race, color, religion, national origin, sex, marital status or physical disability.

Owner warrants that he is the owner of record of the Property or has the legal authority to execute this Authorization. Owner agrees to hold Broker harmless from any liability or damages arising from any incorrect information supplied by Owner or any information which Owner fails to supply. Owner acknowledges receipt of a copy of this Authorization and the attached SCHEDULE OF COMMISSIONS, which Owner has read and understands.

If either Owner or Broker commences any litigation to enforce the terms of this Authorization, the prevailing party shall be entitled to receive a reasonable attorney's fee from the other party hereto.

No amendments or alterations in the terms hereof or withdrawal of this Authorization shall be valid or binding unless made in writing and signed by both Owner and Broker.

The heirs, transferees, successors and assigns of the parties hereto are duly bound by the provisions hereof.

DATED: _____, 19_____   OWNER: _____

ACCEPTED: GRUBB AND ELLIS COMMERCIAL
              BROKERAGE COMPANY

By _____

By _____

Address: _____

By _____   Telephone: _____

CHAPTER 5 / Forms and Legal Documents   73

FIGURE 5.9   Office—Retail—Industrial Income-Expense Summary

_____
Property

_____
Address and City

_____
Listing Number

TNT NO.	TENANT NAME	Bldg. Area Occupied Sq. Ft.	Monthly Rent ($)	Rent Sq. Ft.	Lease Term. Date	Options Footnote #1	(See Footnote #2) Tax	Ins.	Maint.	Last Year's Overage (Dollars)	% Clause Footnote #3	REMARKS
	TOTALS											

(1) An entry of 2-5 or 1-3 for example, signifies two five-year options or one three year option.
(2) L = Paid by landlord; T = Paid by tenant; I = Tax increase clause; TR = Taxes recoverable.
(3) An entry of "5%" would indicate a minimum rental vs. 5% of annual gross sales; or 1½¢ in the case of a gas station would indicate a minimum rental vs. 1½¢ per monthly gallonage pumped.

EXPENSES: (Estimated _____ Actual _____)
          Insurance (Fire & EC–Liability $ _____
          Gas & Electricity   _____
          Water   _____
          Garbage   _____
          Supplies   _____
          Janitorial–Gardener   _____
          Elevator   _____
          Air Conditioning   _____
          Replacement Reserve   _____
          Maintenance & Repair   _____
          Licenses   _____
          Management   _____
          Advertising   _____
          Miscellaneous   _____
          TOTAL ANNUAL OPERATING EXPENSES $ _____

COMMENTS:

Exercise A

1. Is it preferable to use a landlord's own lease form or your office's standard form?
2. a. According to the terms of the tenant representation agreement, how is your commission paid?
   b. Should the owner or the tenant be the one to pay your commission?
3. When should the tenant representation agreement be signed by your office? Why is this important?
4. If a tenant leases space that requires additional work before the business can open, when does the lease become effective?
5. a. In a lease transaction, why is it important to attach the schedule of commission to the commission agreement?
   b. How does this procedure differ in the case of a land sale?
6. What is meant by a recapture clause? Under what circumstances might this clause be incorporated into the lease?
7. Who is responsible for the cost of brochures generated as part of a market coverage for a piece of property?

Answer A

1. *It is preferable to use the landlord's lease form. Your office's standard lease form is the second choice.*
2. *a. According to the tenant representation agreement, you will be paid by the property owner if the owner executes a lease agreement with you. If you are not paid by the owner, the tenant agrees to pay you. Neither the owner nor the tenant, however, is obligated to pay you unless you have a separate agreement with each of them.*
3. *It is very important that your office not sign the agreement until the tenant has returned a signed copy to you. If your office signs the agreement before the tenant receives the form for signing, the tenant may try to make changes in the agreement with regard to commission or certain properties.*
4. *If the leased space is not ready for occupancy, the tenant has either 30 days from the time the landlord completes construction or whatever amount of time under 30 days it takes to prepare the premises for opening the store. The lease begins either on the thirtieth day or on the day the store is opened to the public, whichever is sooner.*
5. *a. In a lease transaction, the dollar amount of the commission cannot be written into the agreement, since the lease term and the exact rental rate are not yet known. The two documents together state that the signer agrees to pay you a commission per the attached schedule.*
   b. The commission agreement suffices for a land sale. The percentage of the total sales price that you stipulate as your com-

mission is written into the agreement. This document alone constitutes a complete contract to pay you a commission based on that percentage figure.

6. *A recapture clause permits the landlord to take back a store and terminate the lease should the tenant not do a minimum volume of business in a prescribed period of time. This clause may be incorporated into the lease to reduce a landlord's risk when dealing with a financially unproven tenant.*

7. *The owner is usually responsible for cost of brochures.*

# Ethical Questions

INTRODUCTION

How you handle yourself in problem situations will depend on how clearly you understand the legal and ethical implications of real estate transactions. In order to fulfill your duty to the client and to protect your reputation, you must always be aware of the possible consequences of your actions or failure to act. Many of the issues you will encounter do not have black and white answers. Rely on your judgment when you have researched a question and can feel secure in your position. If there is any doubt concerning the answer, seek the advice of a more experienced broker.

In this chapter, the broker's responsibility to the seller and to the buyer is discussed, as is the question of cooperating with outside brokers. Following these sections are two sets of questions that describe common situations in which ethical and legal issues are raised. Attempt to answer these problem situations by relying on both the preceding material and your own best judgment.

BROKER'S RESPONSIBILITY TO THE SELLER

A broker who takes a listing becomes an agent of the owner. As soon as the broker enters into the agency relationship, he or she also becomes a fiduciary. Fiduciary obligations include good faith, fair dealing, skill and diligence—qualities that are crucial to the real estate licensee.

The *agency* or *fiduciary relationship* as it operates in the field of real estate means that brokers and salespeople must act toward the principal in the highest good faith. This obligates you to disclose to the principal all facts within your knowledge that bear on the transaction. When the acts of an agent are questioned by the principal, the burden is on the agent to prove that he or she acted in good faith and made full disclosure. Brokers also have a fiduciary duty to use reasonable care and will be expected to show a high degree of skill and diligence.

The real estate licensee is affected by two basic sets of rules. One relates to licensing; it involves the disciplinary proceedings that can be brought against an agent by your state's real estate commission. The second set of rules refers to the obligations an agent owes the principal. These sets of rules are separate and distinct.

How are these rules applied? First, consider the duty to disclose. If the broker is the buyer, of course, he or she must disclose that fact. If a property comes on the market and the broker obtains a listing for less than market value, the broker is obligated to disclose that fact to the owner.

What if the broker knows of factors that will affect the future value of a property? Brokers and salespeople must remain current on all tax legislation and proposed regulations of any kind. If you learn that a property may be rezoned in the foreseeable future, you have an obligation to disclose that fact. Even if you personally do not know that a property will be rezoned, you are liable in this situation as well.

The broker has a duty to use the utmost skill, care and diligence in performing services for the client. If a listing is taken and nothing is done to promote or advertise it, the broker is liable regardless of whether the owner revokes the listing.

BROKER'S RESPONSIBILITY TO THE BUYER

A *cooperating broker,* by legal definition, becomes the agent of the seller and owes the same fiduciary responsibilities to the seller as does the listing broker. The questions are, who has fiduciary responsibilities to the buyer, and does the buyer have the right to insist that those obligations be fulfilled?

Cooperating brokers may find themselves in a very difficult position. If they know that the buyer is willing to pay more, must they disclose that fact to the seller? And if they do disclose it, won't the buyer object? In many instances, the buyer will have talked with and confided in the cooperating broker and will be relying on the broker's skill and ability. The buyer does not expect the broker to breach those confidences, yet the cooperating broker has a fiduciary obligation to the seller.

The legal consequences can be significant. For example, the cooperating broker may know that the property, for some reason, is about to increase in value. This fact would be beneficial to the buyer and is perhaps the reason the buyer wants to purchase the property. Presumably, both the listing and the cooperating broker have the obligation to disclose that fact to the seller.

An unethical cooperating broker may make representations to the buyer that the listing broker and the seller would never make. If the buyer acts on the basis of those false representations and is damaged, he or she can sue not only the cooperating broker but also the listing broker and the seller. Where a cooperating broker and a listing broker work together, the representation of each are held to be the representations of both. Thus, one broker can be liable for what the other says.

These problems are difficult, but there are guidelines to help you cope with them. First, always keep in mind your precarious legal position. Second, and most importantly, always act in good faith, deal with everyone with the greatest care and acknowledge that you are a fiduciary to each principal with whom you deal. Third, always spell out the rights and obligations of all parties involved. For a more thorough discussion of agency issues, please read *Agency Relationships in Real Estate* by John Reilly.

COOPERATING WITH OUTSIDE BROKERS

Most commercial brokerage firms follow the policies on cooperation with other brokers set forth in the code of ethics of their local real estate boards and The National Association of REALTORS®. Mutual cooperation is encouraged with all responsible brokerage firms that operate according to high standards of professional conduct.

Most productive salespeople are cooperative, both within the company and with outside brokers. A high percentage of the transactions made by most successful salespeople are cooperative deals.

You will be working in a relatively small community of brokers who know each other by reputation, if not personally. Since you must be cooperative in order to become a top producer, it is important that you start immediately to build your own good reputation.

Unfortunately, not all members of the real estate profession operate within proper professional boundaries. You should make it a policy to refrain from becoming involved in any way with those individuals or firms. If a salesperson or manager suspects dishonest or unethical conduct by another broker, it is the manager's responsibility to take action to protect the company's legal position and reputation.

If you are cooperating with an outside broker who is unknown or has a questionable reputation, it is particularly important to have that person sign a broker cooperation agreement. This is especially true when working with open listing information. At times, the situation may be reversed, and the outside broker will request that your office sign such an agreement.

To encourage cooperation within the brokerage community, no one is authorized to place advertising that solicits inquiries from "principals only." This will limit the number of people who may express an interest in the property, and it does not represent the seller properly.

Exercise A

1. You have received one or more offers from an outside broker and at the same time developed one of your own on an exclusive listing. How should the multiple offers be presented?

2. You have delivered your offer to a listing broker, but to your knowledge it has not yet been presented to the seller. How long should you wait for the broker to present your offer before you consider applying some sort of pressure?

3. An outside broker asks you to sign a broker cooperation agreement in return for information on property. Should you do it?

4. An outside broker mentions the name of a tenant to you, the listing broker. Does this constitute registration?

5. You have agreed to cooperate with an outside broker on a certain property, knowing full well that the broker does not have an exclusive listing. Must you now negotiate through that broker as long as the property is available?

Answer A

1. *All brokers can submit their offers to the owner in person. The presentations should be made in the order in which the offers were received. If another broker's offer was ahead of yours, that broker will make his or her presentation first. If someone tells you he or she will deliver an offer in person the next day, and you have just received an offer, tell this person that you are obligated to present the offers in the order in which they have been received. Don't ever leave a buyer with the impression that you are shuffling orders to suit yourself.*

2. *This depends on why the offer has not yet been presented. The seller may have been unavailable. However, if the broker has been too busy with other projects, you should insist that your offer be presented as soon as possible. If you get nowhere by applying pressure, ask your manager to assist you in handling the situation.*

3. *No. The broker probably does not have a client but simply wants to maneuver into an advantageous position with respect to commission, then seek out clients.*

4. *No. An orally communicated registration is usually not honored. However, if you happen to mention a tenant's name to a broker you know well and with whom you have already worked, he or she will probably consider it a registration. You should still follow up immediately with a letter.*

5. *Yes. You made the agreement with full knowledge of the broker's listing position. As long as the property is available and as long as you pursue the transaction you described to the broker, you have a moral and ethical obligation to deal through him or her rather than directly with the property owner.*

Exercise B

This exercise asks you to think about some of the ethical problems you will confront in your career. Back up your answers with reasons whenever possible.

CHAPTER 6 / Ethical Questions   81

1. You are in the office and a call is received at the switchboard from a person who got the company's number from a sign placed on a building by another salesperson. Unfortunately, that salesperson is out of the office, and the caller wants more information about the property. You answer the call and help the person as much as possible. Is this now your transaction, or does it still belong to the salesperson who put up the sign?

2. You are in the office and the receptionist asks if you will handle an incoming call from a potential client. You are in the retail division, but the caller needs an industrial building. What should you do?

3. You are looking for a property and mention it in one of your weekly sales meetings. One of the other salespeople says, "I've got the perfect building," and gives you the information on it. It is not listed in any of your company's listing systems and would therefore be considered a pocket listing. What do you owe to the salesperson who gave you the information?

4. If an outside broker has an exclusive listing for sublease, may you contact the owner of the property directly?

5. You cold call on a company and they say, "Yes, I know your firm. I'm working with John Doe of your office." What should you do and say?

6. One of the salespeople in your office has placed an open listing on a property in your firm's inventory system. You receive a call from an outside broker friend of yours requesting information on buildings similar to the open listing. Should you give out the open listing information, or should you check first with the salesperson who entered the building into the system?

Answer B

1. *The person who put up the sign should get the full commission. Help the caller as much as you can, then take his or her name and telephone number and relay it to your colleague.*

2. *You are not a specialist in industrial real estate. Transfer the call to someone in that division. (Always get the name and number of the caller in case the call is accidentally disconnected.)*

3. *Find out immediately why your colleague didn't put the listing into the system. If the answer sounds legitimate (perhaps the listing was received only the previous day, for instance), a 50-50 split is in order. But if the other salesperson has had the information for a week or so and simply does not want to share it except on his or her own terms, either refuse to get involved or take the problem to your manager.*

4. *Yes. The other broker should have already done so; if not, the broker has missed an opportunity that you can take advantage of.*

5. *Introduce yourself as a colleague, not a competitor. Keep your call brief, and try to demonstrate the advantage of working with*

your firm. If you are aware of the retail space inventory of your company, this situation need never arise.

6. *First, check with the lister to see if he or she objects to your handling the transaction yourself. If not, ask the outside broker to sign (or have the broker's manager sign) a broker cooperation agreement in return for the information. Your manager must agree to the broker cooperation agreement. Don't give out the information before you get the signature. There are two keys to this situation: First, any time you are dealing with someone else's listing, check with the lister. Second, never give the outside broker an opportunity to take an open listing away from you. The broker might, of course, find out from some other source that this is an open listing. But you needn't make it easier by giving away the location of the space.*

7

Telephone Techniques

INTRODUCTION

As a retail salesperson, you will find the telephone one of your most valuable tools for doing business. It can be a tremendous time-saver for you, if used properly.

The most important skill to develop is the ability to make initial contacts with owners and users, to qualify and make appointments with those who are in the market and with whom you might do business. You will be able to reach a broader range and greater quantity of retail users and owners in less time than if you made each call in person.

The techniques described in this chapter will help you develop this cold calling skill, understand how to apply it to reach your objectives and learn the general procedures for effective telephone usage.

STRATEGY FOR TELEPHONE COLD CALLS

The objective of telephone cold calls is to make appointments to talk to qualified prospects about their real estate needs. There are seven major steps in the strategy.

1. Get to the decision maker as quickly as possible.
2. Identify yourself, your company, and the division you represent.
3. Explain why you are calling.
4. Describe a benefit of the meeting you wish to arrange.
5. Ask for an appointment.
6. Counter objections.
7. Follow up.

Before you use this strategy, think through each step and plan what you will say for every call. After you have become familiar with the strategy, you should be able to review each step before a call in less than a minute. The following explanations illustrate what each step in the strategy should accomplish.

Get to the Decision Maker

If your purpose is to move a particular listing, or a group of listings, you will call the retail firms you think will be interested in the location and the type of buildings you have in mind. If you are calling to obtain a listing on a vacant building or to inquire about a vacant piece of property, you will want to talk with the owner.

Whether you are trying to find tenants or retail space, you will want to talk with the person who makes the company's real estate decisions. Your office probably maintains a master list of the real estate managers of all major retail users. If you are calling a large company, therefore, you should know which individual to contact. Your office should also maintain lists of property owners. Since real estate ownership is a matter of public record, owners' names can also be obtained from the title company's customer service department.

If you cannot give the name of a particular person when calling a company, chances are you will have to go through a switchboard. In this case, ask to be connected with the person in charge of real estate for the firm. The switchboard operator will probably give you the person's name. If not, ask for it. If you fail to do so, or if the operator simply puts you through to the real estate department, surely the secretary who answers the phone will provide you with a name.

In a small company, the president usually makes real estate decisions. Your initial contact might be a receptionist, not a switchboard operator. A receptionist will generally ask if you have an appointment when you call in person, but will usually put through a telephone call without question. If you do not know a specific individual to contact, simply ask to speak with the president, and get his or her name from the receptionist.

Master the pronunciation of a name before being put through. Mispronouncing a person's name or company's name is no way to begin a conversation, so get the name from the switchboard operator or receptionist. If it is unfamiliar, ask to have it spelled and pronounced, then write it down.

Exercise A

Jim Bardon has been trying to reach Dan Smart, real estate manager for the ABC Food Chain. He has called three times and each time Smart has not been available. He tries, again.

SECRETARY: *Mr. Smart's office.*

BARDON: *Hello. I'd like to speak with Mr. Smart, please.*

SECRETARY: *I'm sorry. Mr. Smart is not available at the moment.*

BARDON: *(Sighing) Okay. I'll call back. Goodbye.*

Evaluate this conversation. Had you been making the call, would you have done anything differently? If so, what?

Answer A

Bardon failed on three counts: He did not ask when Smart would be available, he did not ask Smart to return his call, nor did he ask for the secretary's name. He could, of course, have done either on his first call.

Exercise B

John Hastings is calling Sam Small of XYZ Corporation. He reaches Small's secretary and asks to speak with him.

SECRETARY: *Mr. Small is not in today.*

HASTINGS: *When will he be in?*

SECRETARY: *I expect him tomorrow morning.*

HASTINGS: *All right. I'll call him about 10:00.*

SECRETARY: *May I say who called?*

HASTINGS: *This is John Hastings, Smith and Jones Company, Retail Division.*

SECRETARY: *And what did you wish to speak with Mr. Jones about?*

HASTINGS: *Real estate.*

SECRETARY: *What about real estate?*

HASTINGS: *I want to inquire about his interest in some property I have listed.*

SECRETARY: *I see. May I give him more specific information?*

HASTINGS: *Well, it's a building on the corner of....*

Comment on this conversation.

Answer B

Hastings found out when Small would be available. He set a time to call again. But then he went too far. He began to explain his business to the man's secretary. He might receive a "no" from the secretary, or he might get through to Small. Even if he does get through, he's wasted enough time explaining himself to make another call.

Identify Yourself

Most secretaries will ask who is calling before putting a call through. Your best strategy is to take the initiative. Identify yourself and your company before you are challenged.

The next step is vitally important, for here you get to the heart of your call. You want to establish rapport, but at the same time you want to be brief and move immediately to the purpose of your call.

Explain Why You Are Calling

If you are promoting a location, you will be calling to discover the user's interest in it and space needs now or in the near future. If you are calling a company already leasing a particular spot, you will be trying to discover its needs and future plans. If you have a tenant, you will be calling owners of buildings or vacant land. You will ask them about availability, price and plans.

Remember, many of your telephone cold calls will not result in business right away. But you will have made important contacts and brought yourself and your office to the attention of a good many people. You will have added to your store of knowledge about your territory. No cold call is a complete failure, as long as it gains you even one piece of useful information.

Describe a Benefit of Your Meeting

So far, you have explained that you work for a real estate firm and told the prospect the reason you are calling. If the prospect has responded positively, he or she has a real estate need. Now you have to give a reason for meeting you face-to-face. You have to promise the person a potential benefit for granting you an appointment. State the benefit so that the prospect has an idea of how you can solve the real estate need. You might say to an owner, "I have some tenants who are interested in space in your shopping center."

Ask for an Appointment

After you have persuaded the prospect to meet with you, explain what you plan to accomplish at the meeting and be sure to suggest a specific time. Give a choice of times. This reduces the chances of the prospect flatly refusing you. He or she will feel obliged to explain why a certain day is impossible, and it will be easier to just agree to the alternate time.

An example of this technique is to say, "I would like to get together with you to show you the property and discuss your space needs. Which would be better, tomorrow morning at 11:15 or in the afternoon around 2:45?"

Remember, do not attempt to conduct a transaction over the telephone. The point of cold calling by phone is to make contacts and acquire information. The complexities of the real estate business demand that the details of any deal be discussed in person. The result of the phone call, the appointment, is what really produces business for you.

Exercise C

John Hawkins has just completed a productive cold call. He has found a retailer interested in discussing a location Hawkins has been promoting. Hawkins is now ready to make an appointment.

HAWKINS: *Let's get together and talk about this.*
RETAILER: *Good idea.*
HAWKINS: *How about tomorrow at 3:00?*
RETAILER: *Sorry, I can't make it at that time.*
HAWKINS: *Well... how about 10:00 the next morning?*
RETAILER: *Let's see... no, that's out too.*
HAWKINS: *Well, you set the time then.*

Comment on this conversation.

Answer C

Obviously, Hawkins lost control of the situation. He might recover, but even so he has wasted time and he might destroy what up to that point was a productive cold call. He failed to explain the purpose of the appointment and give the tenant a choice of appointment times. As a result, he allowed the tenant to take command of the situation.

Counter Objections

Make a list of all the objections you think you will receive and develop answers to them. Ask other salespeople with greater experience how they would handle those objections. Also, every time you get an objection you can't answer, write it down and have someone help you develop a response to it. If you keep a record of all these objections and answers, you will have a valuable reference book to use when the going gets rough.

Here are a few objections you might hear:

"The company might need more space, but everyone is too busy to think about it right now."

Zero in on time. Stress the obvious need for long-range planning to save time. To get started on that planning, with your help, would take only a few minutes. If the prospect remains adamantly opposed to considering specific future space needs now, try to get the present square footage and configuration requirements and an estimate as to how much additional space might be needed. At the very least, you can send the person brochures on property that might be suitable to get him or her thinking about you and your company. Later, follow up.

"Cost is a real problem. I can't afford more space now."

This might lead you in one of several directions. First, it is essential that you know the market and the specific area in which the company you are calling operates. It is up to you to demonstrate that a price represents the current market price for whatever type of building, business or location is under discussion. Do not, in your eagerness to make a deal, offer to obtain space for less than the going rate. And never be precise about rates. When you mention a range, your prospect will expect to get the minimum rate.

A company or a person with space to lease, sublease or sell might have a price in mind higher than the market will bear. Here again, you must know the market. It is a waste of time to take a listing at a price you know will prevent the property from moving. Never promise something you are not sure you can deliver. If a person will not accept the realities of the marketplace, you are much better off without the listing.

"This building is just too big for our needs."

Stress your many listings. Ask the prospect what the specific requirements are. Get an appointment to go over those requirements in detail at the present location. It is not wise simply to take a person's word about his space needs, because he or she might be mistaken about them. The prospect may insist, for example, that a 24-foot clearance is needed when in reality an 18-foot clearance would be adequate. You cannot tell, however, until you have inspected the present location.

"I've always worked with National Realty, and I'd just as soon continue with them."

This objection may come up from time to time. Certainly, you will not want to criticize the other firm. Point out, however, the advantages of working with a company of the size, type and location of yours. Emphasize that you and your company have a solid reputation for service. Stress the value of having access to services in addition to the other firm's. If all else fails, send company brochures and follow up.

Follow-up Calls

How many follow-up calls you will make during the course of a transaction, and what their nature will be, depends entirely on the situation. You might make several to gain more information or to set additional appointments as you progress toward closing a deal. On the other hand, a follow-up call might take place well in the future. A company with no real estate needs today might be interested in making a deal tomorrow. Many of the techniques and procedures involved in effective telephone cold calling also apply to follow-up calls.

EFFECTIVE TELEPHONE PROCEDURES

In order to make your phone calls more productive, you should develop a habit of using the following procedures.

1. *Plan.* Know what you are going to say before you put through the call. Make a list of the questions you are going to ask, the information you are going to convey and the agreements you want. Be sure to have all documents or reference materials at hand. Divide your prospects among those you are calling blind, those whom you know have property to move, those who might need more space and other groups. Then, stay with one group until you have exhausted that part of your list.

2. *Set a regular time.* Set aside time for making calls and stick to it as much as possible. Determine how many calls you are going to make during each allotted time and do nothing else. Cold calling tends to be smoother and more productive if you stay with the job until it is completed.

3. *Allow no distractions.* Don't be interrupted or otherwise distracted while you're making cold calls. During the time you allot to them, these calls must be the only business at hand. This principle applies to follow-up calls as well.

4. *Assume that every person you call is busy.* Everybody will be as busy as you are, so get to the point of your call immediately. Don't waste time discussing personal matters or other topics that bear no relationship to the purpose of your call.

5. *Don't break in.* Don't try to interrupt people in the midst of important transactions or conferences. If they are tied up, the secretary will say so. You have a choice: Call back or have them call you. Which should you do?

   That depends. If the person will be available in a short time, or later in the day, identify yourself and tell the secretary what time you will call back. Make a note of the time and be sure to follow up. If the person will not be available until the next day, or later, leave a message and your number so he or she can return your call. Do not, however, state your reason for calling. This is something you want to discuss with the decision maker, not a secretary. It is a waste of time to go through the explanation twice.

   However, do not wait too long for the return call. Jot down when the decision maker is supposed to call you back. If you don't hear from the person by that time, call again.

6. *Tone of voice and speech rate are important.* Your tone of voice and the rate at which you speak can help to establish rapport. Speak confidently, enthusiastically and courteously. Modulate your voice to avoid speaking in a boring, monotone. Adjust the speed at which you talk to that of the person on the other end of the line.

7. *Listening can be more important than talking.* Reading, writing, speaking and listening are the four communication skills. Among them, the last is most often ignored. Few things are more irritating than a person who is not listening to what you're saying. Don't concentrate so hard on your own thoughts that you fail to hear what the other person is saying. Listening becomes especially important when the person begins to show an interest in your call. He or she might have questions for you. Listen. Restate the questions so both of you understand them, then respond. Listening, like cold calling itself, is a skill that can be learned. But it cannot

be learned casually. You have to practice. Remember, you can listen yourself into more appointments—and more commissions—than you can talk yourself into.

8. *Do not interrupt or finish sentences.* Listening is closely tied to these two don'ts. Both behaviors indicate that you are impatient and are not really interested in what the other person has to say. If the individual speaks slowly, be patient. If he or she hesitates in choosing words, don't fill in with your own words. Remember, you are after business. You do not earn commissions by showing how articulate you are.

9. *Avoid technicalities.* The purpose of the telephone cold call is to establish contact, gather information, gain interest and make appointments. It is not intended for lengthy discussions of technical matters. Once the prospect is interested, get an appointment and end the call. Details can wait for the face-to-face meeting.

10. *Keep names confidential.* Keep tenants' names confidential until a transaction is well underway. If you mention your tenant's name or company when calling an owner, he or she is likely to tell others. Your tenant may decide to find another broker, or the owner may decide to go around you and contact the tenant directly. In either case you will lose a commission.

11. *Confirm and thank.* When ending the conversation, repeat the time and the day on which you will see the person. "Fine, I'll be there at 2:00 tomorrow afternoon."

    Thank the prospect. After all, he or she has taken the time to talk with you and given you an opportunity to present yourself, your company, your division and your product. Show your appreciation.

12. *Keep score.* It is a wise idea to keep a record of the calls you make and the number of appointments they produce. Keep trying to improve your score.

PRACTICE IS IMPORTANT

Effective cold calling can be mastered only through practice, but it is practically impossible to learn this skill efficiently by yourself. In the beginning, work with another salesperson. Trade roles now and then, and evaluate each other.

Evaluation does not stop once you are making cold calls on a regular basis. One can always improve. Evaluate each call carefully, especially those that seemed unproductive. See if you can detect what is consistently right or wrong in your approach.

Exercise D

John Bardwell has cold called Henry Steel, real estate manager of a regional hardware chain. Bardwell has learned that the chain is planning no new outlets in the near future and that plans for the following year have not been set. Then:

STEEL: *How are things with Smith and Jones?*

BARDWELL: *Going along very well, thank you.*

STEEL: *Are you a football fan?*

BARDWELL: *Oh, yes.*

STEEL: *What did you think of that game yesterday?*

BARDWELL: *Hey, wasn't that something! That last touchdown....*

Would you say that this cold call was successful or unsuccessful? Why? Would you have done anything different from Bardwell?

Answer D

The call was a success insofar as Bardwell gathered useful information—the possibility that the hardware chain would be in the market the following year. He would note that fact and file the information. On the other hand, he allowed the conversation to drift into irrelevancies, and even joined in. While you cannot completely avoid or ignore the pleasantries, after responding to Steel's question about Smith and Jones, Bardwell could have said, "Thank you, Mr. Steel. It has been nice talking to you."

Exercise E

George Leader of Smith and Jones has interested John Swan, real estate manager of a fabric chain, in a location he has listed.

SWAN: *Where is the building located?*

LEADER: *In the Pinehurst Shopping Center.*

SWAN: *Good traffic flow around that spot?*

LEADER: *Very good.*

SWAN: *Will we have to remodel?*

LEADER: *That depends....*

SWAN: *What about basement and storage space?*

LEADER: *Oh, I'm sure it's adequate.*

SWAN: *Who's next door?*

Evaluate this conversation. Would you have done anything differently from Leader?

Answer E

Leader was not doing badly here, but he was running the risk that the conversation would drift into a lengthy discussion of technicalities, which would have to be gone over again during an appointment. As that conversation began, he should have emphasized in general the positive aspects of the location to Swan, and then obtained an appointment to discuss it in detail.

Exercise F

Sarah Moody has adopted the following procedure for cold calling.

She makes her calls every Tuesday and Thursday morning. The nights before, she prepares and checks over the list of individuals and companies she plans to call. At about 9:15 a.m. each Tuesday and Thursday she begins her calls. When she completes the first one, she places a plus or minus sign next to the name and records any notes. She goes immediately to the next number. By 10:15 a.m. or so, she has completed the list. Cold calls have led to a good many commissions for Moody.

What four rules of effective telephone calling does Sarah Moody appear to follow?

Answer F

1. *She lists the calls she will make at each session.*

2. *She establishes a definite time to call, sits down and makes the calls.*

3. *She keeps score on the calls and maintains a record of comments.*

4. *She goes immediately from one call to another until all scheduled calls are made for the day, because her proficiency is greater when she continues the task until it is completed.*

Exercise G

As George Smith was making his second telephone contact of the day, his secretary came in with a paper to sign. He read it hastily and signed it, in the meantime losing his train of thought with the individual with whom he was speaking. He had to ask the prospect to repeat what he had just said. Five minutes later, a friend came in, scribbled a note about lunch and placed it before Smith. Smith glanced at it, nodded agreement and the friend left. A few minutes later, Smith's secretary placed some papers on his desk. Smith found that his calling time ran 15 minutes longer than usual that day, but he made only his regular number of calls. He seemed to have fewer successful calls than usual.

How would you evaluate Smith's performance that day?

Answer G

Smith, of course, was committing a serious error of telephone cold calling. He allowed himself to be distracted from the business at hand. Set a time for calling, work with a scheduled list of calls and allow no distractions while making the calls.

Exercise H

Dave Forman of Smith and Jones has cold called Marvin Vose, president of a regional fast food chain.

VOSE: *Well, as a matter of fact, we have been....*

FORMAN: *Thinking of opening an outlet in this area?*

VOSE: *No. We've been thinking of reevaluating our plans for the coming year. Right now it looks like....*

FORMAN: *You'll be expanding?*

VOSE: *No. We've about decided to slow down a bit and....*

FORMAN: *Wait a while?*

Evaluate this conversation.

Answer H

Obviously, Forman is not a good listener. He appears impatient and insists on finishing sentences for his prospective tenant. Nor is he a good guesser. If Forman makes a transaction here, it will be a minor miracle.

Exercise I

The following is a complete conversation between Harry Horlick of Smith and Jones and Marvin May, president of a regional drugstore chain. Evaluate both the good and the bad points of the call, then compare your observations with the ones that follow.

MAY: *Marvin May speaking.*

HORLICK: *Good morning, Mr. May. This is Harry Horlick, Smith and Jones Company, retail division.*

MAY: *Yes?*

HORLICK: *We're in the real estate business and....*

MAY: *Yes, Mr. Horlick. I've heard of Smith and Jones.*

HORLICK: *Well, what I'm calling about is this: I've observed that your company has no outlets in the territory for which I am responsible, which includes a section of 25th Street in Oakvale.*

MAY: *That's true. We don't have any outlets along that street.*

HORLICK: *I've done some investigating of the area, and also of the drugstore business and its real estate needs. And I've looked closely into the competition in that area. I have some prime locations that might interest you.*

MAY: *Indeed? Well, I....*

HORLICK: *Might we get together to discuss them?*

MAY: Well, Mr. Horlick, I don't know. Our plans for the future have not jelled yet.

HORLICK: I don't need very much of your time. Naturally you have planning to do; that's very important. I would just like the opportunity to lend my input to that planning. I think Smith and Jones can be of service to you.

MAY: Undoubtedly you can. Still, it might be too early to discuss specific areas.

HORLICK: On the other hand, having specific areas in mind can be very valuable in planning for expansion.

MAY: That's true. But....

HORLICK: I have my presentations in order, and it won't take much time to make them. The main idea is to give you more information to go on for your planning.

MAY: Well, perhaps you're right. Perhaps we should talk.

HORLICK: Fine. Would tomorrow at 3:00 p.m. or Wednesday at 10:00 a.m. be the best time for an appointment?

MAY: I'm sorry, I'll be out of town on both of those days.

HORLICK: Then how about Thursday at 10:00 a.m. or Friday at 3:00 p.m.?

MAY: Make it Thursday.

HORLICK: Fine. I'll see you then. Goodbye.

Answer I

Horlick got off to the right start with this greeting and his identification of himself, Smith and Jones, and the Retail Division. But he did not get immediately to the purpose of his call. With some prodding from May, he did get to the point. Horlick established himself as an alert, professional and quietly aggressive salesperson. He indicated that he was aware of May's company and interested in it. Horlick noted that the firm had no outlets in his area, and established his expertise by informing May that he had investigated the area with May's company in mind. He asked for an appointment at the earliest possible moment, although he did not succeed at that point.

He then turned an objection to his own advantage by pointing out how valuable his input could be to the drug company's planning for the future. Horlick assured May that he had done his homework well, that his presentations were in order, and that an interview would take only a little time. By being persistent, he brought May around. At that point Horlick moved in again for an appointment and offered May a choice of times. When May said he was not available either time, Horlick immediately responded by offering a choice of two other times until he got the appointment.

Horlick could have handled the closing better. He confirmed the appointment, but not in a complete fashion. He should have repeated the day and the time, impressing on May that he would not fail to be there.

On the whole, this cold call was a successful one. The flaws in Horlick's presentation can be corrected with practice and experience.

CONCLUSION

Above all, in making telephone cold calls—as in carrying out any other task as a retail salesperson—you should present yourself as an expert in your business. You won't know all the answers to the questions a prospective tenant, an owner or retail manager might ask during a cold call, but always tell the questioner you can find out and will call back. Follow through on all your promises. Be courteous on the phone, as in all your business dealings. Be persistent, aggressive and confident. The last quality will build as you follow the suggestions for cold calling in this chapter and as the number of cold calls you complete successfully increases.

Exercise J

Answer the following questions.

1. Why might it be easier to reach the person in authority by cold calling on the phone rather than in person?
2. What is the basic objective in telephone cold calling?
3. Should you mention your tenant's name in an initial call to an owner?
4. What are seven major steps in telephone cold calling?
5. If the decision maker is unavailable, should you call back or ask him or her to call you?

Answer J

1. *If you cold call in person, the receptionist might prove to be an obstacle. However, a call will usually be put through without question.*
2. *The basic objective is to set up appointments to talk to qualified prospects face-to-face about their real estate needs.*
3. *No. Tenants' names should always be kept confidential until a transaction is well under way.*
4. *The steps are (a) get to the decision maker as quickly as possible; (b) identify yourself and your company; (c) explain why you are calling; (d) describe a benefit of the meeting you wish to arrange; (e) ask for an appointment; (f) counter objections; and (g) follow up.*
5. *If the decision maker will be available in a short time, say that you will call back and specify at what time. If the person will not be available until the next day or much later, leave a message for him or her to call you, but do not state your reason for calling.*

8

Basic Selling Skills

INTRODUCTION

Some people seem to be "born salespeople." Selling seems to come easily to them, and they are successful with little effort.

Don't be fooled. No one is born anything—except a human being. Selling skills are acquired and they can be defined, analyzed, taught and learned. Those salespeople who perform seemingly without effort have simply honed these skills to a fine edge. But they had to learn them, and they are successful partly because they continue to learn and sharpen their skills.

This chapter is designed to introduce you to basic selling skills applicable in dealing with retail real estate, both buildings and vacant land. The techniques offered will start you on the road to developing selling skills in yourself. After you have completed this chapter you should:

1. understand the importance of leads in selling retail real estate

2. be familiar with general retail users' needs

3. understand the importance of qualifying a tenant initially and as the transaction progresses

4. be able to distinguish between features and benefits and understand how both must be related to prospects' needs and interests

5. be familiar with the use of supporting statements

6. know how to use questions effectively in the selling process

7. realize the importance of completing a transaction with an economical expenditure of time, and understand the skills involved in doing so

THE TASK

The dime store pitchmen hawking a gadget to slice vegetables have a narrowly defined task. They have one item to move, and they can concentrate on that one item's features and benefits while persuading people to buy it. The real estate salesperson's task is more complex. All prospects have definite needs—a family needs a house in which to live, a company needs office space or a place in which to sell products. Needs are peculiar to the individual prospect and must be refined—that is, qualified. Once prospective real estate has been matched to prospect's needs, the prospects generally have a choice—one of three houses, this building or that, one piece of vacant land instead of another.

Yet all of this takes time, and a salesperson's time is a precious commodity. Salespeople must keep transactions moving and bring them to successful conclusions—that is, bring their prospects to a decision—in the most efficient manner possible. Qualifying prospects, building their confidence, developing features and benefits and working toward a successful closing require a great deal of skill.

Who are your prospects? Broadly speaking, they are users and developers of retail shopping centers and the land for those centers. Either they come to you for service or you go to them and persuade them to use the service you offer. Prospects are everywhere. The owner with one of your competitor's signs on his or her building is your prospect. So is a retailer you cold call on Tuesday morning, or the owner of a vacant site you discover as you drive through your territory. And so is the president of a company you meet at a service club luncheon, or the company that reports a 25 percent increase in corporate earnings. However, if you sit and wait for the phone to ring or the door to open, you may obtain a few clients and make a few transactions, but you will never be truly successful.

PROSPECTS' NEEDS

What are the retail prospect's needs? The owner of a building or vacant land has one need—finding a suitable tenant or buyer who will rent or buy at a price sufficient to make the owner's investment profitable. For the retail space user, the list of needs is longer. There are at least 13 needs nearly all users share:

1. a certain number of square feet
2. good traffic counts
3. a certain type of location—neighborhood center, regional center, freestanding, mall, etc.

4. dock facilities (although this does not apply to all tenants)
5. good visibility to the customer
6. utility services
7. high volume retail neighbors
8. fire protection
9. parking spaces
10. easy access to major highway routes
11. ability to generate potential dollar volume
12. a specific tenant mix
13. a sufficient number of customers residing in an area specifically defined

These are general needs; how they are qualified depends on the individual user. Two users seldom have identical needs, even if they're in the same business. Part of qualifying tenants is to define their needs precisely—you must do this both for yourself and your tenants. Strangely enough, many tenants do not really know their retail space needs, regardless of how well they know their business.

In many cases, you begin to size up needs before you meet a prospect. It takes a skilled eye to do it well. A cold call can be a good place to start.

You drive up to the present location of HRH Company and park your car. HRH is a prestige department store with five locations (at present) and the company wants to expand. Before you enter the building to see the real estate decision maker, you observe it from all sides. Among other things, you make notes about the following items:

1. The tenant's store is located in a suburban shopping mall.
2. There is an American flag near the main entrance to the store.
3. The shopping mall is located at the intersection of two major suburban routes, one-half mile from a major north-south freeway.
4. The store is located in an upper-middle-class suburb consisting of private homes and prestige condominium units.
5. The tenants in the shopping mall include:
   - a major national retail chain appealing to bargain-minded shoppers,
   - a number of exclusive jewelry and china shops,
   - ten specialty dress shops carrying primarily more expensive clothes,
   - eight men's stores, again catering to the top-of-the-line customer,
   - two small furniture stores.
6. They have been in their current location four-and-a-half years.

Exercise A

Of what importance to you is each of the items you observed?

Answer A

1. This may indicate that the tenant is oriented exclusively toward the large suburban mall. It would be wise to check the locations of the tenant's other stores to verify this trend.

2. This is of no major importance to you.

3. The tenant needs a location with access to other areas to support such a large store. Where would the freeway bring this retailer's customers from?

4. A location in a wealthy suburb may tell only part of the story. A large mall attracts customers from a large area. From what other cities or towns do the customers come? The answer could give you a good idea of the real clientele on which the business is based and could indicate what type of area would be a likely choice for the new location.

5. The tenant mix in this mall can give you an indication of what other stores will help this business draw shoppers. This information will be important when moving the tenant to a new space. (Tenant mix may be a more vital element to smaller businesses, since large stores are often their own best drawing cards.)

6. Their current lease may be expiring in the near future.

The point is, before you've even met your potential tenant, you've gained some idea of the company's business and its retail space needs. You have begun to qualify the prospect. Keep in mind that qualification of needs is only one element. Normally, you must qualify finances and motivation as well.

FEATURES AND BENEFITS

Determining needs is one step in the process of dealing with prospects. In selecting property to show and in discussing property with prospects, you must also demonstrate your understanding of features and benefits. A feature is a characteristic. A benefit is some desirable quality—economy, convenience, comfort or the like—that results from a feature. A feature is a cause. A benefit is the consequence. They are sales points you must stress in order to motivate the prospect to examine, evaluate, choose and move toward a closing.

Exercise B

Following are some features found in a certain retail building. From each feature, list one or more possible benefits that would appeal to a retail user for whom you are seeking suitable space:

1. one-year-old building
2. one-half mile from freeway exit and entrance
3. grocery chain and discount house are other tenants in the center
4. 250-space parking lot
5. bus stop one block away
6. air conditioning throughout
7. good visibility from the freeway
8. well landscaped
9. lot large enough for expansion
10. competition limited in the area

Answer B

1. *A newer building like this could mean lower maintenance costs and perhaps lower rent.*
2. *This location offers economical and convenient transportation.*
3. *The other tenants will draw specific types of clients.*
4. *This lot provides adequate parking facilities for all shoppers.*
5. *Access to public transportation is convenient for employees and shoppers who do not drive. It broadens the geographical area from which shoppers may come.*
6. *Air conditioning is essential for employee/shopper comfort.*
7. *Good visibility increases customer flow.*
8. *Landscaping attracts customers and gives the business a pleasing public image.*
9. *No need to seek larger space elsewhere as business expands.*
10. *Limited competition increases your sales almost automatically.*

Keep in mind that a feature is worthless if it is unrelated to the prospect's needs and interests—if he or he does not see it as a benefit. You must qualify your prospects thoroughly in order to know what features will be valuable to them.

Exercise C

Give examples of situations in which features 3, 4, and 8 would not interest a prospect.

Answer C

1. *The low-prestige tenants of feature 3 would not be attractive to more exclusive shops.*

2. *Depending on store size, feature 4 might not be adequate.*

3. *Certain prospects might have no interest in landscaping. They may view it as an unnecessary expense and be unable to relate it to the success of their business.*

A primary retail selling skill is to select the appropriate features and relate them to benefits that are appropriate to your prospects and their needs. You must know your prospects. Furthermore, you must know something about the type of businesses in which they are engaged. You will need to:

1. Gain the prospect's confidence, ascertain their most important needs and guide them in adjusting their objectives when necessary.

2. Screen what you tell them to eliminate inappropriate and irrelevant information that can sidetrack discussions.

3. Have a well-organized body of information at hand: knowledge of your territory, the prospects' business, the retail space and land market and each prospect's needs.

You can sometimes use features and benefits to influence prospects. For example, suppose in compiling your list of buildings to show a retail user, you find one that fills his or her needs almost exactly, one that would require very few compromises with the tenant's objectives as you have qualified them. Although time is money to you, you should not try to persuade the tenant that it really is not necessary to look at any other building or piece of land, unless this were a long-time tenant you had served well in the past. In most cases, tenants will trust you to select buildings for them to see, but they will not rely on you to make a selection for them.

Instead, you might show the property in the normal order dictated by your route, not necessarily first or last. However, as you drive toward that particular site, start ticking off its features and benefits, relating each one to the tenant's needs and objectives. The tenant is then more likely to inspect the property with his or her company's occupancy in mind. As you pull up to the property, you can say, "Well, I think this might be the one."

How a prospect responds to features and benefits determines the emphasis you place on each one. A tenant who prefers convenience centers will not be impressed by a large suburban mall. If a tenant is in a discount operation, location near a prestige department store may do nothing for him or her (except possibly in terms of draw), while location on a major highway will. For a user who has no interest in building modification, inadequate dock space will be enough to make the site unacceptable. If a tenant likes a building because of its size or a vacant parcel because of its location, emphasize these points. Such tenants may or may not be interested in the competition located near them.

The point is, skillful salespeople not only qualify prospects to begin with, but they also listen and observe as they go along. Qualification really does not end until a decision is made. Salespeople who listen and observe, who ask questions for clarification and who strive to understand their prospects will be able to shift gears when necessary and play up features and benefits that match the prospects' needs.

SELLING YOU AND YOUR COMPANY

Suppose you've been working with ABC Company to find a larger space, and the transaction is progressing well. At the same time, ABC has notified the owner of its present space that it will not renew the lease. You should immediately realize that this will give you a chance to try to secure a listing on the building.

You call on the owner of the building, Jean Gibson. She says, "I don't know whether I want to lease that building again or not. I just might decide to sell it." You don't care whether she sells or leases. The important thing is that your office has the listing for the building. Whether Gibson decides to sell or lease, point out to her the time-saving benefit of giving you necessary information on the building now. Then, when she is ready to move, all listing information will already have been prepared for the inventory file. You will have acquainted Gibson with yourself and your company, and you will have started her along the road toward using your services. Whether she agrees to give you listing information now or not, don't wait to hear from her about putting the building on the market. Call her within a few days.

On the other hand, suppose you call on owner Charles Valdez for the first time and he says, "Well, I've always dealt with XYZ Realty. They've given me good service and I expect I'll continue to deal with them on this building."

You certainly don't want to criticize XYZ. Agree with Valdez that it's a reputable company and a good competitor. You do, however, want to talk about the benefits to the owner of listing with your company. You should be able to enumerate several of your company's features that can be converted into owner benefits.

Exercise D

What benefits might owners receive from the following features?

1. Many tenants call because of your company's signs.
2. Your company employs salespeople in the retail division.

Answer D

3. Your firm enjoys a record of fine service to owners and other tenants and a long list of satisfied customers.
4. You are working with a number of retail users looking for space.

1. *Signs mean that a building will be well promoted. The fact that many tenants call in response to signs means that the promotion produces results.*
2. *Many retail salespeople will bring the building to the attention of many tenants.*
3. *A record of good service and satisfied customers indicates that your company is likely to satisfy this prospect as it has so many others.*
4. *The fact that your company has many tenants interested in space means more than one tenant probably will look at the building, thus enhancing the chances of moving it.*

Reinforcing statements are sometimes necessary to buttress prospects' acceptance of benefits and to relate them to their needs. Such statements support the reasons why it is an advantage for prospects to deal with your company. They also help them to relate this advantage directly to their needs. Reinforcing statements can lead prospects to accept a particular site.

A property you are showing might have the feature of being exceptionally well-landscaped. This benefit could contribute to employee morale and help the company's public image. You might reinforce the landscape observation with, "These days, a good public image is important." But be careful that you have qualified your prospect here. Be sure that public image through landscaping is important to him or her.

Or you might say, "As you can see, the traffic count on this street is very high" (a feature). "This allows more potential customers to see your business" (a benefit). "And, of course, the more people who see your store, the more who will patronize it" (reinforcing statement).

Exercise E

If a building requires only minor modification (a feature), and would then be just right for your tenant (a benefit), what might you use as a reinforcing statement?

Answer E

Your statement might be one of the following:

1. *"To suit your purposes, this building would require only minor modification."*

2. "With minor modification, this building would be just right for you."

DRILL QUESTIONS

In most cases, one question and one answer will not yield all the information you need to be of maximum service to your prospects. Drill questions are those that plumb for more information as you qualify your prospects and move transactions along to satisfactory conclusions. For example, you might ask Sandy Farwell how many square feet she needs. After she replies, you could then ask if that space is about what she has now. Farwell's answer to that question should suggest at least that the business is growing and that it might well continue to do so. She might need more additional square feet now than you originally figured.

Other questions you might ask are:

1. "Which do you need, a freestanding building or one in a shopping center or mall and why?"

2. "Tell me about your parking needs."

3. "What type of sign will you use to identify your company to the public?"

When you ask a tenant if his or her business requires a freestanding building, the tenant might well respond, "No, but it's what I want." Here you have distinguished one kind of need from another, although in the prospect's mind want and need might mean the same thing. You have learned that, regardless of cost or other considerations, a freestanding building is what the tenant will have.

Salespeople who use drill questions to qualify prospects will save a good deal of time and effort. As they make presentations, they ask more questions to qualify the prospect further. For example, as you drive away from one building and on to another you may ask:

"How did the layout there strike you?"

"I liked it."

(Drill) "How did it compare in your mind with that of building A?"

"I like it better, although I like the parking arrangement in A better than that in B."

Exercise F

What might a further drill question be?

Answer F

You might ask: "Which would you trade away, the selling space or the parking area?"

A building or space seldom fits a tenant without some compromise on original objectives, requirements and desires. It is vitally important that you gather information on possible compromises, taking your cues from your tenants' responses and using drill questions to clarify the situation and help guide tenants to a decision. Keep listening for indications of refinements in their priorities, noting particularly whether priorities seem to shift as they look at buildings.

On another occasion, you might observe to tenant John Frye that the building he is viewing certainly has a well-landscaped front; but Frye merely grunts. Your objective then is to discover how important landscaping is to him. You might ask if he is especially interested in landscaping or if landscaping is a low priority with him.

Exercise G

Suppose Frye responds: "I think a company can waste a lot of money having to maintain extensive landscaping. A little grass, maybe. That's enough." Would you drill further in this case? If so, what might you say?

Answer G

It would be wise to find out how strong Frye's feelings on the matter really are, and to determine whether extensive landscaping would rule out a building. He may merely be expressing a personal opinion, accepting landscaping at the same time as a public relations gesture a company must make. On the other hand, avoiding extensive landscaping may be a firm policy of his.

An item like that in the example might not ordinarily come up during the initial tenant qualification process. Drill questions help you learn more about your prospects and how you might successfully serve them.

SELLING TO THE RIGHT PERSON

This subject is covered in detail in the chapter titled *Showing Retail Property*. Because it touches on basic selling skills, it also merits some discussion here.

It may seem mere common sense that the right person to sell to is the one who contacts you or the one you contact through a cold call, a brochure or in some other way. But in retail selling this is not always the case.

When making a cold call you might be directed to a person who is involved in company real estate problems as a recommender rather than a decision maker. While such people can be valuable to you, they are not the ones who make final decisions.

Skillful salespeople will go about their task in a roundabout way, asking, for example, "Who besides yourself is involved in company real estate decisions?" Or they might say, "How has your company handled real estate decisions like this is the past?" This oblique approach helps to smoke out the information you need. If the person to whom you're talking is not the right one, find out who is. The most direct way—and usually most skillful and productive—is to ask who is involved—names, positions and so on.

When you're dealing with a national or regional company whose headquarters and decision makers are in another city or state, your initial and most frequent contacts will probably be with a local representative. Here again, you must qualify this person's position within the company hierarchy and discover the extent to which he or she recommends and makes decisions. Even if the representative is only empowered to make recommendations, you will still want to qualify him or her just as you would an ultimate decision maker, for this person's recommendation will be a necessary first step toward doing business.

With a national company, you will probably present properties to more than one person when the time comes. One or more people might come into town to join the local representative in viewing lots or buildings. Once you have the group assembled, you'll have no trouble identifying the decision maker. If the group separates to look at various aspects of a building or site, you stay with the decision maker for the simple reason that until the key person is convinced, there is no transaction. So don't waste your time. Zero in on the decision maker.

Answer subordinates' questions too, of course, but be extremely tactful. Do not alienate them or make them look foolish. If you do, they can see to it the transaction is not completed. This, of course, applies to any dealings with subordinates—before, during and after presentations.

HANDLING OBJECTIONS

Knowledgeable salespeople realize that a building or site will seldom fit a tenant's needs perfectly. Some compromise in tenant objectives is almost always necessary. Skillful salespeople lead their tenants to the compromise and obtain their acceptance of it with a minimum of time and effort.

First of all, however, prepare by qualifying both your tenants and the properties equally well. Never waste time showing buildings or sites you know will not suit tenants on the off chance that you might be wrong. In other words, do your homework and anticipate objections. Sometimes, of course, the unanticipated occurs. Take advantage of all kinds of situations, helping your tenants to clarify the issues and move toward a decision.

Exercise H

Consider some examples:

1. Tenant Carol Goodwin decides that a building without a loading dock will not really do, thus ruling out a building that in other respects fits her needs pretty well. How do you respond?

2. Tenant David Turner believes he needs more parking space. What would you do in this case?

Answer H

1. You might simply indicate where an opening for a dock could be made. Also, you would certainly want to play up the features and benefits the building already offers the client, which would help move her toward accepting the idea of modification.

2. Again you would discuss modification, assuming there is sufficient space around the building to extend the parking lot.

Before you even bring up the subject of modification, before you show tenants any properties at all, you have to know if they are willing to modify a building if necessary. Second, you must know if they are financially able to modify. It is pointless to discuss modification if either of these conditions is not met.

You will also have to deal with objections when you talk with owners about putting up your company's signs on buildings and sites not listed with your firm. Frequently you will need to bring a great deal of skill to bear during the process of persuasion.

In trying to obtain a total blanketing of your territory with your company's signs you will encounter a variety of situations. Each situation presents you with slightly different problems; handling them is covered in the chapter titled *The Use of Signs,* which you will want to study carefully. Within the context of this chapter, however, there are general arguments you will use in every one of these situations to persuade owners that their buildings need your company's sign. You will play up your company's features and their benefits to owners. You will need to know them thoroughly.

CLOSING THE TRANSACTION

Your objective in showing a tenant buildings and sites is to bring a transaction to a satisfactory conclusion. Only then will you realize your overriding goal—your commission.

You move toward a closing with two assumptions in mind, that the tenant will choose one location from among the sites or buildings you have shown, and that the initiative for moving toward a closing lies with you.

Since the initiative is yours, now is the time to lay out the titled fact sheets you prepared earlier on each site or building (on this and other aspects of preparation, see the chapter *Showing Retail Property*). This will give your tenant an opportunity to review the buildings and compare them. And now is the time to ask questions. You might ask which properties impressed the tenant and which ones he or she didn't like, and why.

Your objective is to narrow the choices as quickly as possible. You have taken notes on your tenant's comments and responses as the presentation has progressed, so you have some ideas about which sites or buildings impress the tenant and why. You can control the situation, exercising your skill to lead him or her toward a choice.

Exercise I

Suppose tenant Tom McDermott wavers between two sites, either one of which would suit him well. What might you do in this case?

Answer I

Suggest that McDermott make a conditional offer on one of the sites. Most owners will accept an offer conditional to further inspection of one or more items from a serious tenant, even though that means that the property will be off the market for, say, 30 to 60 days. The important thing is that you have put your tenant in a proper frame of mind to negotiate a transaction. Nothing will help your cause more.

What price should a tenant offer, regardless of whether the offer is conditional or firm? Here you must exercise considerable skill, for the price should be the tenant's decision, not yours. You might review the current retail market, discuss the asking price and go over any modifications that might be necessary. But remember, you are helping the tenant, not telling him or her what to do. If the tenant insists that you suggest a price lower than the asking price, do it, but make sure he or she understands that the owner might not accept it and might not make a counteroffer. Above all, persuade the tenant to be realistic about an offer in terms of the building's features and benefits, the asking price and the retail market in general.

Never under any circumstances tell a tenant you can get a property at a certain price. You might be lucky, but chances are you will not be, and you will end up losing a tenant in the process.

Because time is money, you want an immediate decision and an offer from your tenant once the properties have been discussed and choices narrowed. Suppose, however, the tenant wants to think it over, get more information or discuss the situation with others in the company. The tenant has this right, but there are things you can do to get him or her interested again in closing the deal.

1. Caution the tenant not to wait too long, for the property he or she likes might be sold or leased in the meantime.

2. Pin the tenant down to a certain time for a decision—no more than a week.

3. Assure the tenant that you will call if you do not hear from him or her by the time promised.

4. Ask for the tenant's notes and have them copied so you can review them, particularly those on the buildings or sites in which the tenant has expressed interest.

At the same time, you will want to note any questions or additional information the tenant requests. Get the information and follow up with a phone call.

At worst, none of the buildings or sites your tenant inspected really appeal to him or her. This might happen through no fault of your own. However, the chances are good that you did not qualify your tenant carefully and thoroughly or exercise sufficient care in selecting buildings or sites for him or her to inspect. In this case, blame for wasted time—both yours and the tenant's—would lie at your door.

CONCLUSION

In all phases of your dealings with tenants, you will have demonstrated your awareness of their needs and requirements, and you will have applied your expertise in finding the best possible solution for them. The goal of any real estate relationship is completing a successful transaction. Assessing needs, guiding tenants to make adjustments in their objectives if necessary, using drill questions and reinforcing statements and knowing how to respond to objections are all essential to moving prospects toward a decision.

A transaction is in progress until it is finalized. At every step along the way you should check and recheck that progress and keep the prospect informed of the current situation. This is important no matter what the nature of the transaction. Letters should regularly be sent to tenants documenting locations that have been shown, any decisions made and changes that have been discussed. Such letters should be sent to the person you have identified as the one authorized to sign a binding agreement. Do not neglect to send copies to all significant people in the company who, although they do not have the final word in the matter, might still have an effect on the decision.

Remember that putting forth that extra effort lets your prospects know that their interests are important to you. The manner in which materials are presented to prospects warrants attention. For example, make an appointment to meet with a tenant personally when you have prepared a site presentation. Always hand-deliver such documents and allow enough time to answer any questions that the tenant may raise.

When you present a site plan or a market survey, make certain that the appearance of the material, as well as its content, is professional. The binder holding the material is the first thing prospects see: A heavy cover of good quality will impress them more than a flimsy, inexpensive one. The contents should be organized so that the information can be read easily. Prospects expect professionalism in real estate salespeople. A lack of concern for these details can cost you a transaction and a commission.

Attention to details also means responding quickly to prospects' request for extra information, such as a further breakdown on demographic statistics or a last-minute recheck on the square footage of a piece of property. Be ready and willing to offer the additional service. Taking a prospect to lunch may put your relationship on a more amiable basis and facilitate further contacts.

When a transaction is ready to be finalized, review the highlights of the progress that has been made and stress the points won by your prospect in negotiations. Remember that no matter how near at hand the closing may be, there can still be precarious moments when the tenant or landlord may reverse the decision. Continually reinforce the advantages to both sides of completing the transaction.

Exercise J

1. Name at least ten needs typical of retail users.
2. Why is qualification of tenant needs so important?
3. What is the difference between a feature and a benefit?
4. Under what circumstances are features of no importance to a prospect?
5. What is the importance of a reinforcing statement?
6. What is a drill question, and of what importance is it?
7. Why is it important that you sell to the right person?
8. How can you prepare yourself to meet objections to a property?
9. When you discuss the price of property with a tenant, what is the one thing you must never do?

Answer J

1. *Possible answers include: (a) a certain number of square feet; (b) good traffic counts, (c) a certain type of location—neighborhood shop, regional center, etc., (d) good visibility to customers, (e) utility service, (f) high-volume shoppers, (g) fire protection, (h) parking, (i) easy access to major highway routes, (j) ability to generate dollar volume, (k) specific tenant mix and (l) sufficient numbers of customers residing in an area specifically defined.*

2. *Tenants' needs must be qualified so that real estate can be matched to those needs. Qualify the tenants' needs not only for yourself, but for the tenants themselves. They may not always know their specific real estate needs.*

3. *A feature is a characteristic. A benefit is some desirable quality that results from a feature and will provide an advantage to the tenant in terms of economy, convenience or comfort.*

4. *Features are only important if they can provide a benefit to the prospect.*

5. *A reinforcing statement may be used to strengthen a prospect's acceptance of a benefit and to relate that benefit to the tenant's specific needs.*

6. *Drill questions are used to plumb for more information. They are necessary in qualifying the prospect thoroughly and in moving a transaction along to a satisfactory conclusion.*

7. *You are wasting your time if you are not selling to the right person. You may convince a subordinate, but you have no transaction until the decision maker is convinced and ready to sign.*

8. *Prospect objections can best be handled by anticipating them, by qualifying the prospects and their buildings or sites thoroughly and by being ready to use skillful persuasion.*

9. *Never tell a tenant that you can get a property at a certain price.*

9

Time Management

INTRODUCTION

As a real estate salesperson, you will find that time is your most important resource. Although you are responsible to those for whom you work, for the most part you operate as an independent. You must manage your time to achieve the maximum return in commissions on your investment. Each hour, day, week and month must be planned and used productively. Remember, lost time is lost money.

As you proceed through this section you will find ideas, suggestions and examples that you can use to develop your own time management system. At the beginning, you may want to borrow a system that can eventually be modified to your own personal use.

PLANNING

Management of your time begins with proper planning. It is not feasible to plan every available minute, but the known activities can be planned. This will help you to cope with unknown or unexpected circumstances as they arise. Effective planning is your best insurance for success.

In laying out goals for yourself, keep in mind the following characteristics.

1. Your goals must be *attainable*. Be realistic with yourself and establish your objectives according to your capabilities. You will

never achieve success if your goals are always out of your reach. The feeling of success is extremely important in establishing a continued pattern of growth and development.

2. Your objectives, on the other hand, must be *challenging*. If they can be achieved too easily, the objectives are probably not meaningful.

3. Your objectives must be *specific* and *measurable*. They should be stated in quantifiable terms—numbers, dollars, percentages and time. Each objective must have a specific target date associated with it.

4. Your goals must be *compatible* with the objectives of your office. The successful accomplishment of your individual objectives must contribute to the goals of each group within the entire firm.

5. Finally, your objectives must contain provisions for *control*. That is, at regular intervals you should compare your actual performance with your plan objectives. This requires that your goals be in writing.

Once you have prepared your written objectives for a given period of time, you will then have to:

1. Determine the activities you will have to perform in order to attain each goal you have set for yourself.

2. Gather the resources needed to perform those activities.

3. Carry out each activity by using your skills and self-motivation.

4. Continually compare your plans to your actual results and adjust your plan where indicated.

Long-term Goals

Begin by establishing broad, generalized, long-term objectives for yourself. You can then work backward to the specific short-range goals—annual, monthly, daily, hourly—necessary to achieve these overall objectives.

Your long-term goals should be for a period of five to fifteen years into the future. They should cover a variety of categories and include both business and nonbusiness areas. You will find that your goals on a long-term basis will be interdependent and, as such, should cover all aspects of your life.

Some of the areas you should consider are financial, family, recreation, travel, cultural, social, educational and retirement. List below ten long-term goals for yourself. Be sure to set specific target dates for each.

Long-term Objective *Target Date*

1. Achieve an income of $ _____ by _____

2.

3.

4.

5.

Long-term Objective *Target Date*

6.

7.

8.

9.

10.

This is not an easy task to complete, but it is the most important aspect of organizing your time, since it is the basis on which you will build your system.

Go back now and organize your ten long-term objectives in order of priority. Consider the relative importance of each goal and the time frame you have allowed for each one.

Priority *Long-term Objective* *Target Date*

1.

2.

3.

4.

5.

6.

7.

8.

9.

10.

Your next task is to support the long-term goals with specific interim goals—activities and steps that will lead to their successful accomplishment. You will want to ask yourself:

1. What is the most effective way of reaching my goal?

2. What knowledge and ability do I already have to assist me in reaching the goal?

3. What skills and additional information must I obtain to achieve the goal?

4. What are the specific steps I must plan to reach the goal?

Using your five highest-priority long-term goals, establish three interim goals for the accomplishment of each. This is the third time you will have restated these long-term goals. Did your list change in any way as you rewrote it? If you have given real thought to these exercises, your goals will have been modified with each successive writing. When you begin the exercise below, you will be completing your final statement of your long-term objectives. Be sure you have established realistic target dates.

	Priority	Long-term Objective	Target Date

1.
    a.
    b.
    c.

2.
    a.
    b.
    c.

3.
    a.
    b.
    c.

4.
    a.
    b.
    c.

5.
    a.
    b.
    c.

What you have just completed is the first step in effectively organizing your time—establishing your long-range objectives. This activity should be completed annually, in writing, and include a periodic review (at least every six months) of these objectives.

Figure 9-1 shows a suggested form to follow in writing your long-range objectives. You may choose to modify or redesign the form to suit your particular needs at some future date.

Short-term Objectives

Once you have determined where you want to be financially, professionally, socially and educationally over the next five to ten years, lay out specific goals for yourself in the next year. Do not extend your short-term objectives beyond a one-year period.

Review the characteristics of objectives discussed earlier in this section—they apply to all plans that you set for yourself. Short-term objectives will be more specific and must also be assigned target dates.

It is extremely important to compare your actual performance with your planned objectives. You can do this by building in a weekly tally of quantifiable activities such as cold calls, listings and closings. Measure

FIGURE 9.1 Long-term Objectives

Date Prepared _____

Objective	Target Date	Completed Date

your progress on a monthly basis by comparing actual achievement to projected achievement.

As each objective is attained, note that fact on your annual plan. You will then be able to adjust your activities to reflect deviations from your plan. Review your short-term objectives on a quarterly basis and make modifications as required.

Exercise A

Your short-term objectives might state that each month you will list five retail properties to achieve your objective of 60 listings this year. However, during March you were able to list only three new properties. From your monthly control figures you note that your annual total is now at 12 listings. How will you adjust your objective for listings? What other objectives will require modification? How?

Answer A

You could have lowered your annual goal, but a better method would be to raise next month's goal to seven listings to make up for the two you missed this month.

Your major goal may require modifications if this is an interim goal. How you modify it will depend on your particular goal. You may find that you have to alter your original goal to make it more realistic.

In support of your long-term financial objective, write your short-term income objective. This will then have to be supported by short-term interim goals. List those, also.

Objective	*Target Date*
Achieve $ _____ in commissions earned	_____
a. _____ sales (by month)	_____
b. _____ listings (by month)	_____
c. _____ cold calls	_____
d. _____ ad calls	_____
e. _____ sign calls	_____
f. _____ client follow-ups	_____
g. _____ new prospects qualified	_____
h. _____ listings shown	_____
i. _____ new business developed	_____

Using the short-term objectives form in Figure 9–2 write short-term objectives for your five major long-term goals. Be sure to include sufficient details to support the accomplishment of these objectives.

FIGURE 9.2 Short-term Objectives

Date Prepared _____

Objective	Target Date	Completed Date

Time Organization

You should now have two valuable documents in your files—long-term objectives and short-term objectives. With these clearly stated plans, you can organize your time for each month, week, day and hour. This will ensure the successful achievement of your goals.

Tickler System

To your system of time organization you should now add a prospect and call control *tickler* file. As pictured in Figure 9-3, this file will be a prime source of input for your monthly, weekly and daily planners.

The hardware for the tickler file includes:

1. three-by-five-inch index cards
2. file for cards
3. twelve monthly dividers
4. five weekly dividers
5. seven daily dividers

Arrange the monthly dividers in sequence beginning with the current month. Place the five weekly dividers in the current month (first through fifth). Place the seven daily dividers in the current week (Sunday through Saturday).

Each prospect, customer and follow-up is placed on a file card. Record the name, address and telephone number in the upper left-hand corner. On the right-hand side, put the next contact date. The bottom portion of the card should contain brief notes regarding the contact. File the card in the appropriate month, week or day for follow-up.

Each month, sort and file the cards by the four or five weeks of that month. At the beginning of each week, sort and file the cards for that week by the appropriate date. When you have completed each contact, refile the card according to the next contact date.

This tickler file system will automatically contribute to your success and profits. It will give you easy control of what day, date and time you are to call on or follow up on a contact. And, most important, it permits you to have at your fingertips all essential information regarding any given account.

```
Name _____  Dates:
Address _____
        _____
Telephone _____
Comments:
```

FIGURE 9.3 Tickler File

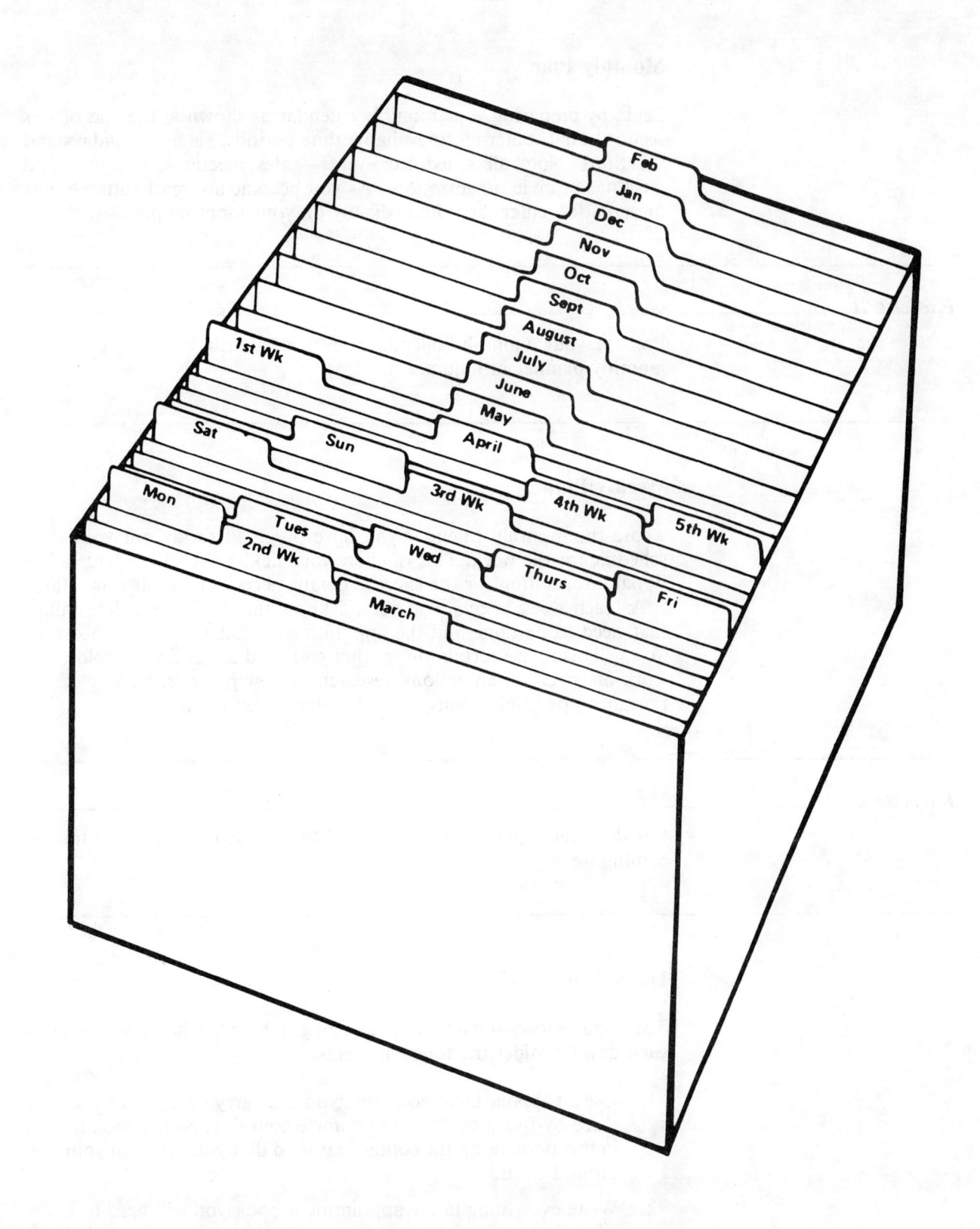

This system is most effective when you develop the habit of keeping full notes on what you intend to do on the date you have selected for making your contact.

Monthly Plan

Begin by preparing your monthly calendar as shown at the end of this section. First, enter all unavailable time periods, such as holidays and vacations. Note all scheduled events—sales meetings, seminars and meetings of civic organizations. As you become aware of future events or activities, enter them immediately on your monthly planner.

Exercise B

Prepare your monthly calendar for next month by completing the monthly planner in Figure 9-4.

Weekly Plan

Use the monthly calendar you have prepared to lay out your time schedule for the week. This is where your tickler file will provide additional information for the specific details necessary in this time plan.

As each week begins, you should know the most immediate things that need to be done and the appointments that you have scheduled. You will also have certain things that you need to get done—cold calls, work on specific transactions, research on new projects, reading of important trade publications, correspondence and the like.

Exercise C

Use the weekly planner in Figure 9-5 to lay out your schedule for the coming week.

Daily Plan

The night before, or early in the morning, schedule what has to be done each day. Consider the following facts:

1. Use an appointment book that you can carry with you or use your three-by-five-inch cards to organize your day. Note appointments in this book or on the contact cards so that you can plan your day around them.

2. Write everything in the appointment book you will need to know when you get back to the office—notes, appointments and phone numbers.

FIGURE 9.4 Monthly Planner

Month _____   Year _____

SUNDAY	MONDAY	TUESDAY	WEDNESDAY	THURSDAY	FRIDAY	SATURDAY

FIGURE 9.5 Weekly Planner

	MONDAY DATE ____	TUESDAY ____	WEDNESDAY ____	THURSDAY ____	FRIDAY ____
MORN.					
AFTER.					
EVE.					

3. Set aside part of each day for specific tasks. For instance, you may plan to cold call on Wednesday morning. Block this out in your appointment book and stick to it. Don't make any appointments for this time slot. If you do not stick to your schedule, you'll find you're not allowing enough time for cold calling, surveying an area or working on specific projects.

4. When setting appointments, allow enough time to arrive early. In many cases you will be seeing top executives, people who are too busy or too important to wait for someone who is late for an appointment. Many unexpected things can happen, so always give yourself plenty of time. In fact, try to be about ten minutes early for appointments. The people you are seeing will appreciate it and know they are dealing with a serious broker.

5. Appointments should be scheduled on a geographic basis. Make certain that you have plenty of time to get from one place to another. Unrealistic estimates will upset your entire schedule. As your geographic area expands, make sure that you are not scheduling a meeting at 10:00 in the morning in a far-off location and another at 5:00 in the same place. Instead, leave an hour or two between the appointments and do site location work.

6. When you make an appointment, ask yourself if you really have to go to that meeting. Unnecessary appointments waste too much of your valuable time.

7. Develop self-discipline. Sit down and make the telephone cold calls when you have them scheduled. Get out into the field, even if it would be easier to sit at your desk. And stick to your schedule. Don't make a marginal appointment if you should be doing something else that will allow you to produce business even if it isn't related to a specific transaction.

8. Make certain that you're not doing something at the wrong time. Don't catch up on your reading at 10:30 in the morning when you could be scheduling appointments or making cold calls. Write letters and do your reading early in the morning or late in the evening when you cannot do other work. Do paperwork and administrative duties at times other than when you could be out talking to people, initiating business or keeping your transaction moving.

   Your days will eventually follow a pattern. For instance, you may come in early in the morning to make calls; spend the majority of the day in the field; and use the early evening for reading, correspondence and administrative duties.

9. Qualify your prospects regarding how much time you should spend with them. A number of individuals that you will deal with are on salary and can afford to waste a little time. As a commissioned salesperson, you simply cannot. When you are starting out, write down how long each appointment took. At the end of the day, total up the number of hours you spent with the prospect and evaluate the use of that time—how much closer did it put you to a completed transaction? In addition, you must immediately qualify people who come in off the street. If they are not qualified, keep your conversation to a minimum. Look at each appointment in terms of the dollars it can earn for you.

Ask yourself at every meeting why you are there. What does it mean to you in terms of dollars? If you are working on a specific tenant or a specific piece of property, there is probably a direct relationship between time spent and commissions earned. If the appointment yields important information regarding a transaction, it is valuable. This does not always apply to appointments with chain tenants. Because of the possibility of multiple transactions, it may be worthwhile to spend more time with them on a social level. You can develop the relationship so that they will come to you when they plan to locate at other sites.

10. Check your schedule hourly, or you'll find at the end of the day you've missed things. After one task is done, check it off. When the day is over you can find out what you've missed and make plans to cover it some other time. The same is true for checking what you've accomplished on a weekly or monthly basis. Make certain everything on your list has been accomplished. Transfer all important notes and phone numbers to their appropriate places.

It is a common unhappy fact of the business that many new salespeople, after several weeks on the job, begin to feel disorganized and start to fumble for things to do. If they had begun by planning their days and weeks, they would not have this problem. One method of developing your planning skills is to talk to salespeople who have been in the business for some time. Ask them what their goals are and how they plan their time. If you don't know who to approach, ask your sales manager to recommend someone.

Exercise D

Choose a day from the weekly schedule you prepared and plan that day on an hourly basis. Use the form in Figure 9-6.

ORGANIZATION

Organization is integral to effective time management. If you organize your work, you will go a long way toward completing more transactions more effectively.

The following is an outline of good organization habits for new salespeople. Setting up and maintaining the system is easy and invaluable.

Pending Files

For each transaction pending, prepare a file folder with a typed label listing the name of the transaction. File these folders in the file cabinet closest to you so that they will be the most accessible. Staple the business cards of the people involved in the transaction on the inside of the file folder, or write their names, addresses and phone numbers.

FIGURE 9.6 Daily Planner

Date _____   Activity   Comments

7:00 a.m.
7:30
8:00
8:30
9:00
9:30
10:00
10:30
11:00
11:30
12:00 noon
12:30
1:00
1:30
2:00
2:30
3:00
3:30
4:00
4:30
5:00
5:30
6:00
6:30
7:00
7:30
8:00
8:30
9:00
9:30
10:00 p.m.

Every time you talk with someone connected with the venture, jot down a brief summary of what you discuss. A good place to record this chronological history is on the inside left page of the file folder. This is very important, especially if a transaction starts to fall through. If a tenant says that you didn't discuss a particular point, you can pull out your note and say, "Yes, Mr. Jones, we did discuss it at 10:00 A.M. on June 15th." This provides a strong buffer for you if there is any dispute. In fact, this type of notation is admissible in a court of law or arbitration.

You may wish to design a form on which you can enter all of the pertinent information about each transaction, such as:

1. property involved
2. owner's name, address and phone number
3. prospective buyer or lessee's name
4. rent
5. taxes
6. maintenance
7. insurance
8. size of space
9. length of lease
10. landlord's improvements
11. tenant's improvements

On the form, keep track of all the developments—what was discussed, whether or not the tenant has agreed to pay the taxes and so on. Note the date and the item discussed to minimize disputes as lease negotiations progress.

If you do not use a specific format like the one mentioned for recording information, keep all notes and letters to tenants and landlords in chronological order in the file.

Tickler Files

Once a month, analyze each transaction pending file to see if a deal can be completed. Move in-between transactions to a tickler file. Be honest with yourself so that you can concentrate on deals that you have a realistic expectation of closing.

Once every two months or so, go through the tickler file. If some transactions have become more feasible, put them back in the active file. Take out the unworkable ones. If you have any questions about which ones to discard, discuss the matter with your sales manager.

Since timing is critical in real estate (for instance, in the development of sites for neighborhood shopping centers), put these sites and information of this type in the tickler file. There might soon be an announcement of a major housing development in that area that would make the transaction workable. Stay on top of things—when the timing is right, you can complete the transaction.

Timing is also important regarding drug, supermarket and discount chains. You should maintain a tickler file on future sites for these tenants. To gather information, get together with home builders and find out what their building patterns will be. Then find out which areas they have designated as commercial sites. Ask the developer if you can submit the site to a possible chain. If the potential tenant refuses it, go back after the site has been developed and resubmit it.

Another possible candidate for the tickler file is a lease that will be expiring, whether in the next three months or in five years. Put all the pertinent information on a lease survey form, place it in the tickler file and follow up on it at the appropriate time.

Escrow Files

When a transaction is completed, put everything that pertains to it in an escrow file. Sort out information that might pertain to other transactions—leads and so on—and put them in the tickler file. The law requires that the escrow file be retained by the company for five years.

SKILLS FOR EFFECTIVE TIME MANAGEMENT

Managing your time and reaching your goals are skills you can learn easily, and they will be useful in all aspects of your life. The skills listed below are varied and require considerable self-analysis on your part. Learn how to use them, and you will be well on your way to effective time management.

1. *Increase alertness.* The routines you have designed for yourself may become so habitual that they dull your alertness to the issues at hand. You can break out of these ruts by changing routines, practicing alertness and cultivating interests centered around observation.

    Change the way you drive to work in the morning or perhaps the place you eat lunch. When you alter your routine, you will find yourself noticing things more carefully or seeing the same sights in a new way. Don't let one routine replace another; continue to change your habits.

    Make it a daily point to practice alertness and sharpen your powers of observation. Be attentive to the words, facial expressions and gestures of clients; notice the clues they give in pauses and body language; evaluate more carefully the obvious conditions in an area in which you are cold calling. Habits save energy by requiring less than your full concentration, but they also make you lazy. You may miss what is happening around you.

    Develop an interest based on careful observation. For instance, a hobby such as photography will sharpen your observational techniques. A camera will pick up things the most trained observer would miss. If you photograph the buildings in your area, you will get a greater feel for their architecture, size and use. A photograph of a skyline can reveal patterns in the development of a city or town that you never would have considered before.

2. *Increase your available energy.* It is obvious that the well-tuned, healthy individual is way ahead of the field in the areas of alertness and energy. Energy creates more energy, and inactivity breeds inertia. Work to improve your exercise habits. In addition to developing your physical resources, learn about your own energy peaking levels. Some people are "morning people"; others really wake up only after the sun goes down. Learn about your own peculiarities and then schedule as many of your activities as you can around them. Do routine work when you are "down" mentally, and creative work when you are "up" mentally. Creative work, besides being the most valuable, also taxes more of your skills and alertness.

3. *Increase your knowledge and range of experiences.* Again, management of time is management of yourself to achieve your best efforts. Your personal storehouse of knowledge from formal and informal sources is the bank of information you will apply to your entire life. For instance, your knowledge of up-to-date management methods and techniques may aid you in making improved management decisions. Or your knowledge of some section of the country as you travel through it and converse with the residents may aid you in discovering a possible property development opportunity. The uses of your knowledge and experience are limitless.

4. *Locate your energy losses.* To understand how to locate just where your energy (and, therefore, your time) is being dissipated, you must first understand that you operate on a variety of levels. You have an internal *thinking* level, which is made up of a variety of observations and conclusions about life. You have a level of *emotions,* based partially on your own experience. Your third level is a *physical* one, which includes your health and diet. These levels often overlap, and negative factors at one level will very likely affect all three.

    In addition, you are controlled by certain elements in your environment, such as the building you work in, the number of hours you commute to work or the pollution count on a certain day. Unfavorable environmental factors can seriously affect your energy level and use of time.

    These factors are discussed in more detail below. Examine them as they relate to your life, and determine where your energy is going. Remember, negative factors result in lost energy, and therefore, lost time.

    - Thinking level—Negative factors may appear in your thoughts as absolutes. Thus, something is always wrong, never done or obviously right. Or they may appear as generalizations such as, "That side of town simply has no development opportunities left." Other negative factors are clued by the words "should" (critical), "must" (tense) and "but" (defensive). None of these words is automatically wrong or proof that you are losing energy through negative thought. However, when you catch yourself using one of these terms, you'll probably find you're using the whole group of them.

    - Emotional level—Are you letting your anxieties and worries get the best of you? Do things bother you too much? Do you think,

"If I have to deal with that man one more minute, I'll drown him."? Look at yourself closely. Are these factors the true cause of your temper?

Anxiety is fear in disguise. What's really worrying you? Are you afraid of not being able to complete a transaction you've been working on for six months? Have an honest dialogue with yourself and find your answer. Analyze your problem squarely—is it real, will it definitely happen or is it something that may not happen but would be upsetting if it did? Real problems must be dealt with before they destroy your time-giving energy. Imagined problems should be recognized for what they are and discarded.

- Body level—Men and women in good physical shape have the strength and energy to devote themselves to life. Such people are truly the only ones who gain all the benefits each day has to offer. Live up to the best within you, and you will obtain the greatest energy level. Watch your diet and keep yourself physically fit through a regular program of exercise.

- Environment—There are many unpleasant elements in the world that you cannot avoid. You can't stop thunderstorms, pollution or traffic congestion. Every now and then the air conditioning will break down on a 100° day in the office you're showing. These factors all sap your energy, but there are elements of your environment that you can control. You do not have to live in the next county and drive an hour to work unless that is really important to you. There is no reason why you should spend every day eating your lunch in the same dreary place, or every evening in front of the television set. Change what you can in your environment to make things easier and more pleasant for yourself and to give you more time.

5. *Court the unfamiliar*. Most of us judge the strange and unique harshly and often reject what we don't understand. Yet it is a proven fact that our greatest opportunities for growth lie in the unfamiliar. Give yourself the chance to grow.

6. *Know when to stop*. This will save you time on many problems. You know that when you keep on grimly searching for a solution you can waste many hours that could be spent on something else. If, after a reasonable time, a solution does not present itself, put the problem aside until later. Otherwise, you will exhaust your energy and lose your alertness.

   In addition, when trying to solve a seemingly insoluble problem, attempt to develop new ideas. This is in keeping with your aim to court the unfamiliar.

7. *Stay in contact*. Don't tune anyone out. Try to keep an inward and outward silence, and listen. You'll be surprised at what you learn. Make certain that you really listen to what clients have to say to you, and that you are not tuning them out because of a poor presentation of their needs or some other distraction.

8. *Simplify*. Eliminate excess baggage from your work and your life.

9. *Delegate authority*. The individual who has to do all the work is inefficient. For example, if you make up an entire site presentation

package, you are helping neither yourself nor the staff in your office that could assist you. Don't overburden yourself with details. Allow your secretary or other assistants the freedom to develop their skills to the best of their abilities.

10. *Make decisions.* Indecision is the world's greatest time killer.

11. *Don't waste time on worry or regret.* If you did something badly, or didn't do something you were supposed to do, acknowledge it. Worry changes absolutely nothing. It is negative, self-defeating, and time-consuming. Only when you move forward and take positive steps will your life and work be of value to yourself and others.

12. *Drag yourself out of slumps.* It is easy to let yourself slack off if things are going poorly, or even if they're going too well. Make cold calls in person for two or three days. Get out in the field and meet people. Turn a slump to your advantage.

13. *Manage your money.* Worrying about money is one of the easiest ways to waste time. When you are working on creating transactions, make certain you have some small bread-and-butter ones interspersed with your larger transactions to help offset feast-or-famine situations.

14. *Select what you read carefully.* There are many excellent books and periodicals available in the real estate field that can help you stay up to date with the industry and your community. They can increase your range of knowledge and effectiveness immeasurably. Also, become familiar with some business publications; they, too, will keep you up to date in the field. Ask yourself:

> Is this book or magazine article about a subject I wish to explore at this time?
> What are the author's qualifications?
> Is the style of the book or article easy to read, or is it so confused that it is not worth my while to pursue it?
> Am I reading this for its value or as an escape?

Review your file and paperwork organization, and ask yourself the following questions.

- Have you set up transaction-pending files?
- Are these files in alphabetical order?
- How often do you review these files?
- Have you set up tickler files?
- What kind of information goes into your tickler files?
- What do you do with the information in a file once a transaction is completed?

As you progress through the day you scheduled in Exercise D, check off the things you have accomplished. Have you done everything you intended? What do you see as your greatest time management problems? How can you overcome these problems?

Exercise E

Evaluate how effectively time is being used in each of the following situations.

1. Jack feels that nothing ever gets done right unless he does it.
2. Helen has been trying for four hours to figure out how to get the Smith Company and the Jones Corporation together on a lease, but so far she has come up with nothing. But she's determined she's going to sit there until she does.
3. George is always making comments like, "You should have done it the other day," or, "I would have done that report, but...."
4. Eleanor feels especially alive in the mornings, so she tries to plan her most important client meetings then. In the afternoon her energy gradually drops off—at 5:00 she'll be reading trade publications and answering mail.
5. Carl feels secure in his lifestyle. He gets up at the same time every day, eats the same breakfast, drives Elm Street to Oak Street to Sycamore Street to work, eats lunch at the greasy spoon around the corner every day when he's in the neighborhood and goes home promptly at 5:00 every day via Sycamore to Oak to Elm.

Answer E

1. Jack has not learned how to delegate the small tasks to his assistants. Jack's life is undoutedly one long, losing race against time.

2. If Helen has already spent four unproductive hours on the same problem, chances are she will be no closer to a solution the next morning even if she does sit there all night. Helen needs to leave her problem alone for a while, turn to other tasks, and come back to it later. She will probably be able to approach it from a fresh perspective then.

3. George spends a lot of time pointing out errors in other people's decisions and defending past failures of his own. Neither is productive. George wastes time.

4. Eleanor wisely plans her daily routine around her own energy pattern, scheduling creative activities for the time of day she feels most energetic and routine tasks for her down period.

5. Carl may feel secure, but chances are both he and his thinking are in a rut. Carl ought to get up one morning at 4:30 to go for an early drive; change his breakfast habits; find a new route to work; change his restaurant pattern; and find still another route home in the evening.

10

The Use of Signs

INTRODUCTION

Placing a sign on a building or a vacant parcel of land is an effective way to advertise a property. Real estate companies spend a considerable amount of money every year on signs because signs generate business, and business generates money for the company and for you, the retail salesperson.

Retail divisions of real estate companies do not rely on signs as heavily as industrial divisions do, particularly with respect to buildings. One reason is that industrial users frequently drive around the general area in which they wish to locate and then contact a broker whose name they noticed on signs and buildings. Retail users, on the other hand, more often depend on the broker to find locations that fit their criteria. They come to town not to look around on their own, but to be shown properties that might suit them.

Signs placed in poor locations tend to bring in fewer qualified leads. You are after tenants who will make many transactions involving large amounts of money. You may waste a considerable amount of time on small, one-time transactions if you have signs in poor locations or where there are many vacancies.

However, keep in mind that signs in good locations will mean business for you. Therefore, you must convince property owners to let you place your company's sign on their buildings or land.

Where do you start? As a new salesperson, you will learn to place your company's signs anywhere and everywhere you can. This practice will accomplish three goals.

First, you will gain a greater understanding of your selling area and begin to develop judgment about the best locations for signs.

Second, having signs erected will give you confidence when you talk to tenants and owners. In addition, retail users to whom you are showing property will be impressed with the size and effectiveness of your company when they see your company's signs on many different locations. It is usually easier to erect signs in less preferable areas, but you should use discretion about what areas will give you maximum exposure and still be good properties.

Third, and most important, your mistakes at the beginning are not likely to be costly. You will be gaining experience and getting to know a great many owners, managers, and tenants. As you gain more confidence, you will be better able to identify good locations and persuade owners to let you place your signs on their property. This skill will help you to attract more business and increase your earnings.

You will encounter several different situations regarding signs on buildings or land:

1. a property with only the owner's "for sale" or "for lease" sign
2. a property with another broker's sign, with or without the owner's sign
3. a property with only two signs—yours and the owner's
4. a property with many signs, but not yours
5. a property with many signs, including your sign
6. a property for sale or lease with only your sign on it

The best situation, of course, is one in which the building or land has your company's sign and no other. Second best is your sign and an owner's sign. Third best, and a distant third, is a property with many signs, including one from your office. This situation reduces your company's credibility and should be avoided whenever possible.

CONTENTS OF THE SIGN

When potential tenants observe your company's sign, what do they learn about the property it advertises? Not much, ideally. You want them to know only that the location is available, not whether it is for sale or lease, how many square feet it contains or what price the owner is asking. They also learn the name of your company and the phone number.

The sign might also show your name. In this case, tenants will call you. If the sign is not personalized and a tenant calls, the receptionist will check the inventory system and connect the prospect to you. If you are out and the tenant must know more about the location or perhaps inspect it right away, another salesperson will handle the situation. You can settle the commission later. If the tenant can wait, he or she will leave a number or call back.

A rider is the term used to describe additional information on a real estate company's sign. The best sign is one that holds only your name as a rider, but sometimes other riders are unavoidable. For example, if an owner wishes to lease only part of a building, he or she might insist that the sign state the amount of space available. The owner also might want the sign to state whether the property is for sale or lease.

Ideally, signs should remain uncluttered. Any suggestions or requests (with one exception, which will be discussed later) for riders other than your name should come from the owner, not from you. You'll want to agree to such riders only when it's impossible to do otherwise. A sign's objective is to bring in business. If it says "for sale" and the prospective tenant wants to lease, he or she won't call you. Neither will the prospect call if the amount of space mentioned on the sign isn't right. But once the person calls, you can learn what he or she is looking for. Even if that particular property doesn't suit the tenant, you'll be able to assemble a list of sites that can fulfill the company's needs.

Project signs are sometimes used on major shopping centers. To attract small users, consider specifying on the project sign the major tenants who will anchor the center. Frequently, the developer also wants the sign to carry his or her name. Before committing yourself, try to have the developer share in the cost of the sign.

TECHNIQUES FOR PERSUADING OWNERS

Exercise A

Salesperson Ruth Donovan has learned that a certain building is for lease, but there is no sign on it. She calls the owner.

DONOVAN: *I discovered that your building is for lease, yet there is no sign on it to let interested people know that.*

OWNER: *It's listed. That's enough for me.*

DONOVAN: *Surely you want to cooperate with the brokerage community, though.*

OWNER: *I am cooperating. The property's listed. It's not an exclusive. I just don't want it cluttered up with a lot of signs.*

How should Donovan respond?

Answer A

In this case, the salesperson's main task is to sell her company. Donovan should stress her firm's reputation, the diversified services it provides, its many satisfied customers and how all of this will benefit the owner.

Donovan could also play on the embarrassment factor. She could explain to the owner that real estate salespeople are embarrassed to show properties that do not hold their company's sign because this undermines tenants' confidence in them. Tenants might wonder how much rapport Donovan has with this owner and how good a deal she can put together if the owner won't even allow her to put up a sign. Good rapport with both owner and tenant is essential. Donovan should point out to the owner that a lack of rapport with tenants will diminish the chances of concluding a satisfactory transaction.

Donovan should also avoid making the owner choose between a yes or no. As the owner begins to be persuaded, she should assume an affirmative response and move on to a discussion of where the sign should go.

Exercise B

Suppose that after Donovan has made all her points, the owner says, "You may be right, but if I let you put up a sign, I'll have to let all the others put their's up too, and the building will look cluttered."

How should Donovan respond to this argument?

Answer B

There are three ways to handle this argument.

First, she can sell her company's capabilities. Then use the following analogy.

"How many doctors do you go to—four or five? You don't go to that many doctors because you know that you won't be able to establish good relationships with all of them or get the services you need. Why go to three other brokers? Our firm can provide all the services you need and, in the process, establish a good working relationship between your company and ours. I am willing to go out of my way to help you if you will allow me to put my company's sign up there without anyone else's."

Second, Donovan can try to get the owner to agree to a sign rider reading "exclusive sign rights." This is one instance in which the salesperson, not the owner, might suggest a rider. An exclusive sign right is not the same as an exclusive listing. It simply means that Donovan's will be the only broker's sign on the property, enhancing her chances of making a transaction and earning a commission.

Third, Donovan might obtain what amounts to an exclusive sign without the rider. This involves simply telling the owner that she will write to the top dozen or so brokers and tell them that the owner doesn't want any more signs on the property. She'll want to send the owner a copy of this letter.

Exercise C

Now Donovan has her sign up. Has she overlooked anything? What steps should she take next?

Answer C

The next steps are extremely important. Donovan should (a) try for an exclusive listing; (b) find out if the owner has other property for sale or lease and (c) learn whether the owner has other real estate needs. Remember, referrals to other divisions in your company can mean increased commissions for you. These steps should be standard operating procedure any time you're talking with an owner.

Exercise D

Consider another situation. An owner has only his or her own sign on the property. Although the salesperson's approach here would be much the same as when there is no sign at all, the owner's sign alone does carry a particular implication, even when it contains the phrase "broker's cooperation welcome." What is that implication?

Answer D

Regardless of the wording of the owner's sign, the lack of any brokers' signs implies the owner's hope to sell or lease the property without any professional assistance. The only motive for this is to avoid paying a commission.

Property for Sale or Lease by Owner

Even if the owner denies this intention, explain how potentially damaging the owner's intention to sell or lease his or her own property can be to relations with the brokerage community. Point out that the owner's chances of moving the property without a broker are slim. Few tenants will want to deal directly with a principal. They need a buffer, a person to negotiate for them. Besides, retail users often wish to remain anonymous until the last possible moment in a transaction and prefer to work through brokers for this reason.

Some users, of course, will deal directly with owners. These people often hope to lower the rent or sale price by eliminating a broker's commission. Owners who go along with this court trouble. The myriad of details handled by a broker will be sure to cause difficulty for owners.

A broker's sign informs the brokerage community that the owner is serious in inviting cooperation. This argument for a broker's sign is impossible to refute. It forces the owner to back up his or words by allowing you to erect your company's sign. Such action hurts the owner in no way; on the contrary, it helps him or her a great deal.

The owner may respond, "If I let you put a sign up, I'll have to let others, too, and soon the place will look junky." If you've been paying attention, you'll know how to counter that argument.

One Broker's Sign

Now consider a situation in which there is one broker's sign on the property, with or without the owner's sign. If there is no exclusive listing rider on the sign, call the owner. If the listing is not an exclusive, tell the owner you would like the opportunity to list the property and put your sign up. If it is an exclusive, emphasize that you will be happy to cooperate with the exclusive broker. The important point here is that you always call the owner first, thereby precluding the possibility of having to split a commission with another broker simply because he or she has a sign on the property.

If the listing is not exclusive, try to persuade the owner that it's misleading to have only one broker's sign when the listing is open. Another sign—*your* sign—will eliminate all ambiguity. It will automatically alert the brokerage community that the listing is open, thus enhancing the owner's chances of moving it. Furthermore, the owner will no longer be bothered by inquiring phone calls. Of course, your sign will increase your chances of earning a commission. You'll have done both the owner and yourself a service.

Once again, if the owner objects and says that allowing you to put up your sign means letting everyone else do so, offer to write letters to all brokers, except the one whose sign is already posted, telling them no new signs will be permitted.

Remember, whenever you're asking an owner for permission to put your sign on a building, assume that the answer will be yes. Lead the owner through arguments in favor of your sign and then say, "Shall I put our sign to the right or left of yours?" Or, "Shall I put our sign to the left or right of ABC Realty's?" Avoid asking a question that might result in a flat refusal. Offer placement choices instead.

Exercise E

Here is the most stimulating and challenging situation you might face—a property has many signs, but yours is not among them. You call the owner, Susan Snyder, to ask for permission to place your sign.

YOU: *(after telling the owner what your company can do for her, conclude):* And I think we could fit our sign right here, to the left of yours.

OWNER: *Well, I don't know. The place is plastered with signs. It looks cluttered. I've been thinking of calling all those brokers and telling them to take their signs down.*

How will you respond?

Answer E

You can be fairly certain that the owner is unlikely to get around to requesting all the brokers to take down their signs. So you must use judgment in this case.

You can ignore the owner's comment and sell her on your company's reputation, size and record of success. Aim to persuade her that your sign on her building would greatly enhance her chances of making a lease or sale. It's not a question of what difference one more sign would make. The point is, the one sign that can do the most good is missing. Chances are you'll persuade the owner that your sign should be on her property.

Exercise F

Suppose the owner is serious when she says the property looks junky with so many signs. Assume also that she means it when she says she's going to have all the brokers remove their signs. What can you do to persuade her to make yours the exception?

CHAPTER 10 / The Use of Signs   141

Answer F

Your own judgment here is of paramount importance; only you can size up the situation. But you might offer to do the owner's job for her. Offer to write to the brokers represented, as well as to others, telling them the owner wants the present signs removed and wants no more erected. Be sure the owner gets a copy of your letter.

And be sure to stress one other point. Tell the owner what will happen after the brokers receive the letters. Tell her they will call, that they will be unhappy and will threaten not to show the property or even threaten to remove it from their list. Assure the owner, however, that although the brokers will be unhappy, they will continue to promote the property. It's safe to assume that they're interested in commissions. The main point is, you've forewarned the owner.

Exercise G

However, even if this ploy works you have not attained your goal. What is that goal? How might you attain it?

Answer G

You're not after an equal chance to move the property. You really want to increase the odds in your favor. You want your sign up and as few other signs on the property as possible.

It is likely that the signs will be those of major companies. However, one might represent a small company, perhaps a firm you've never heard of. It may be there because someone in the company is the owner's friend. And so you proceed:

"We'll take the signs down, but we don't really want them all down. We don't want to give the impression that you're not cooperating with the brokerage community, nor do we wish to confuse anyone. Let's leave ABC's sign up. Now, shall we put ours to the left or the right of it?"

You will have your sign up, and you will have it up against the weakest competition. Within a couple of weeks (and if this is not the case by then, get on the phone to competitors about their signs) just your sign and ABC's will adorn the property. Because your sign is on many more buildings observed by users looking for retail space, you're more likely to get a call than ABC.

The technique just described won't work in every case. You must exercise your judgment about when to use it.

Don't forget that each sales talk will occur under slightly different circumstances. You have to play each situation by ear, at least in part. Keep a record of what works and what doesn't in any given situation, and try to discover why. Gradually you'll weed out mistakes and faulty judgment and develop your own successful style.

Don't be put off. In spite of all your arguments in favor of your company's sign, the owner might still say no. But that is not the end of it. Keep going back, in person and by phone. Be persistent. Eventually the owner will get to know you. He or she might grow weary of your persistence and let you put up your sign just to get rid of you.

Remember, completing a transaction—be it a sale or lease—is the name of the game. With a sign up, especially if it's alone or against weak competition, you have a much better than even chance of completing the deal. The more signs up, the better your chances.

SIGN REQUISITIONS

Some companies use standardized sign requisition forms. Find out what your form looks like, what information you will be required to fill in and where all copies are to be sent.

You'll probably have to provide copy for the sign indicating when the property is available; whether it is for sale, lease, sale or lease or build-to-suit; and when to call for information. If the sign is to contain extraordinary copy, company policy might be that the owner or developer pay the cost, or that the cost be borne jointly by the company and the broker. Find out what your company's policy is.

You will probably also have to indicate whether the sign will be erected on posts, a fence, the building or an illuminated freestanding sign. In the case of the building, note whether the building is wood, brick, or concrete block.

Street address and cross-streets, as well as any distinctive features of the building or the area, may also be asked for.

Find out when you expect the sign to go up. Then check it to verify copy and location.

11

Retail Promotion

INTRODUCTION

Real estate promotional efforts are not aimed solely at selling or leasing specific pieces of property. This is an important objective, but promotional efforts also have broader, more inclusive goals. One is to bring in prospects, people who call in response to a promotional piece. Although they may not buy or lease the property they originally call about, these prospects are prime candidates for future properties. The salesperson's job, then, is to qualify them and proceed toward a possible transaction. A second general purpose of promotion is to create and keep before the public an image of your company as a reputable and active real estate firm. This will help salespeople obtain listings.

TYPES OF ADVERTISING

Since promotion is company-oriented, the annual advertising budget is a company-level concern. Generally, promotional efforts are paid for by the company, not by individual salespeople. In cases of large properties, the owner or merchants' association may pay for some or all of the promotional effort.

Four types of promotional effort will be discussed here. They are:

1. classified ads

2. display ads
3. brochures
4. letters

Retail divisions generally do not use classified ads. Sometimes they will run display ads. Only on occasion will they rely on letters to promote property. Heavy emphasis is on brochures and site submittal packages. (Submittal packages will be discussed in the chapter titled *Site Presentation*.)

Classified Advertising

Of all forms of advertising, *classified ads* are the least expensive per line of copy. However, the true cost of advertising is the cost per reader who is actually qualified to take action on the product the company is offering. Classified advertising represents a scattershot approach, aimed at the public in general, many of whom are not interested in retail real estate. It is also short-lived. Few people read yesterday's classified ads. Most important, many users of retail space, especially large chains, do not look at classified newspaper ads to find property for sale or lease. They are more likely to read classified ads in specific trade journals or trade papers such as *The Wall Street Journal*, and display advertising is even more popular with such users.

Display Advertising

Display advertising (see the example following) is placed throughout a newspaper or periodical, although a specific ad may be designated for placement in a specific section of the paper. For example, the financial section is often an appropriate place to position an ad for commercial or industrial real estate.

The display ad allows much more flexibility in format. Borders around the ad, pictures, maps and other embellishments can be used. The cost per line generally is higher than in classified advertising. Display advertising might be used in the case of a large retail property or a shopping center development. However, display advertising has the same limitations as classified advertising in reaching the qualified prospect.

Brochures

A brochure is a specially designed and printed piece that is mailed to a select group of people who constitute the market for particular properties. Two sample brochures are reproduced in this chapter. A brochure may be directed to a single property or may cover a vacant shopping center. The brochure ordinarily contains a picture of the property in question, brief copy and a map. It sometimes includes an aerial photograph of the property.

Brochures have the longest life of any type of promotion. They tend to remain in the offices to which they are mailed. They also can serve as calling cards for the retail salesperson, so always carry several to leave

FIGURE 11.1 Display Ad

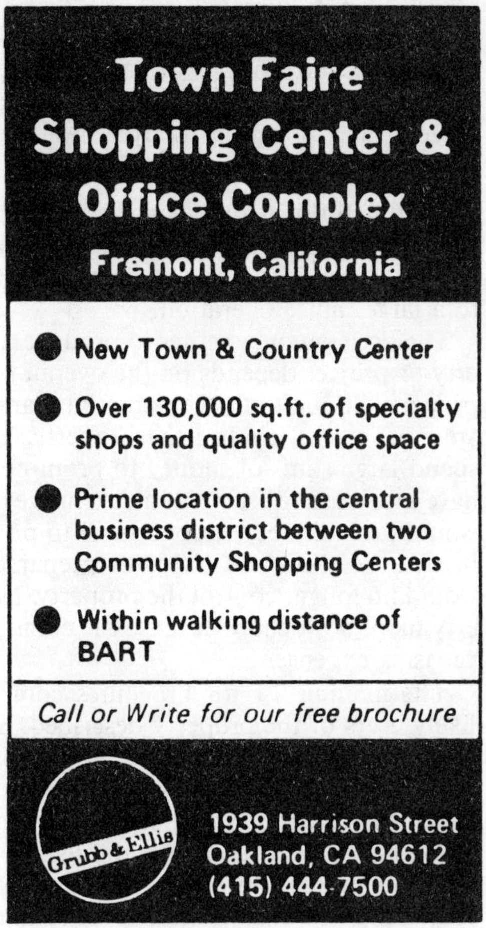

Town Faire Shopping Center & Office Complex
Fremont, California

- New Town & Country Center
- Over 130,000 sq.ft. of specialty shops and quality office space
- Prime location in the central business district between two Community Shopping Centers
- Within walking distance of BART

Call or Write for our free brochure

Grubb & Ellis
1939 Harrison Street
Oakland, CA 94612
(415) 444-7500

---

with companies when cold calling or making face-to-face contacts with prospective tenants.

An effective brochure has certain essential characteristics. The design should be eye-catching to attract attention. The copy should be brief and to the point. The brochure should say little or nothing about the lease or sale price because you want the tenant to come to you for further information. If the prospect decides against the property because of the figures in the brochure, you lose the opportunity to provide comprehensive service and to suggest alternate properties.

The brochure should point up special features of the property, such as current census statistics, traffic counts, proximity to other major development and anchor tenants already secured. It should also include your company's name and/or logo. If it deals with a single piece of property, it should include the salesperson's name, address and phone number. All brochures should carry a disclaimer, which might read:

> This statement, and the information it contains, is given with the understanding that all negotiations relating to the purchase or leasing of the property described above shall be conducted through this office.

The above information, while not guaranteed, has been secured from sources we believe to be reliable.

Another version of a disclaimer is:

The information contained herein either has been given to us by the owner of the property or has been obtained from sources we deem reliable. We have no reason to doubt its accuracy, but we do not guarantee it. The prospective buyer should carefully verify the above items of income and expense and all other information contained herein.

Although this feature is not essential, a brochure may also contain a suggestion as to which users might have a particular interest in the property. For example, a vacant supermarket would be especially appealing to a large fabric operation.

The decision on whether to produce a brochure for a particular property or project depends on the overall promotional budget, the type of property in question, the potential market for it and the length of time your office will control the property. Your company will not want to spend large sums of money to promote property on which it does not have an exclusive listing. If an exclusive had only a 30- or 60-day term, it would probably be uneconomical to promote the property by brochure because by the time one was prepared and distributed, your office would no longer control the property. Nor would a small piece of property merit a brochure because the commission would not justify the advertising expense.

The mailing list for brochures comprises companies that are most likely users of the property described. Special lists can be obtained for brochures that deal with special purpose buildings. For example, you would use a list of restaurateurs for a promotional mailing describing a potential restaurant location. Depending on the property, a brochure might have a wide mailing, although this is an expensive method and returns are not usually high. A firm might decide on a wide mailing for a large property that would appeal to national and regional users. More frequently, brochures will be mailed to local or regional users.

Another important mailing list contains the names of active brokers and salespeople of retail property. By mailing brochures to them, you can solicit their cooperation, which will increase the exposure of your property.

As a salesperson, you must furnish information for brochures, since you are the one who knows your listing best. You should know what features to emphasize, but it is best to verify all information with the owner or developer and perhaps the merchants' association. Design and layout of the brochure are normally assigned to commercial artists.

Letters

Letters are addressed to the narrowest market of all and are the most expensive form of promotion. They are conversational, short and to the point, and they usually cover a package of other promotional pieces describing particular types of property. Promotional letters state why the property is important, describe it briefly and end by asking for some action on the reader's part or by promising some action on the signer's part. Ordinarily, letters are addressed to 100 or fewer people. If a list has more than 100 names, a brochure is generally a better medium than a

FIGURE 11.2 Brochure A

OXFORD CENTER NOW LEASING

SPACE AVAILABLE:
26,000 Sq. Ft. Retail.
10,000 Sq. Ft. Professional office.
16,000 Sq. Ft. Medical suites.

PARKING:
341 cars.

TRAFFIC FLOW:
20,000 cars Third Ave.
5,000 cars Oxford.

POPULATION:
100,000 City of Chula Vista and surrounding area.

LOCATION:
Ideally located at the Northwest intersection of Third Avenue and Oxford Street.

FOR ADDITIONAL INFORMATION CONTACT:

Ed Pope
Res. 282-0978

Grubb & Ellis

Grubb & Ellis Co., Real Estate
110 West A Street, Suite 1000, San Diego, CA 92101
Telephone (714) 236-1177

FIGURE 11.2 Brochure A (Concluded)

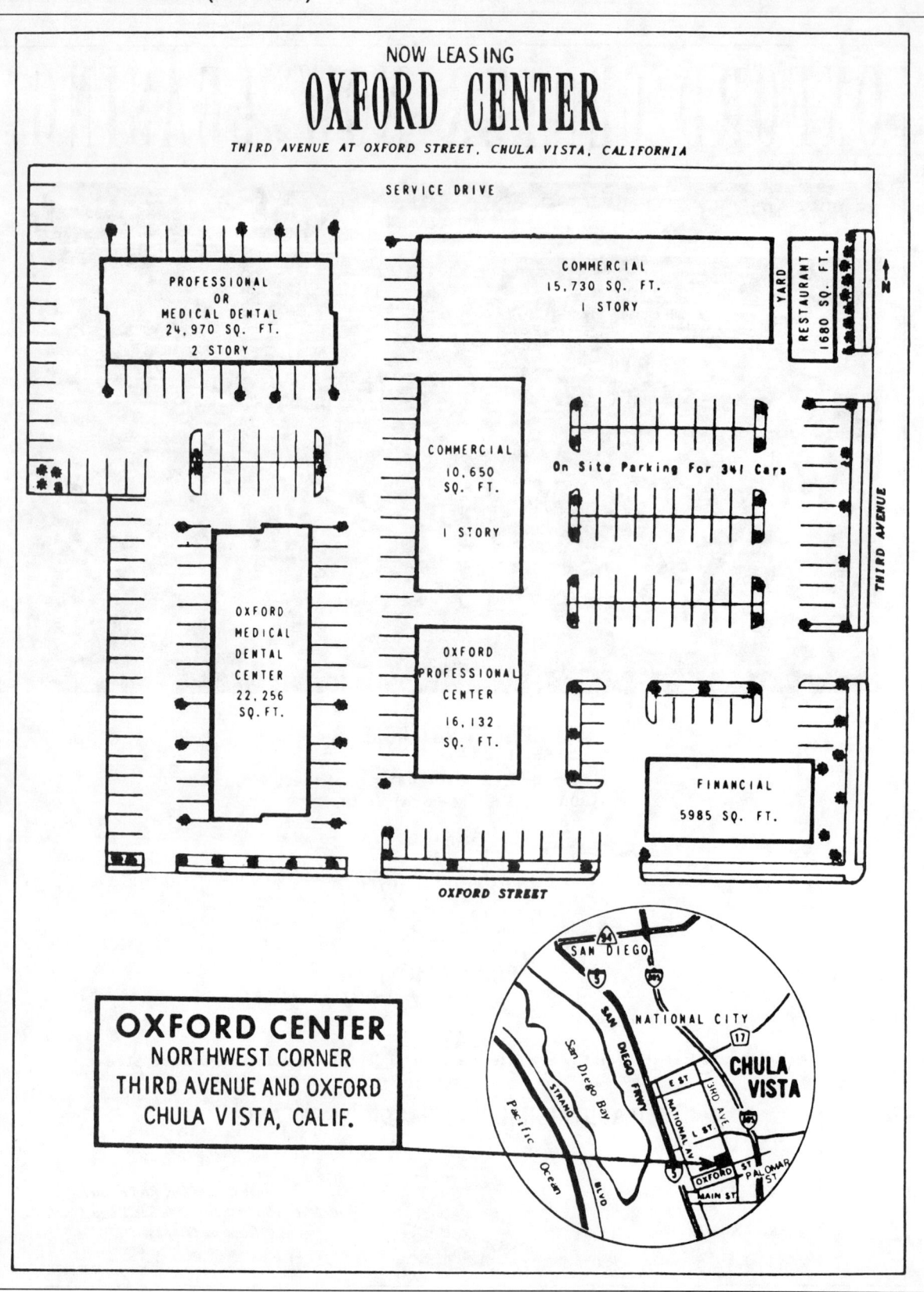

letter. However, letters are best to use when you are submitting site packages to prospective users or buyers. Together with site submittal packages, letters are probably the most widely used form of promotion in the retail division.

THE SALESPERSON'S FUNCTION

Promotion is one of the services a salesperson offers a prospective seller or lessor. Your ability to provide this service will be limited by the overall promotion budget.

A retail property salesperson has other promotional responsibilities besides providing accurate copy for ads and mailings. You must bring into the company the kind of property that makes promotion worthwhile. Be prepared with a list of properties comparable to those promoted through advertising, brochures and letters. When a promotional effort draws a response, you will be ready to present alternative sites if a particular property does not suit the prospective tenant.

Exercise A

1. What are the purposes of promotion?
2. Why do retail brokerage firms place a major emphasis on brochures?
3. Why should a brochure say nothing about sale or lease price?
4. What are your responsibilities with respect to brochures?
5. What influences the decision to produce a brochure?
6. What are the essential characteristics of an effective brochure?
7. Examine Brochure A in the text. On an ascending scale from 0–10, rate each characteristic you have identified in question 6 above. Do the same for Brochure B, which follows the questions.
8. Overall, which brochure would you rate higher? In what ways do they differ?

Answer A

1. *The purposes are to move a particular property, bring in prospective tenants and keep your company's name before the public.*
2. *Brochures are used because ads, especially classified ads, are generally not an effective medium for attracting attention to retail property. Letters are also largely ineffective and are too expensive.*
3. *You want the tenant to contact you directly for that information. This will give you the opportunity to determine what services you can offer.*

150   Successful Leasing and Selling of Retail Property

4. *You are responsible for providing accurate copy, stating what you would like to feature, bringing in listings worth advertising and being prepared to show comparable property.*

5. *The likely commission on a sale or lease, the state of the promotional budget, the size of the building (which influences the commission), the length of time your office controls the property, the type of property and the likely market for it all affect the decision of whether to produce a brochure.*

6. *A brochure should be characterized by catchiness, brevity, special features, company name, salesperson name, disclaimer and ambiguity as to price and location.*

7.
	A	B	
catchiness			*(opinions will vary)*
brevity	*8*	*7*	
special features	*10*	*0*	
company name	*10*	*10*	
salesperson name	*0*	*0*	
disclaimer	*0*	*0*	
price ambiguity	*10*	*10*	
location ambiguity	*0*	*0*	

8. *Brochure A rates higher on several counts. It contains details on special features missing in Brochure B and it has more interesting graphics.*

Exercise B

Read the following descriptions of property. Then indicate what items you would eliminate in a brochure describing each property.

1. This property is located in Hayward. It is a shopping center of 120,000 square feet. Stores in the center range in size from 6,000 to 20,000 square feet. None of the property is presently leased. The center has a lighted, blacktopped parking lot with parking for 1,000 cars and city water and sewers. The traffic count is 30,000 cars per day. There is room for further expansion of the shopping center once present facilities are leased and prove successful. It is located near Grand and Lake, in one of the faster-growing areas of the county, five minutes from the freeway interchange. A larger shopping mall is located in the area.

2. This is a freestanding restaurant building located on the main artery between downtown and the most affluent suburbs. It has failed as a restaurant in the past due to poor management and promotion rather than location or the facilities. It contains 9,000 square feet, with parking for 60 cars on a lighted, blacktopped lot. The building is two years old and has been vacant for four months. It has a completely equipped kitchen, including utensils, and a small office in the rear. Chairs, tables, booths, dishes and silverware are still in the store.

3. This is a retail facility in a downtown location, containing 4,000 square feet with a 40-foot frontage. It is a half-block off the main

CHAPTER 11 / Retail Promotion 151

FIGURE 11.3 Brochure B

FOR LEASE
36,000 SQUARE FEET

GENESEE PLAZA SHOPPING CENTER
San Diego, California

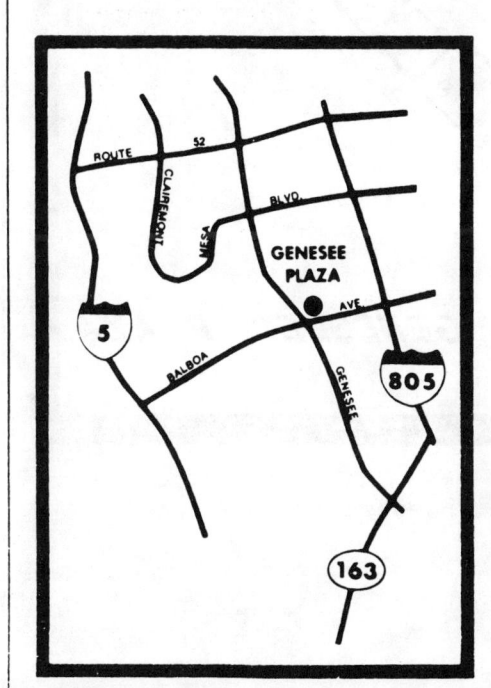

This is a 47 acre shopping center now developed with an 100,000 sq. ft. FedMart store, banks, restaurants, and retail stores located at the northeast corner of Balboa and Genesee Avenues.

CONTACT: George Adams or Rob Schaefer

- Prime retail location in one of San Diego's major regional shopping areas.
- Population: 82,500 in 2 mile radius.
- Traffic Flow — Balboa, 34,000 cars/day; Genesee, 20,000 cars/day.
- Space Available — 2,400 sq. ft. to 36,000 sq. ft. in 1200 ft. increments.
- Available: October 15, 1973.

Grubb & Ellis

110 West A Street
San Diego, Calif. 92101
(714) 236-1177

FIGURE 11.3 Brochure B (Concluded)

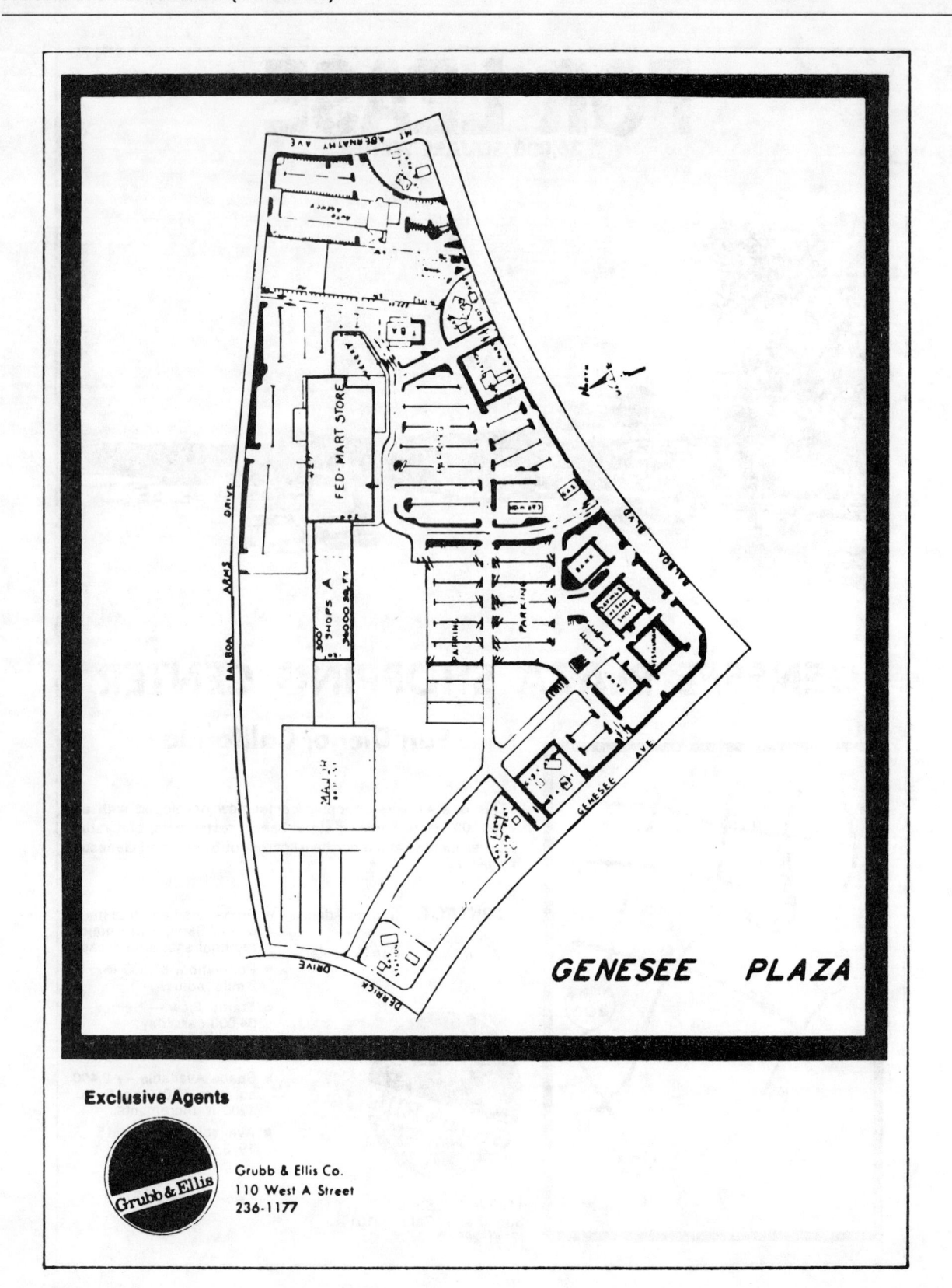

CHAPTER 11 / Retail Promotion   153

downtown street, and contains a full basement storage area. There is a hardware store on the east side and an office supply store on the west. The store was previously used as a gift and card shop. The lease is for five years. Some store fixtures are still available. The traffic pattern is erratic, depending on the time of day and the season.

Answer B

1. *You would probably not want to mention that none of the property is presently leased. A prospective tenant might wonder if there are certain drawbacks to the property that have kept retailers away. Also, stating that expansion is possible once present facilities are leased and prove successful has a negative tone and does not inspire confidence in the shopping center. Finally, rather than saying that stores range in size from 6,000 to 20,000 square feet, you might say that stores are available in a full range of sizes.*

2. *You would not want to mention that the building failed as a restaurant due to poor management and promotion rather than because of location and facilities. This sounds as if you are casting around for blame and some suspicion will inevitably fall on the location. For like reasons, it would be unwise to mention that the building has been vacant for four months.*

3. *Several points in this description should be eliminated, such as previous use of the store, the types of adjacent users, the fact that it is half a block from the main street, the erratic traffic pattern and the specific lease term of five years. Any one of these points could make a user decide, sight unseen, that this particular facility is unsuitable.*

12

Showing Retail Property

INTRODUCTION

You will probably show property to many retail users. They will be taking time out from a busy schedule, so be prepared to show them sites that fit their specifications, and be ready to discuss the listing and move toward completing a transaction. There are three steps in showing retail property:

1. preparation
2. presentation
3. follow-up

After completing this chapter, you should understand the details involved in these three steps. You should also know the procedure for showing retail property and the pitfalls to avoid.

PREPARATION

The first rule in showing retail property, and a vital part of your preparation, is to qualify your tenants. Among other things you will need to know:

1. What do they sell?
2. How many square feet are they looking for?

3. Are they interested in a freestanding or shopping center property?
4. What is their rent range?
5. What kind of neighbors do they want—or object to?
6. How many locations will they want in a given area?
7. Do they have a minimum for traffic count, and is it auto or pedestrian?
8. Who are their competitors and how near will they locate to them?
9. Do they require demographic information such as type of population and median incomes?
10. What are their parking needs?

You can determine tenant's requirements over the phone. As you talk with them, you can be thinking of suitable locations. After you have gathered the information you need, set a time for them to visit the sites. Half a day is usually sufficient for showing several properties.

The next step is to match tenant specifications to listings. As you comb the listing file (explained in the chapter on inventory), select listings allowing a range differential of 500 to 1,000 square feet, unless a tenant is adamant about a particular square footage. Although space is usually one of the tenant's primary considerations, it is far from the only one. You want to provide as wide a range of choices as possible within the tenant's limitations.

How many listings should you select? This will depend on:

- How many locations the tenant wants in a specific area.
- How far apart he or she wants the outlets to be.
- How many sites are available that fit the tenant's specifications.

For example, if the tenant needs 20,000 square feet of building and parking, you might have only two or three suitable locations to offer. If, on the other hand, the tenant wants 2,000 square feet in a neighborhood shopping center, you might come up with 15 or 20 appropriate listings.

Next, check the listings to be sure they are up to date. Call the owners to verify the price, availability, current taxes and other information on listings. If the building is occupied, find out when the tenants will move and how much time they will have. Allow some leeway here. A move can be delayed for a number of reasons and if a tenant cannot get out on a specific date, your transaction might fall through.

You'll need keys to show the buildings, so have them made well in advance of your appointment with the tenant. Be sure the keys work and there is lighting at the location. To avoid any surprises, inspect the property yourself shortly before showing it to the tenant.

Plan Your Route—Then Drive It Yourself

Every property has good and bad points. Naturally, you want to stress the good points. If a property has an industrial area on one side, for example, and a residential neighborhood on the other, bring the tenant to the location through the residential area. Retailers are particularly concerned with residential back-up. Approach the site so that you can make a right turn into the property. Most tenants are concerned about the entrance to and exit from a location, so you want to avoid left turns (unless the property lies on the left side of a one-way street). Lay out the route that saves you and the tenant the most time.

Although you want to set up a tight schedule and stay with it, don't cut corners. Allow sufficient time for presentations. Be sure to tell your tenants if more than half a day is needed to show all the properties they want to see. Then, as you progress, plan not to hurry them. A broker who fails to allot sufficient time for showings can lose business. If you fail to show tenants all the properties they wish to see, some other broker might show them the remainder. If that happens, you've wasted your time.

The only way you will know how much time it will take to travel the route you've laid out is to drive it yourself and time it. Tracing your route on a map will not only make it easier for you to follow, but will also give the tenant a layout of the area. The map should indicate where competition is located. Include a fact sheet giving information on zoning, necessity for local special-use permits and traffic counts if these are important to the tenant. Traffic counts can be obtained from planning and highway departments. Be sure the figures are current. If no counts exist for a location, you will have to count traffic yourself, or have someone do it for you.

The tenant will also want information on the type of population in the area, its median income and other demographic characteristics, which you will include in your fact sheet. You can obtain such data from the planning department, state sales tax figures and U.S. Census Bureau publications.

It's a good idea to compile fact sheets containing descriptions of all the properties—location, size, facilities, background on the merchants' association and so on. However, do not give this information to the tenant until all the properties have been shown.

Showing to Local Users

The main difference between showing properties to national or regional chains and to local tenants is that the local people usually know the area. You can go further with qualifying them on the phone. You can inquire if they are familiar with a particular intersection, commercial strip or shopping center. Are they interested in these locations? Why or why not? What rent are they paying? Do they know the rent ranges in the area you are discussing? Are they willing to meet the rent if it is higher than what they are paying now?

Ordinarily, local users will not need to see as many locations as out-of-town users, simply because you can qualify them more thoroughly on the phone. You will need less time for showing, and that is certainly to your advantage. Regional or national tenants, however, can represent several transactions for you because they will probably plan to open a number of new outlets each year. They are well worth the time you devote to them. Local users, as a rule, will represent only one or two transactions. You will want to spend less time with them.

A third difference between local users and regional or national users is that business with local tenants will usually be completed more quickly. In many cases, one person will make the decision. Several people will usually be involved in a decision about regional or national outlets, and the decision will be made on a high level. Consequently, weeks—even months—might pass before a transaction is approved.

What About Owners?

Some owners and developers want to be present when you show their property. If the owner insists, emphasize that your time and the tenant's are valuable. Explain that he or she must adhere to the schedule you have set and not become involved with the presentation in any way.

Owners generally do more harm than good during a presentation. They tend to talk too much, and they cannot usually present their property to its maximum advantage because they are not trained salespeople.

Exercise A

How might you persuade an owner not to accompany you when you show his or her property?

Answer A

Explain that showing the property is your job, the task for which you have been trained. Assure the owner that you'll get in touch with him or her if there are any questions you can't answer. Emphasize that you are the expert and that you know what you're doing. The objective is to complete a transaction, and you are the one to do that. If the owner is still adamant about being present, make it clear that all you want him or her to do is to unlock the door and stand aside. The owner is to volunteer no information and ask no questions. Above all, he or she must remember that tenants usually wish to remain anonymous until a transaction is well along. Tenants think of you, the broker, as a buffer between themselves and the owner.

THE PRESENTATION

You are now ready to make your presentation. You should do the driving because you know the route and the area. Make sure your tenant has a note pad and pen to jot down observations about each property. As you drive, the tenant can study the map you have made of the area where you will be showing locations.

Don't worry about conversation as you drive the presentation route. It will not help you earn a commission. You can test a tenant's desire to talk by asking a question that can be answered with more than a simple yes or no. If the tenant chooses to respond with a one-word answer, you had better save conversation for later.

What happens at a location? What dialogue occurs? This depends on the retailer. In many cases, tenants will not be especially concerned about space and other physical aspects of the location, such as bathrooms and the heating system. They will know that you are offering locations that meet the physical specifications agreed on during initial qualification. A national or regional tenant might not wish to inspect the building at all. On the other hand, a local user will probably want to look closely because it may be the only one of the few locations he or she will be occupying.

Regional or national tenants will probably be more interested in who the tenants are, the number of people at the location and the number of cars in the parking lot. They will try to get a feeling for the atmosphere of the location and of the general business area itself. You must be prepared to talk about how other tenants seem to be doing, the market area, trends with respect to new shopping centers or the development of new commercial strips—in other words, factors that will affect business should the tenant locate in this particular area.

Exercise B

Suppose a tenant asks a question you can't answer. What should you do?

Answer B

The best thing, of course, is to say, "I don't know." Some salespeople in their eagerness to do business, are tempted to make up an answer. Faking can cause you to lose a transaction. Simply tell the tenant you don't know the answer but will find out. Make a note of the question and tell the tenant when you will get back to him or her with the information. If you do not have the answer at the time specified, call the tenant and say so. Don't leave him or her hanging. Don't let the tenant get the slightest impression that you're not interested in his or her needs. This goes for all tenants—local as well as national and regional.

What about instances in which you're promoting a project for which you are responsible? Will your techniques be different?

Not really. You have an obligation to promote your project, but a tenant might not want the location. In that case, be sure to have alternatives. Let the tenant know that the property is your listing. If you can't sell your project, direct the tenant to another location.

When dealing with regional or national tenants, you will often have to show locations more than once, and you might have to show them to groups. Normally, your first contact will be with a nearby company real estate director or manager. This person's recommendations will go up the corporate ladder to be considered by others. Several people might come to town to narrow choices and go into greater detail on certain locations.

Exercise C

What should you do if you are showing a shopping center or commercial strip to a group and the members split up to examine different aspects of the site?

Answer C

> *Stick with the decision maker. This person may be the head of the company's real estate department, the company president or some other officer. He or she will be instrumental in the decision.*
>
> *You want to stay with the decision maker because you want to be available to answer questions and assess his or her reactions. Also, when the others come back with objections—and generally they will, if for no other reason than to impress their superior—you will be ready with answers. A minor objection can become major if it is not handled immediately and properly. On the other hand, a major objection can become minor only if you've done your homework and your preparation has been thorough.*

When handling objections, be tactful with everyone. Meet objections easily and smoothly. Bruised feelings, even in a subordinate, can mean the loss of a tenant's business.

FOLLOW-UP

Once your showing schedule is completed, give your tenants the fact sheets mentioned earlier and suggest that they transfer their notes to these sheets. They can then match their comments to the physical facts about each location. Tell them you withheld the sheets until now because you wanted them to see all the locations first. They could then form their own impressions and avoid eliminating any sites solely on the basis of physical description.

Since your prime objective is to complete a transaction, try to get the tenants' commitment on which locations to pursue further. You will get some indication of what they are thinking from their reactions and remarks along the presentation route. They may have already decided on one location. In some cases, you might be able to persuade the tenant to make a bid on a location immediately, even if the deal is not completed. The presentation of a bona fide offer, even with conditions, takes a property off the market for a specified period of time. For example, the offer can be based on such conditions as tenants' satisfaction with a building's physical aspects or a remodeling agreement reached with the owner.

Rent Schedules

Never tell a tenant that you can get a property at a certain price. You may know that the price can be negotiated, or you can quickly find out from the owner, but don't put yourself out on a limb by quoting a specific figure. If you are not able to deliver, you will lose the tenant.

Rent for retail locations generally goes by square foot, often tied in with a percentage of gross sales. For example, an owner might ask six percent of gross sales. This may be too high a figure for a particular tenant. However, the tenant may do a sufficient volume of business that a lower percentage on gross sales will provide the same amount of rent. Checking with the owner and getting back to the tenant is part of your follow-up procedure.

Rents on retail outlets vary from area to area. Part of qualifying your tenants is determining the range in which they fit. Some tenants, particularly those from out of the area, are inclined to be unrealistic about rents. Perhaps they have been operating within a lower rental range than the one in your area. You must persuade them, early in the game, that they will pay higher rents if they insist on locating in a certain area. Some tenants will not fully understand this until they are ready to make a bid. In such cases, you might find yourself doing a special selling job to save the transaction.

Remember, do not, under any circumstances, tell a tenant that you can get a building or a vacant lot for a particular price. The best you can do is take the tenant's bid to the owner and try to negotiate. Do not, however, leave the tenant entirely on his or her own to determine a bidding price. If the tenant's figure is unrealistically low, say so. A bid that is too far under an owner's asking price may be flatly rejected, with no counterproposal from the owner. Each situation is different. You must be the judge, based on your qualification of the owner, the tenant, and your knowledge of the area and the market.

Exercise D

If current rents in an area range between three and six percent, what should you tell your tenant?

Answer D

If you give the tenant a range, you've made a mistake. He or she will remember the low figure and forget the high one. You might have trouble finding a transaction at the low price. Don't suggest a range; take the top figure. Then if you settle somewhere between low and high, you'll have been of service to your tenant.

On the other hand, your tenant may be familiar with rental ranges and want to aim at the low figure. You're wise here to persuade him or her that this is probably unrealistic. Convince the tenant that it's best to aim for the high figure and hope to close a transaction somewhat below that.

A specific price is only one of several things you should never promise tenants. Others include specific types of remodeling or refinishing, extra power and so on. Such items frequently depend on negotiations with the owner. Tenants must be aware of this. Some owners will remodel to suit and amortize the cost over the leasing period from the rent. Others will insist that remodeling is the tenant's concern. However, what they tell you in the beginning might not hold true forever. An owner might be strongly against doing any remodeling, yet if you present an attractive tenant whose outlet will mean money in the owner's pocket, it might change his or her mind.

The main point is, don't promise anything.

Moving Toward a Close

If you have shown a tenant a number of buildings and he or she is indecisive, you can help reach a decision. Borrow the tenant's notes and copy them. Then compare the sheets, looking for common factors. Probably two, three or more locations will appear suitable with respect to neighbors and general business atmosphere of the area. Concentrate on these with your tenant, and help narrow the choice to one. Nudge him or her toward a decision. The end result might be a compromise on rent and other location features. The main point is to serve and satisfy your tenant.

Always follow up the showing with a letter to the tenant. The letter should include a list of all the locations you showed and your thanks for the time spent with you. The list of locations serves two purposes: It indicates that you are interested in the tenant and have his or her needs in mind, and it protects you from any tendency on the tenant's part to do business on his or her own for a location you have shown. A tenant who has been shown ten locations, each under a different ownership, will probably not take the time and trouble to try to find out who the owners are in order to make a transaction without you. But it is particularly important to protect yourself in a shopping center situation because it is fairly easy for the tenant to identify the owner of a large shopping center.

Also, make sure you follow up on questions or give additional information by letter or phone. Stay with the tenant. If no decision is made within a certain amount of time, contact him or her periodically and find out how deliberations are progressing. Offer to be of further assistance, and try to discover when the tenant expects to reach a decision. You're not through with any tenant until a transaction is closed.

If you prepare for every showing carefully, follow the procedures in this chapter in making presentations and then follow up, you will have served your tenants well and opened the way for future business with them.

SHOWING VACANT PROPERTY

There is little difference in procedure and technique between showing vacant property and showing buildings. Two important factors, however, do apply only to vacant property. One is the question of who will finance construction—the owner or the prospective tenant. In either case, you must qualify the party financially. Financial qualification is covered in the chapters on qualifying tenants and owners.

The second factor regards timing. Does the tenant need to occupy the building within a specific time to prepare for a season, such as Christmas? If the new building cannot be ready within the time specified, then it may be better to steer the tenant to a building that already exists.

A FINAL WORD ABOUT LOCAL USERS

Many calls off signs from local people will turn out to be nuisance calls. Perhaps a person has always wanted to be in the restaurant business and calls about a certain location. You may think you have a potential transaction, but you could be very wrong.

Until they learn better, new salespeople often take these calls and make appointments to show the locations. The would-be tenants never appear, because they were not really serious in the first place. The best way to handle these calls is to invite such tenants to your office to discuss their plans, their real estate needs and the location they are calling about. If they are serious, they will meet with you, and you can qualify them further. If they are not serious, they won't show up, and you've saved yourself a great deal of time and energy.

Remember, every phone call does not mean a transaction and a commission. You must qualify every tenant as quickly as possible. Your first concern is whether or not the tenant is serious, particularly if the call comes from an individual who is acting on impulse. If local companies call, you rarely need to question their intentions. Certainly regional or national retail users who are looking for new outlets are legitimate customers.

Preparation, presentation and follow-up are all equally important. Overriding all three steps is the idea of service—service to fulfill tenants' needs, to complete transactions and to bring you commissions.

13

Site Presentation

INTRODUCTION

Showing retail property and developing retail site presentations are two different functions. Usually when you show property you are dealing with a particular available building and a particular retailer whom you have qualified and who will, under your guidance, make a physical inspection of the property. On the other hand, a site presentation in many cases deals in futures, frequently with a neighborhood or regional shopping center proposed or under construction. The object of site presentation is to stimulate retailer interest, which will lead to an appointment for showing. Developing a presentation package usually involves compiling, organizing and presenting data on a site's geography, traffic flow, demography, income levels, competition and so on. The information may be time-consuming to obtain, but it is vital to a retailer's decision to relocate or open additional outlets.

Presentations may be brief or lengthy, depending on what you are promoting. All, however, will contain three components:

1. site identification and description
2. area description
3. terms of site availability

This chapter will introduce you to these components, explain them in detail and show how site presentation is related to you as a retail salesperson.

At the end of this chapter is a sample site presentation package for a shopping center development. You may find it helpful to study it as you read through this chapter. Compare its contents with those items discussed as essential components of a good presentation, and determine which of these components are present in the sample and which are not.

SITE IDENTIFICATION AND DESCRIPTION

You will be concentrating on different retail groups, depending on which site you're promoting. Site identification and description usually begins with a large area map, sometimes but not always reinforced with an aerial photograph. The aerial shot shows buildings and thus indicates population density; it gives clients a bird's-eye view of the site. When using an aerial photograph, outline the site to orient the clients, indicate the adjoining streets and include an arrow pointing north.

Your area map will show tenants their present locations (if they are in the area), locations of competitors and traffic arteries. Draw one-mile or two-mile radii from the site and from each of the tenant's other locations. You will present detailed data on population, income and traffic flow later.

Occasionally, you may want to indicate all retail outlets in the area. The names of retailers can be printed on a special, made-to-order map. But if you are using a highway map or a general map obtained from a newspaper or chamber of commerce, you will probably have to list the retailers separately and key them to numbers or letters on the map. This will certainly be true if the area contains many retail outlets.

Utilize chamber of commerce sources, information from local newspapers, chain store directories or the yellow pages of the telephone directory to locate tenants' present outlets and those of the competition. The best way to obtain information about retail outlets in the area, however, is to survey the area personally. Drive along the streets, particularly the main arteries, and make your own list of outlets and their locations. In this way, you will have up-to-the-minute data for tenants.

Population data can, of course, be obtained from Census Bureau publications. Be sure that you're using the latest estimates, updated between census years. Newspapers and chambers of commerce may have more up-to-date figures than Census Bureau sources.

Assessor's Map

Your presentation package will include an assessor's map showing the size and dimensions of the site and the street on which it is located. The map will also indicate street width, any media strips and the length of the portions of the street or streets that run along the site. In some cases, you will want to include the assessor's map for adjacent or nearby property to give a more complete picture of the site. The assessor's map can be found in your office, in title companies and in the county assessor's office.

It is a good idea to include a proposed site plan along with the assessor's map or the actual site plan if you are dealing with a completed or proposed shopping center. The layout need not necessarily be scaled, but the various parts should be shown proportionally.

Given the following data, construct a proposed shopping center layout:

1. site size: approximately 20 acres
2. dimensions: 1,200 feet along one street, 725 feet along another
3. proposed outlets: discount store—100,000 sq. ft.
   food store—30,000 sq. ft. with 25,000 sq. ft. of drugstore adjacent
   two freestanding pads—5,000 sq. ft. each
   shops—totaling 35,000 sq. ft.

Zoning

You must know how the site is zoned or master-planned, or if it is a planned unit development or "PUD," and include the information in the presentation. Zoning places restrictions on property use, and the wrong kind of zoning or PUD regulations can restrict the types of retailers to whom you make presentations. Incidentally, there is a difference between a zoning change and a zoning variance. A change means a permanent alteration in the legal use of the property. It involves a political appeal and takes time to obtain. A zoning variance, on the other hand, is temporary and refers to a particular parcel. Sometimes, for example, a zoning boundary variance is needed to accommodate a certain parking ratio. Variances usually are not difficult to obtain. Zoning information can be gathered from local planning departments of the government municipality.

Utilities and Improvements

Tenants will need to know if utilities are present at a site or whether it will be necessary to bring them in. Also, have on-site and off-site improvements such as curbing, sewers, and gutters been provided, and are there any assessments for them? On-site improvements refer to the contour of the site and how it has been changed. Off-site improvements involve such items as easements, the relationship of the property to other properties, street lighting and street interfaces. Public works departments, the city engineering department and utility companies themselves are sources of information for on-site improvements. Data on off-site improvements can be obtained from the public works department.

AREA DESCRIPTION

For obvious reasons, the size of an area's population is of considerable importance to a retail user. Population growth is equally important, particularly for chains that must plan ahead and make intelligent decisions about the future. Determining customer population, however, is not simply a matter of discovering how many people live within a certain linear distance from the site. Today, distance is less significant than travel time, retailers are interested in how many people live within a certain number of minutes of the location.

Retailers, of course, want more than just raw population data. They also want to know the area's population trends and income level. Although this information is usually available from local sources, you can make your own estimates based on figures in Census Bureau tract books.

Information on income levels is of utmost importance to retailers. Well-to-do people spend only slightly more for food than do middle-income people, and high-income families tend to be smaller than others. Consequently, a food chain might not wish to locate in a high-income area, where there would be fewer people, and hence less volume, than in a middle-income or a lower-income area.

Exercise A

Would a restaurant chain real estate manager feel the same way? What about a laundromat chain?

Answer A

A restaurant chain might have an opposite preference, since high-income people tend to dine out more frequently than other groups. A laundromat chain would probably prefer to locate in a low-income or middle-income area with a high population density.

Sales Forecast

The sales projection is another vitally important factor in a retailer's decision to locate at a particular site. Forecasting generally involves taking the population of an area and casting data based on average expenditures per person per week for food, clothing and the like, sometimes weighted in terms of income level. Data on average expenditures can be obtained from various federal government agencies or derived from sales tax figures. Tax data are available from chambers of commerce, Federal Reserve banks, state internal revenue departments and boards of equalizations.

Business volume, of course, bears a direct relationship to the rent a retailer will pay for a location, since rent is generally figured as a percentage of sales income.

Accessibility

Regardless of an area's population, a site is worthless if people cannot get to it, or if only a few people use the roads that pass by it. A traffic analysis is of great importance to a site presentation package.

Traffic counts are available from planning departments and city traffic and state highway departments. These counts may not exist for your

CHAPTER 13 / Site Presentation   169

site, or they may be outdated. In that event, you'll have to count traffic yourself.

A traffic count must be made whether the site is in an urban or a suburban setting. The difference is in *what* you count. In an urban area you generally count people on foot. In a suburban location you count cars. You may refine the car count if you wish; for example you may record how many men, women and children are in each car, or how many cars are from out of state. Refining a count in these ways sometimes requires two or more people.

You may want to gather traffic data on collector streets as well as on main arteries. Collector streets are those feeding traffic into major thoroughfares. These thoroughfares include state and federal highways designated as streets in metropolitan areas. Whether you count collector streets or not depends on the particular site and tenant.

Exercise B

Answer the following questions.

1. For a city location, under what circumstances may you wish to distinguish between the gross number of men and the gross number of women passing a certain point?

2. Will the day of the week on which a traffic count is taken influence the results in any way? If so, how?

3. Will the time of day be a factor in a traffic count? If so, why?

Answer B

1. You may wish to do this if you are promoting a location to a particular retailer, such as a hardware or sporting goods dealer or a fabric or cosmetic outlet.

2. Saturday is usually a big family shopping day, and Thursday, Friday and Saturday are important food shopping days. During the school year, Saturday is an important day for children's clothing stores. Therefore, for maximum usefulness, traffic counts should be taken every day of the business week.

3. Of course, traffic will be heavier during rush hours than during off-peak hours in both urban and suburban settings. A noontime count in a city business district will record many people passing a given point, and most of them will be thinking about food more than anything else. Traffic counts should be taken at various times during the day.

Count traffic in both directions at each site; if it is a corner location, note turning traffic as well. Check the speed limit. If the location is in a 50-mile-an-hour zone, it might lose some of its appeal to certain retailers. Note whether there are median strips that would make left turns into the site difficult or would force traffic to exit in one direction only, thus diminishing the location's accessibility. Check to see if planning or highway departments intend to make changes, such as installing a median strip, changing the speed limit or altering the arrangement and timing of traffic-control signals. These factors might affect access to the site.

Competition

Retailers are as interested in a study of competition in an area as they are in traffic analysis. They must decide whether they can compete with a particular store at or near the site and whether the trading area itself will support another business such as theirs. Retail real estate salespeople ordinarily do not have the time or the resources to make a thorough analysis of competition. They often lack information about any retailer's estimate of his or her share of the market, for retailers customarily keep this knowledge to themselves. Still, retail division salespeople must gather some data on competition and include them in the presentation package.

You can pinpoint competition with the aid of telephone directories, lists of chain outlets or chamber of commerce lists. But since any source of information is dated to some extent, you must examine the area in person to be sure of what you are dealing with. The data on the competition and its strength needed for your presentation include its exact location, whether it is part of a shopping center or in a freestanding building, its building space and appearance.

Only personal observation will indicate the strength of a competing store. This means you will need to visit the competitor's location at various times of day and on various days of the week. Observe how many cars the parking lot contains. If customer traffic is slight most of the time, the competition would not appear to be strong. However, if the location does well during peak and off-peak periods, this could be a problem for your tenant.

Many retailers also want to know about outlets that will complement their business at a particular location. Drugstores and liquor stores are often found next to or quite near supermarkets. A sewing machine dealer would find it advantageous to locate next to a fabric shop and vice versa. Pay attention to possible complementary locations. They can help to promote a site.

TERMS OF SITE AVAILABILITY

We come now to the final component of the site presentation package. When promoting single buildings you will usually be dealing with a rental situation. In new areas, availability might be in terms of sale, build-to-suit, or ground lease. Lease terms will vary. Chains, for example, will want a minimum term of ten years and sometimes as many as 25 years. Exact figures generally are not used in the presentation package because rental rate, escalation clauses, and so on are normally negotiable.

CONCLUSION

If you are dealing by mail, you should ordinarily submit one site at a time to possible tenants. A personal presentation might allow for the examination of two or more sites, but keep in mind that your objective is to *sell* tenants, not to confuse them. Avoid discussing too many sites at one time.

Your company will want tenants to know that its associates can gather and present site information in an interesting and concise fashion, with the tenant's interest uppermost in mind. This chapter has discussed the highlights of site presentation packages. You will come across more details and refinements in the presentation process as you work with more experienced retail salespeople.

FIGURE 13.1　Site Presentation

ELEVEN-ACRE COMMERCIAL DEVELOPMENT
SEC HIGHWAY 111 & CLINTON STREET
INDIO, CALIFORNIA

DEVELOPMENT: Approximately 120,000 square feet of retail space including a supermarket, drug store, home improvement center and retail shops with pad locations for financial institutions, restaurants and other freestanding users.

DEMOGRAPHICS:

RADIUS	POPULATION AT COMPLETE BUILD OUT OF PRESENT TRACTS**	INCOME* MEDIUM	AVERAGE
1 mile	12,308	20,715	29,737
2 miles	17,001	24,737	27,803
3 miles	25,419	19,928	23,506

　*Estimates by Urban Decision Systems, Inc.

**Based on housing tracts provided by the City of Indio and County of Riverside. (See enclosed for detailed lists). Population based on 3.1 persons per dwelling unit.

*TRAFFIC:**

	Average Daily Traffic
Highway 111 (west of Clinton)	15,900
Highway 111 (east of Clinton)	17,500

Clinton Street, City of Indio has no current figures, however, it is estimated to be 1,000.

47th Street, City of Indio also has no current figures, however, it is estimated to be 1,000.

The funds to construct a traffic signal at Clinton Street and Highway 111 have been appropriated. The signal is scheduled to be completed by late September 1989.

*City of Indio Traffic Department.

RETAIL SALES: The Indio area ranks number 1 in retail sales in all of Riverside County.

Indio	$17,664
Corona	17,319
Riverside	16,905
Banning	15,050
Beaumont	15,035
Palm Springs	11,763
Hemet	10,858

Source: Editor & Publisher Market Guide.

Indio ranks first in Riverside County and sixth in California in estimated sales per household:

　　　　　　　　Indio　　　　$22,503

Source: Editor & Publisher Market Guide.

Indio ranks first in Riverside County in estimated food sales per household:

　　　　　　　　Indio　　　　$4,926

Others listed:

Hemet	$4,121
Beaumont	3,766
Palm Springs	3,021
Corona	

Source: Editor & Publisher Market Guide.

FIGURE 13.1 Site Presentation (Concluded)

REMARKS: Indio is a well-established trading area for the Coachella Valley, Salton Sea area, and as far east as Arizona. This is evidenced by the higher retail sales averages relative to other cities in Riverside County.

This site is on the "going home side," which is significant considering that much of Indio's residents are employed in North Valley, e.g., Palm Springs, etc.

The higher-income areas of Palm Desert, Indian Wells and La Quinta have easy access due to this site's close proximity to west Indio versus the more congested areas downtown.

With the curve in Highway 111 immediately in the front of the site visibility is enhanced, especially for the going home, eastbound traffic.

The importance of shopper traffic on 47th Street will become more important in two ways:

The south Indio residential traffic (where much of the new residential growth is) has 47th Street as a cut-off. This south Indio residential traffic saves 1¼ miles on 47th Street and is a perfect stopping place for shopper traffic.

47th Street provides easy access to Highway 111, thereby avoiding the traffic congestion and ingress and egress problems at Monroe and Highway 111.

This site represents the last parcel of commercial property over eight acres and signalized within the city limits of Indio.

DEVELOPER:
STEVE BROWN DEVELOPMENT COMPANY
1303 Avocado Street
Newport Beach, California 92660
(714) 640-1770

EXCLUSIVE AGENT:
Jeff Jones
GRUBB & ELLIS COMPANY
4299 MacArthur Blvd.
Newport Beach, California
(714) 833-2900

FIGURE 13.2 Desert General Corporation Site

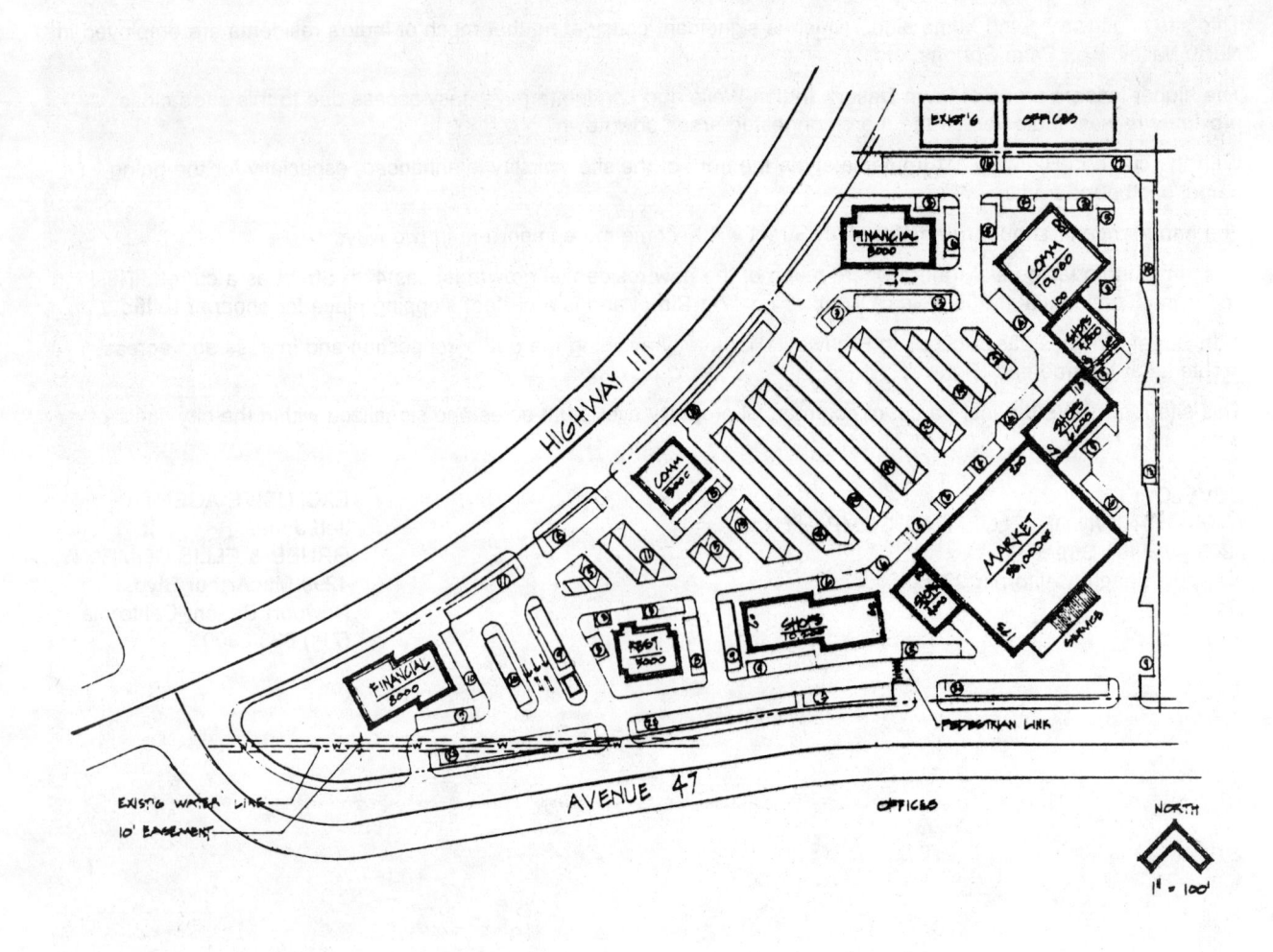

resume:

SITE AREA	494,200± SF
BUILDING AREA	96,600 SF
SITE/BUILDING RATIO	4.1 TO 1
PARKING	581
PARKING RATIO	1 CAR/166 SF

HIGHWAY 111 & AVENUE 47
INDIO CA.   DESERT GENERAL CORP

FIGURE 13.3 Site

176 Successful Leasing and Selling of Retail Property

FIGURE 13.4 Property Site

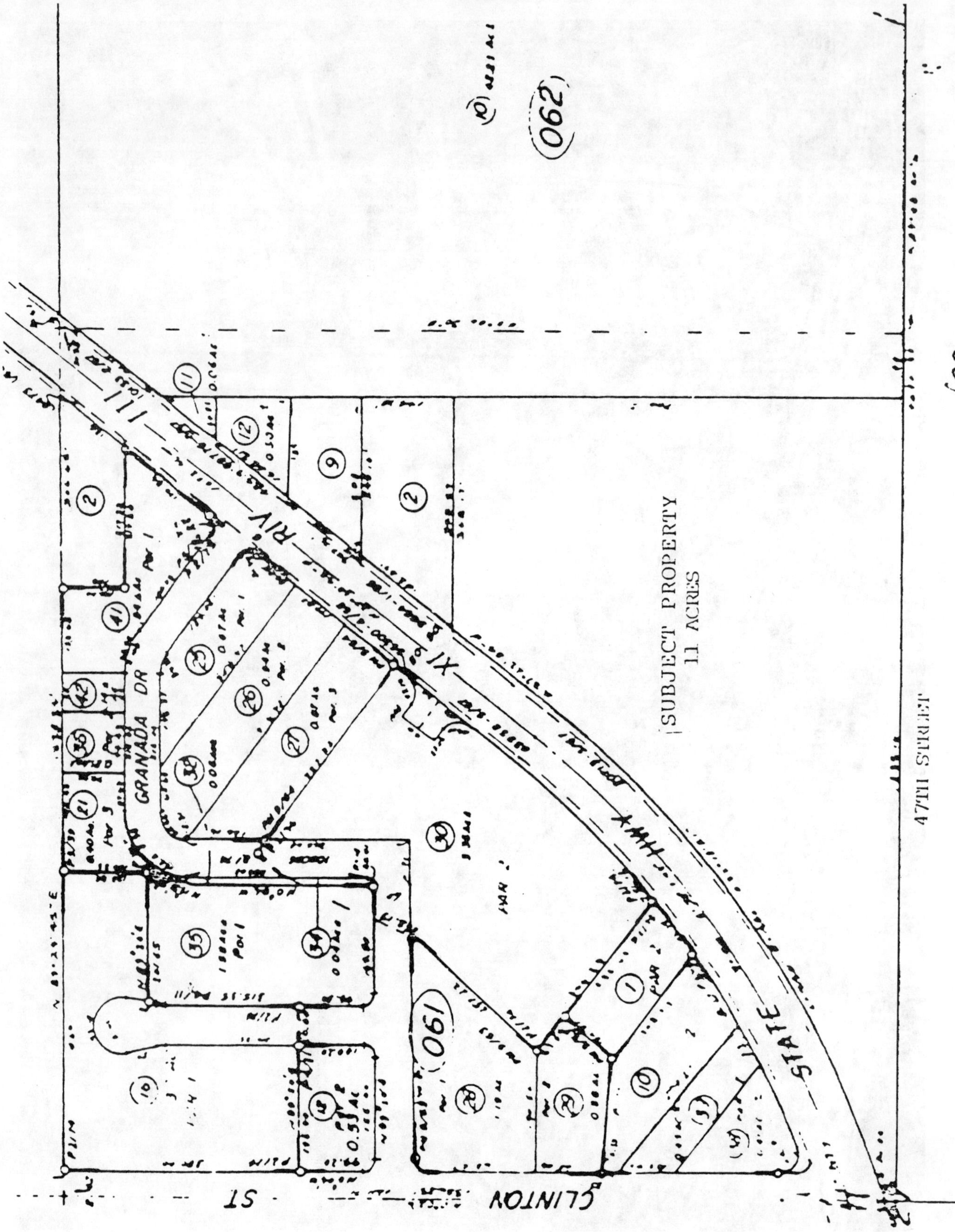

FIGURE 13.5 One-Mile Radius Developments

NUMBER	NUMBER OF UNITS	DEVELOPER	TYPE OF HOUSING
51	68	John Wessman	multiple family
28	87	Lewis Homes	single family (87 under construction)
50	51	Villa Serena Apartments	senior citizens housing
52	100	George Marizicola	condominiums (permits issued May 1979)
53	34	Del Mar Estates	multiple family
33	39	Beam Development Co.	single family (36 permits issued)
36		104 acres planned for	single family
65	232	Paul Southers Alice Sakai & J. Sherman	mobile home park
58	73	Expansion of Bermuda Palms Mobile Home Park	mobile home park (in plan check)
15	185	Danco Development	single family
64	160	Rancho Casitas	mobile home park (permits issued July 1979)
66	350	Al Levin Heritage Mobile Home Park	mobile home park (permits isued April 1979)
61	152	Burger Incorporated	mobile home park (grading permit issued)
59	486	BNB Financial	mobile home park (grading permit issued)
45	189	Coachella Land Development	condominiums (tentative tract approval)
19	155	Pacesetter Homes	single family (tentative tract approval)
20	40	Regent International	single family (33 permits pulled-Phase I)
37	163	Lewis Homes	single family
26	113	Lewis Homes	single family (permits issued June 1979)
25	72	Indian Palms Country Club	single family
70	22	Moran Properties	single family (preliminary plan)
17	133	Mize Company	single family (tentative map approval)
40	356	B.N.B. Financial Corp.	condominiums
76	124	James White Oil Co.	condominiums (tentative map approval)
79	32	Dedo Mouldings	apartments
TOTAL	3,416		

FIGURE 13.6 Two-Mile Radius Developments

NUMBER	NUMBER OF UNITS	DEVELOPER	TYPE OF HOUSING
32	115	Norman Dreyfuss	single family (tentative map approval)
31	350	King & Associates	single family (phase I completed Jan. 1979)
44	59	Main Street Development	single family (tentative map approval)
41	68	One Hundred 13 Corporation	condominiums (tentative map approval)
18	55	One Hundred 13 Corporation	single family (tentative map approval)
22	10	One Hundred 13 Corporation	single family (tentative map approval)
21	15	One Hundred 13 Corporation	single family (tentative map approval)
62	506	Breit Feller	mobile home park (tentative map approval)
39	135	One Hundred 13 Corporation	condominiums (tentative map approval)
42	112	One Hundred 13 Corporation	condominiums (tentative map approval)
35	49	Wheatley Corporation	single family (tentative map approval)
29	85	Lewis Homes	single family
63		Breit Feller	RV park (tentative map approval)
34	66	Bruce Development	single family (near completion)
49	51	Main Street Development	condominiums (tentative map approval)
54	13	Carl Cox	condominiums
57	60	Clayton & Clayton	apartments (permits issued Jan. 1979)
43	59	Main Street Development	condominiums (permit issued)
30	177	Suntree Development	single family (completed June 1979)
44_1	120	Indian Palms Country Club	condominiums (56 permits pulled)
46	169	Howard Dworkin	condominiums (tentative map approval)
38	181	Main Street Development	condominiums (tentative map approval)

FIGURE 13.6 Two-Mile Radius Developments (Concluded)

NUMBER	NUMBER OF UNITS	DEVELOPER	TYPE OF HOUSING
11	78	Guy Wilson	condominiums (ready for permits)
55	126	Rolando Properties	condominiums
78	150	Arthur Goyer	condominiums
77	210	One Hundred 13	condominiums (permits issued July 1979)
TOTAL	3,019		

FIGURE 13.7 Three-Mile Radius Developments

NUMBER	NUMBER OF UNITS	DEVELOPER	TYPE HOUSING
24	40	Zellner Corporation	single family (tentative map approval)
23	175	O'Brien/Dunn	single family (tentative map approval)
47	40	Guyer/Brookhurst	apartments (tentative map approval)
60	66	Miller Partnership	mobile home park (tentative map approval)
8	187	Desert Palace Incorporated	single family
4	224	La Quinta Gates	single family
6	150	Marzicola Development	single family
3	2,045	ATO Development	condominiums & single family
81	392	Palmer Development	mobile home park (tentative map approval)
TOTAL	3,319		

SUMMARY

The figures and data above were taken from the City of Indio's *Report of Development,* dated August 1, 1986. This report is available upon request from Grubb & Ellis Commercial Brokerage Company.

1 mile – 3,416 New Housing Units
2 mile – 3,019 New Housing Units
3 mile – 3,319 New Housing Units
   TOTAL 9,754

FIGURE 13.8 Proposed Developments in County

DEVELOPER	LOCATION	NUMBER OF UNITS	STATUS OF PROJECT
1) Landmark Development	West of Eisenhower, north of Calle.	592 units detached & 27 holes of golf.	Final tract map approval.
2) La Quinta Gates Property	West of Washington, north of Eisenhower.	404 Condo's and Single family.	Hearing in June, 1979.
3) ATO	East of Washington, north of 50th Street.	2,045 Condo's & single family, plus resort hotel & 36 holes of golf.	Specific plan approved.
4) La Quinta Gates	East of Washington, north of 48th Street.	224 Single family	Final map approved.
5) Lewis Homes	East of Washington south of 50th Street.	356 Single family	Hearing for tentative map.
6) Marzicola Development	South of Highway III, west of Adams.	150 Single family	In process.
7) O'Neal Development	Jefferson and 56th Street.		Preliminary plan in process.
8) Desert Palace Incorporated	NWC of Jefferson and Miles.	187 Single family	In process.
9) Desert Palace Incorporated	NEC of Jefferson and Miles.	142 Single family, 152 Multiple family.	In process.
10) AC Dock Steders	West of Washington and Darby.	202 Condo's	Map approved.
11)			
12) AMCA Development	SWC of Country Club and Washington.	600 spaces, Mobile home park	Final map approved.
13) AMCA Development	Adjacent to #12 above.	296 Apartments	Final map approved.
14) Affiliated Construction	42nd and Country Club.	960 Condo's and Single family.	Final map approved.
15) Danco Development	SEC Sheilds & 46th.	185 Single family	Final map approved.
16) Donald Scanlin	North of 44th, West of Palm Desert Country Club.	512 Single family	Final map approved.
82) Covington Brothers	West of Washington south of 42nd Street	51 Single family	Tentative map.

182   Successful Leasing and Selling of Retail Property

FIGURE 13.9   Map

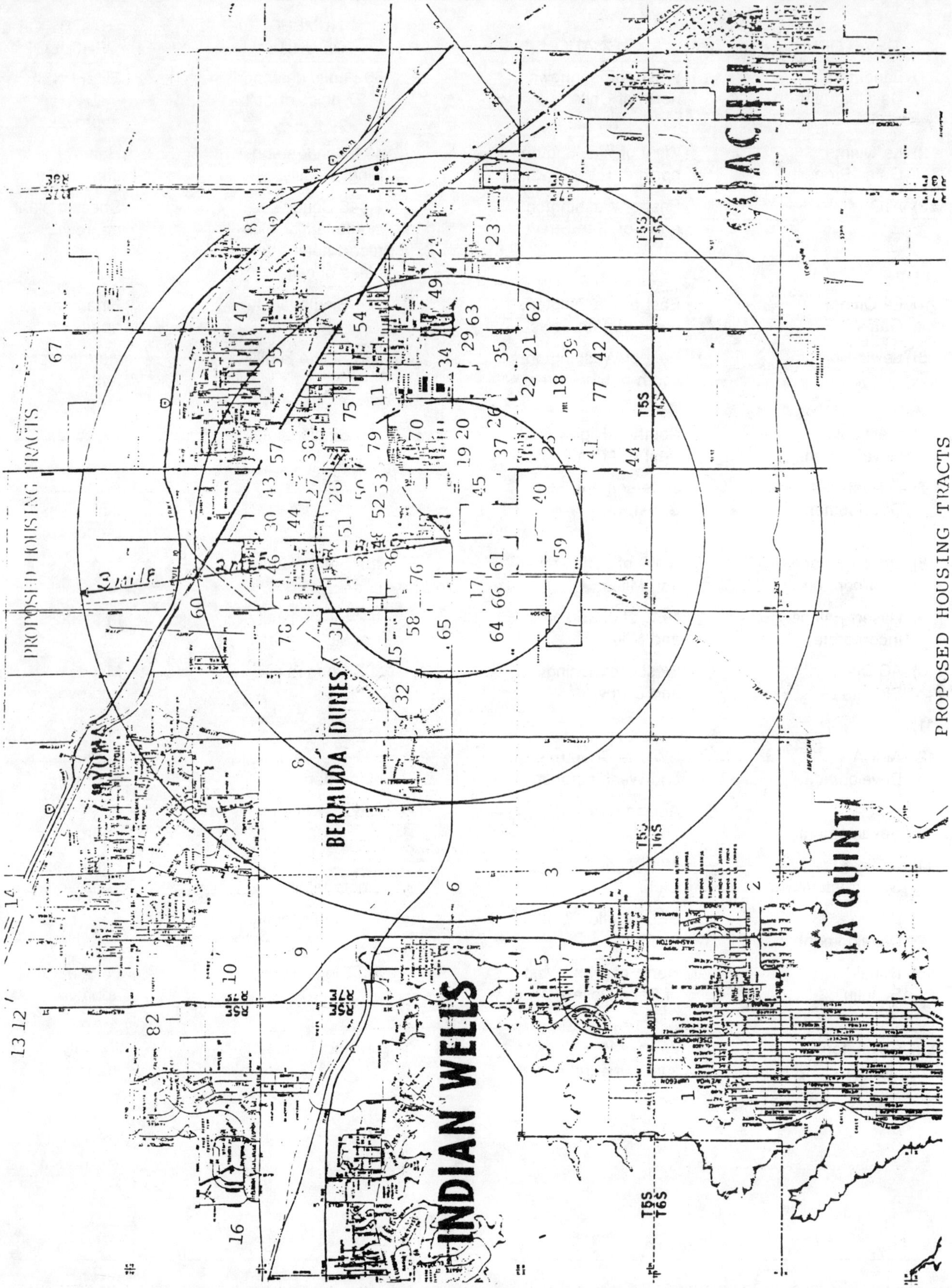

FIGURE 13.10 Map

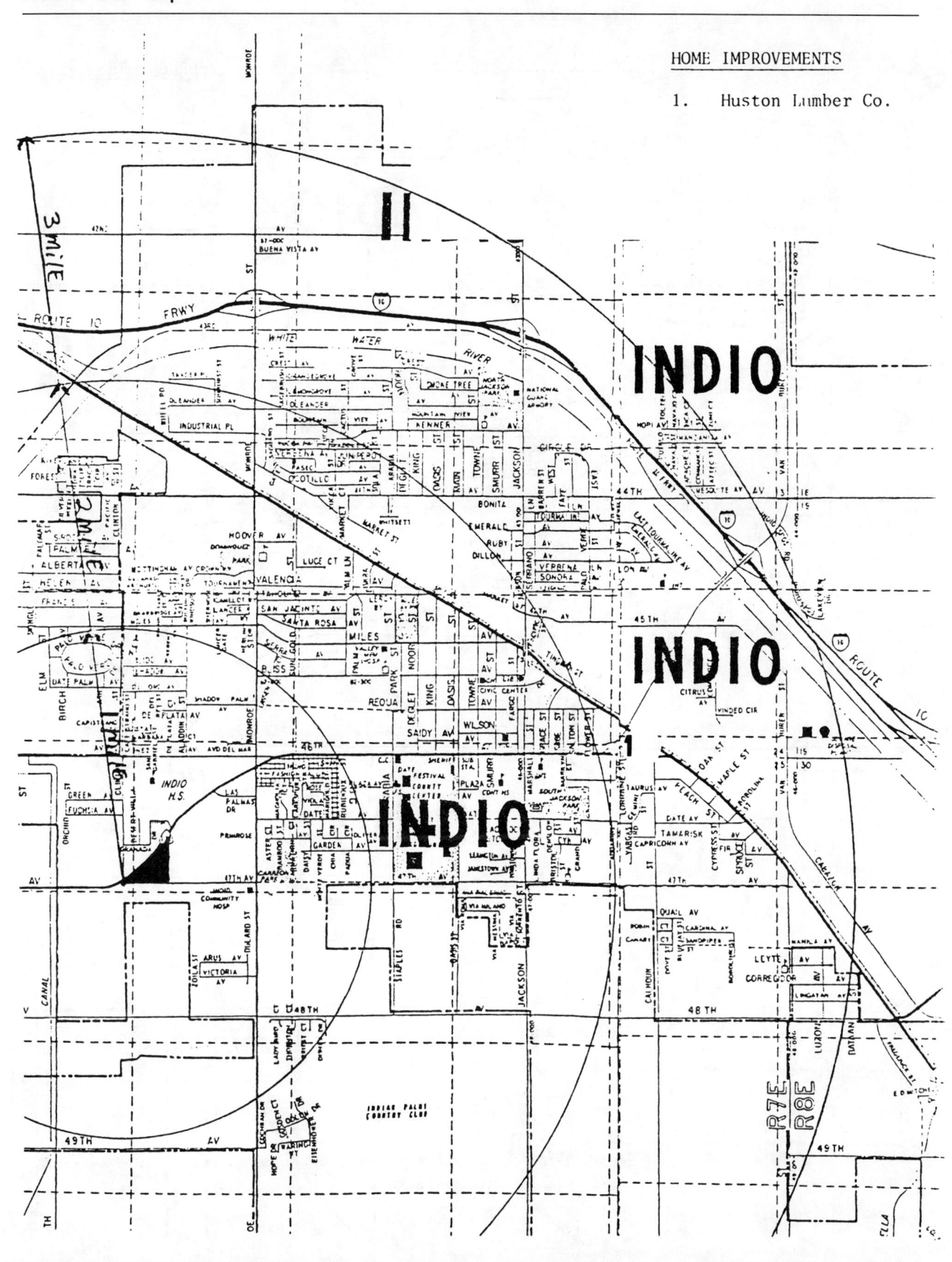

HOME IMPROVEMENTS

1. Huston Lumber Co.

FIGURE 13.11 Map

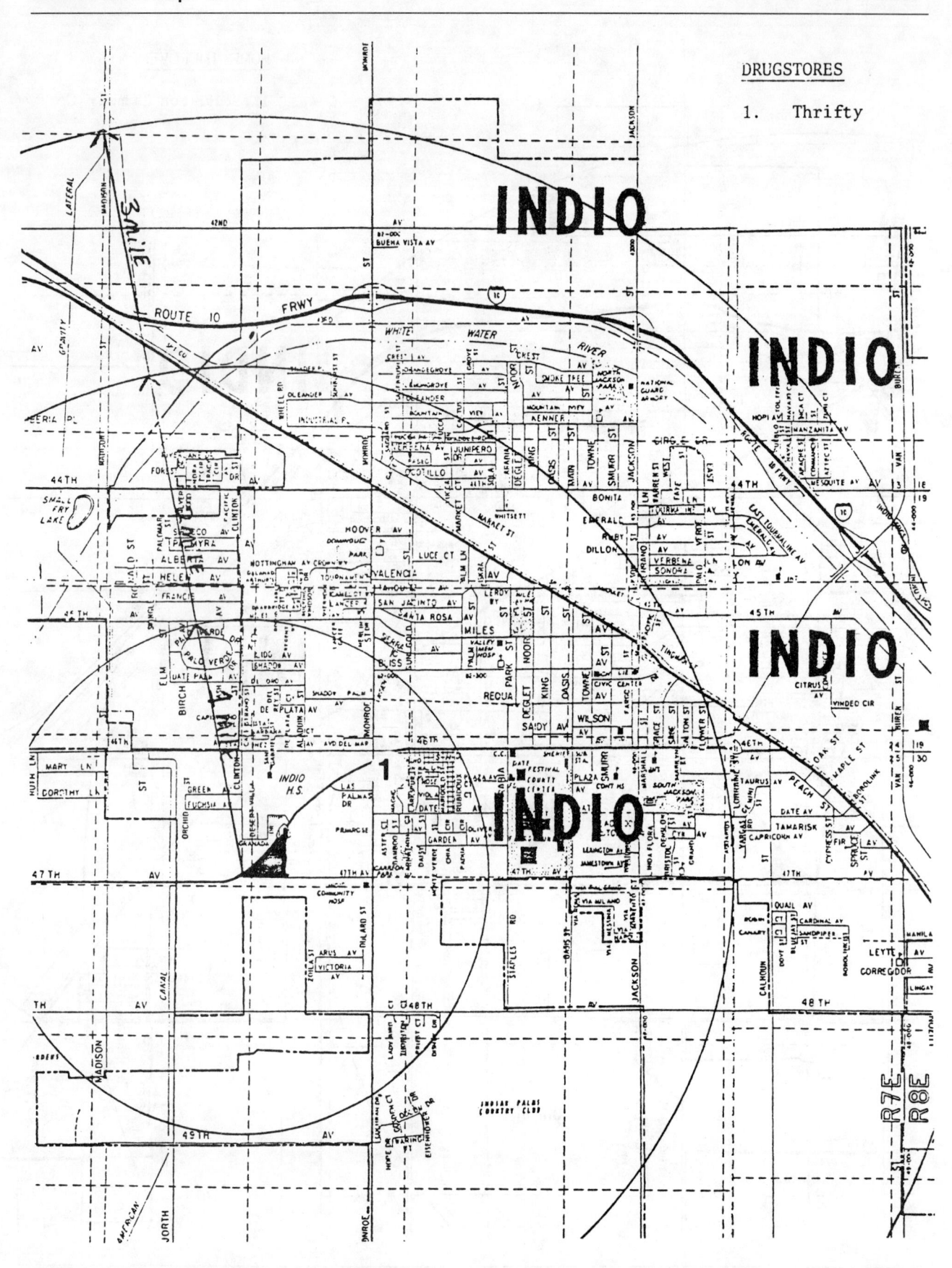

CHAPTER 13 / Site Presentation 185

FIGURE 13.12 Map

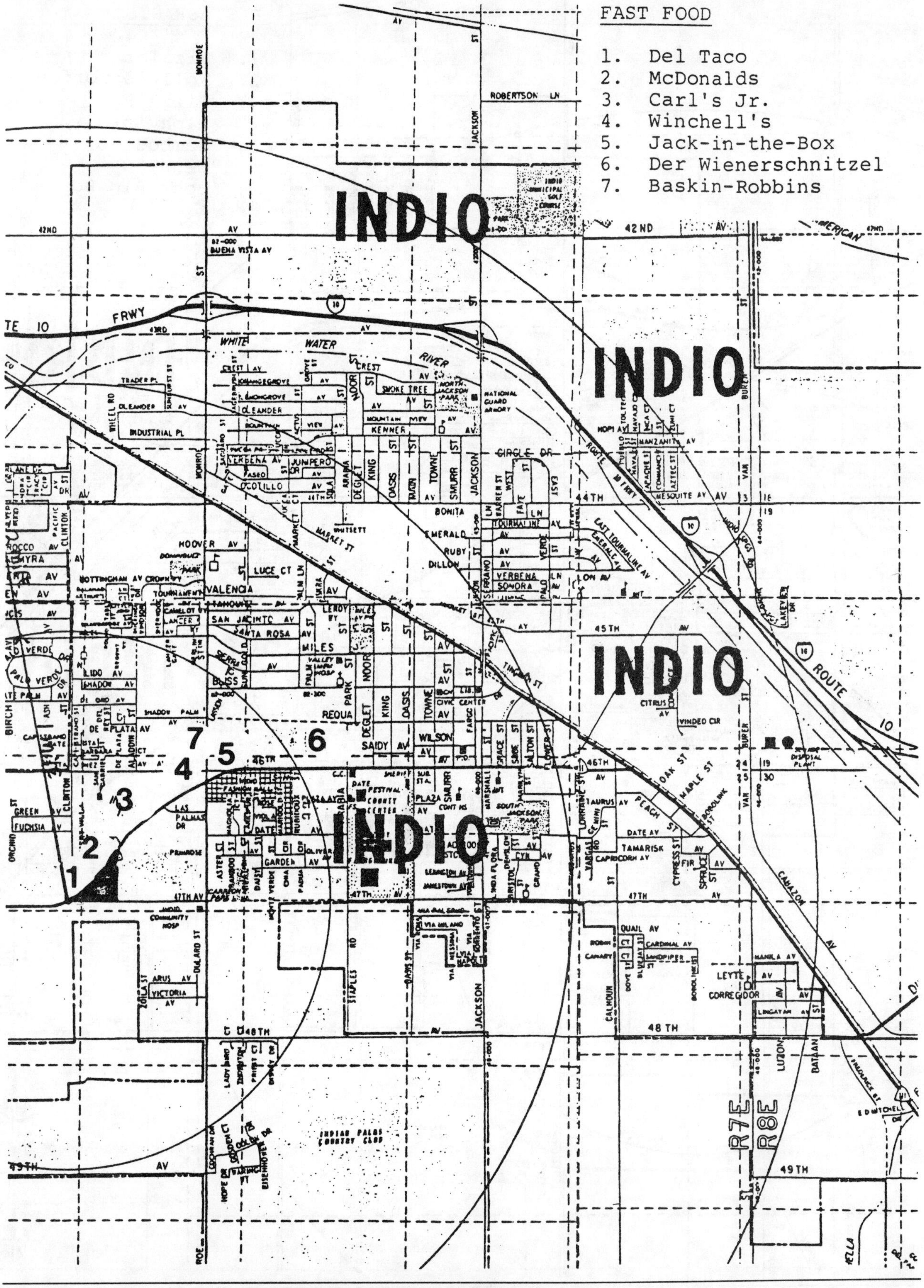

FAST FOOD

1. Del Taco
2. McDonalds
3. Carl's Jr.
4. Winchell's
5. Jack-in-the-Box
6. Der Wienerschnitzel
7. Baskin-Robbins

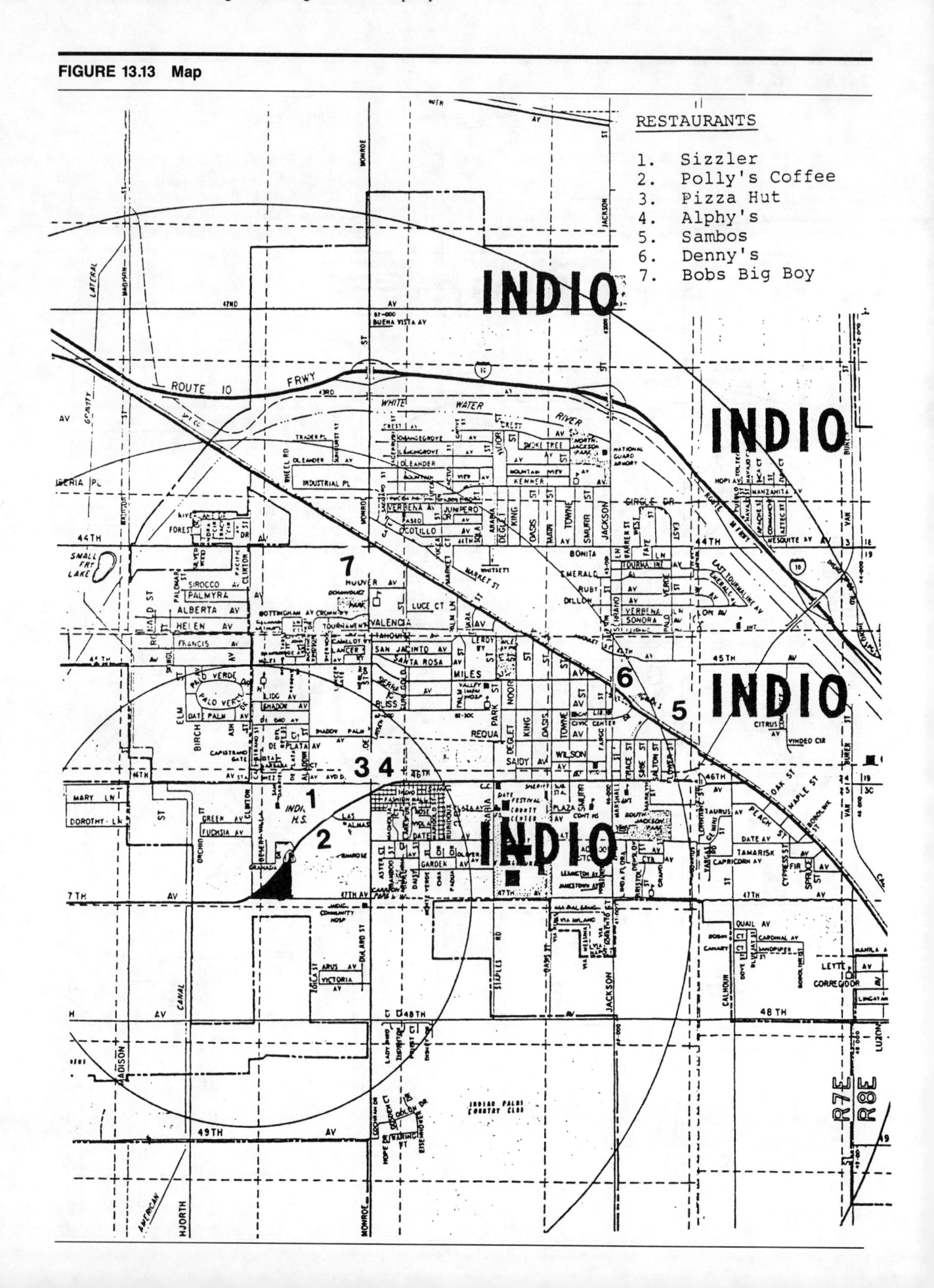

186 Successful Leasing and Selling of Retail Property

FIGURE 13.13 Map

RESTAURANTS

1. Sizzler
2. Polly's Coffee
3. Pizza Hut
4. Alphy's
5. Sambos
6. Denny's
7. Bobs Big Boy

FIGURE 13.14 Map

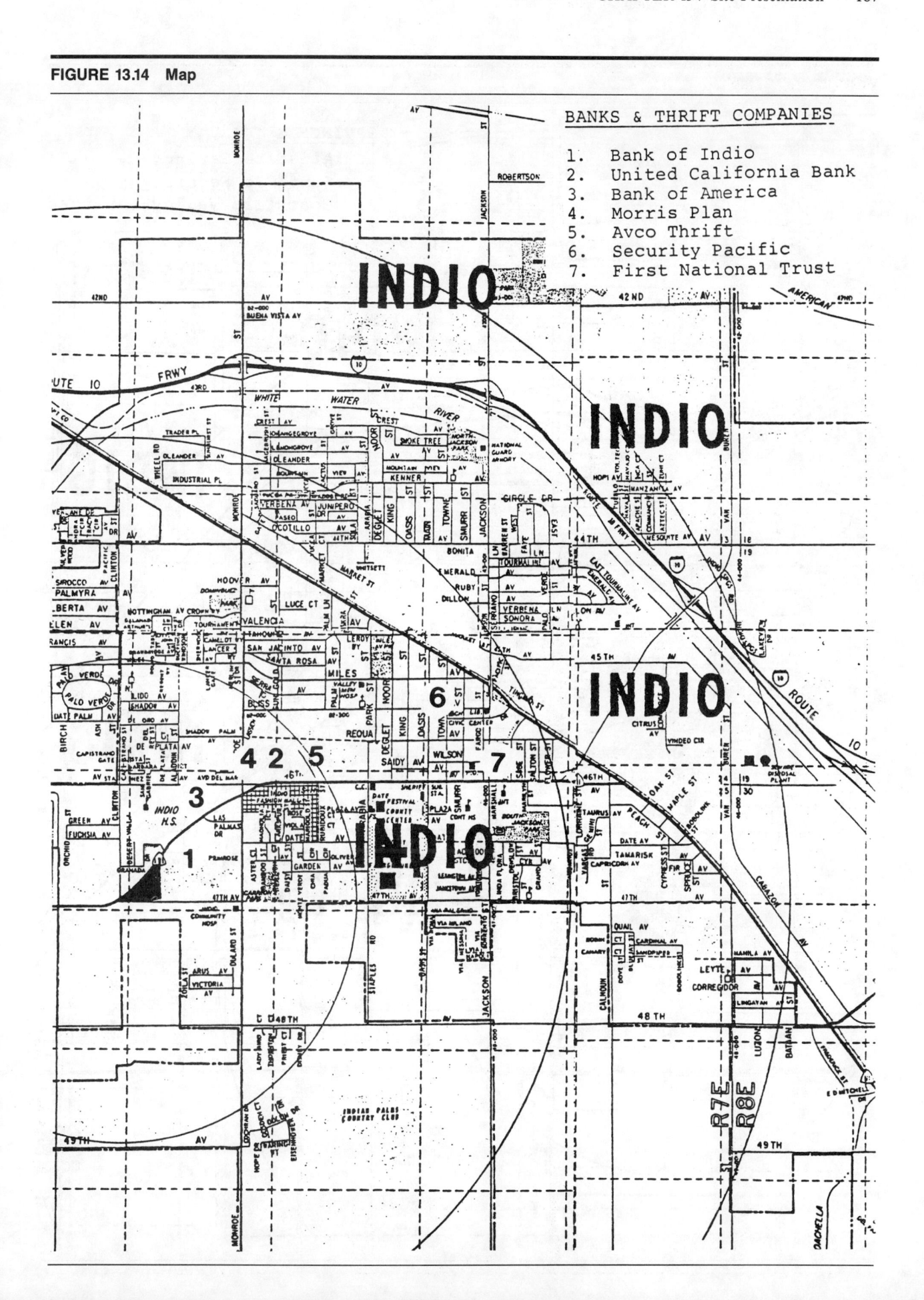

BANKS & THRIFT COMPANIES

1. Bank of Indio
2. United California Bank
3. Bank of America
4. Morris Plan
5. Avco Thrift
6. Security Pacific
7. First National Trust

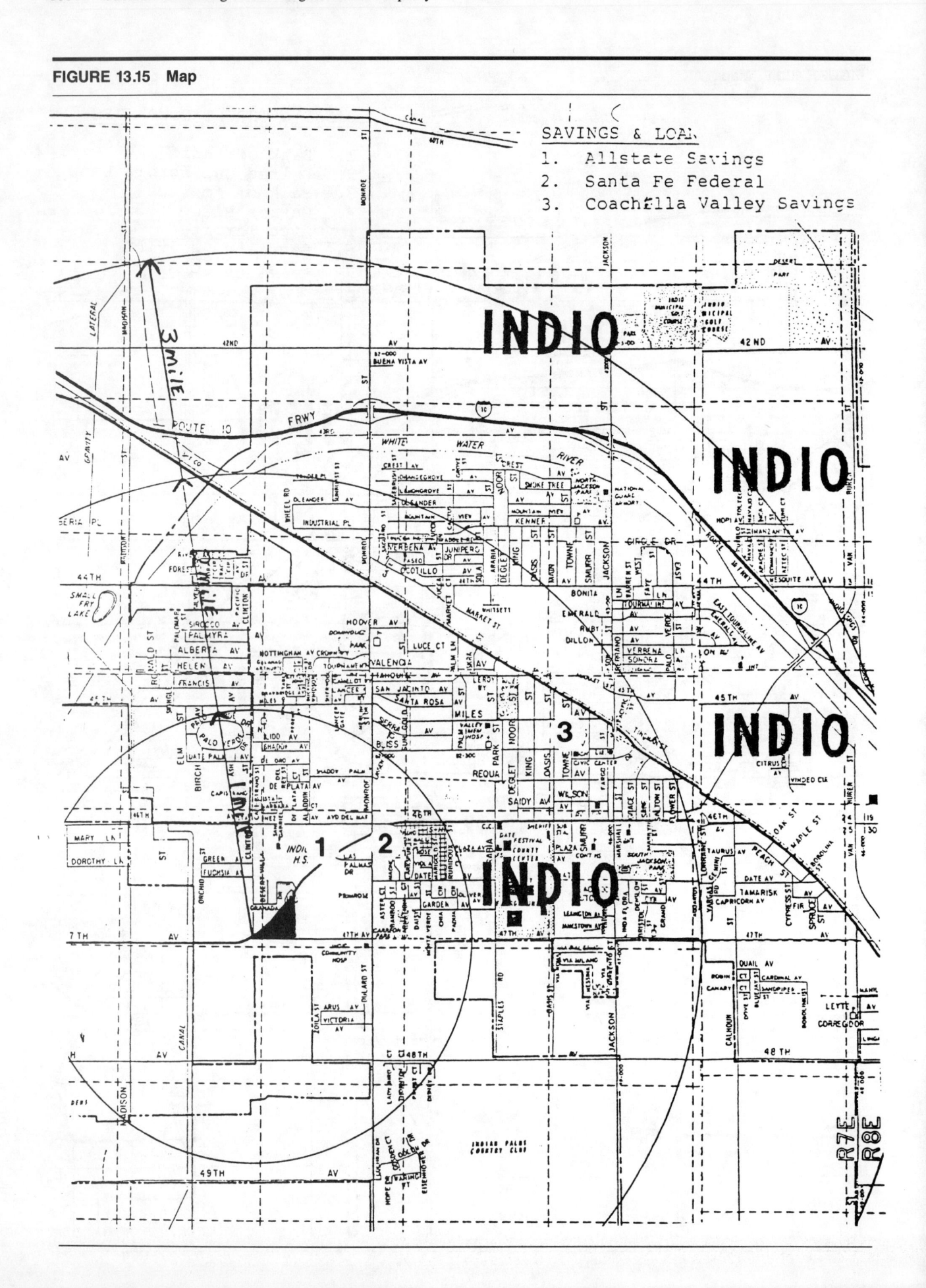

188 Successful Leasing and Selling of Retail Property

FIGURE 13.15 Map

CHAPTER 13 / Site Presentation 189

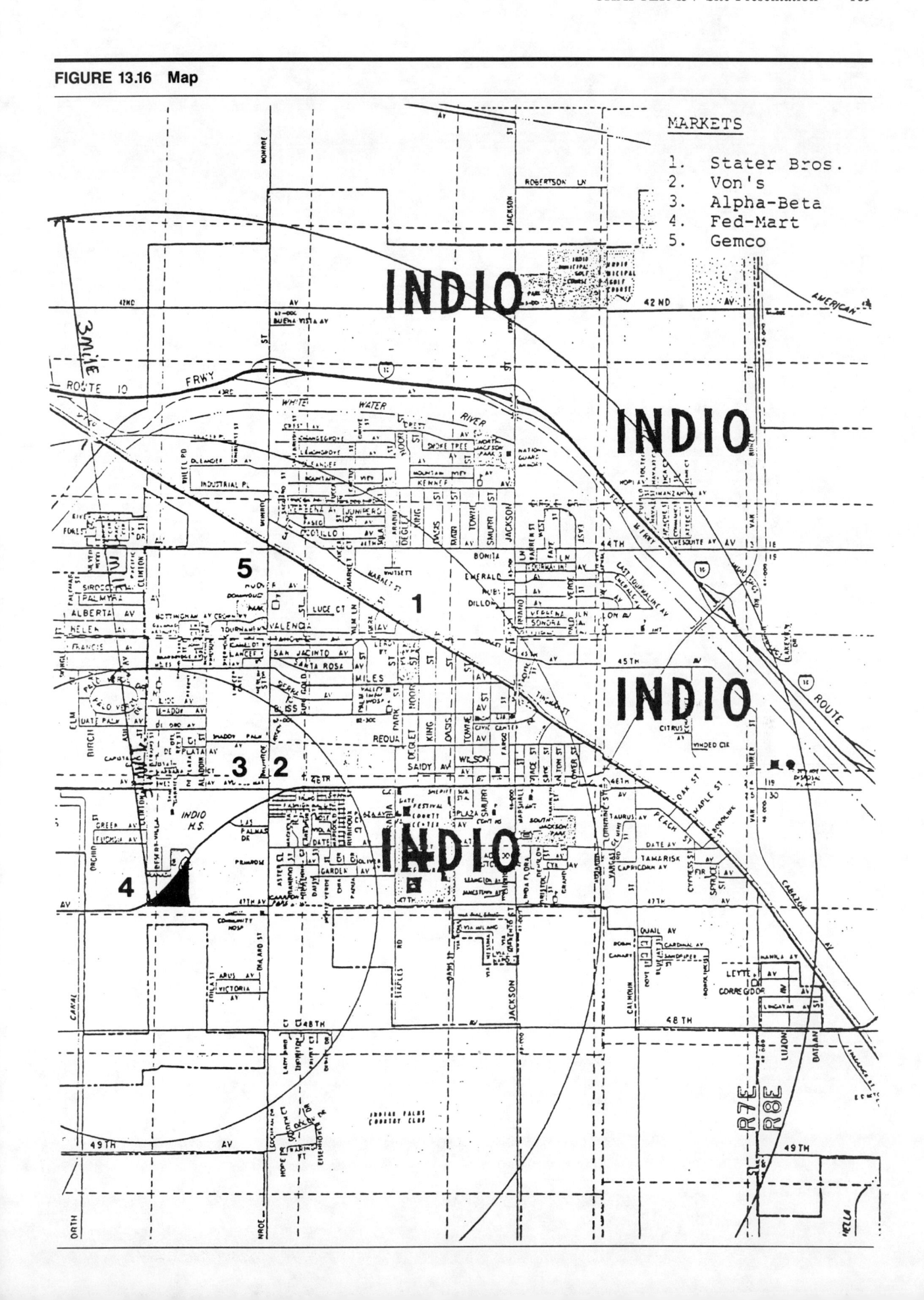

FIGURE 13.16 Map

14

Local Developers

INTRODUCTION

Developers create or "manufacture" the space that you will market and retailers will occupy. Becoming acquainted with the developers in your area is one of your major priorities. Generally, developers will be eager to meet with you because as a new salesperson in a retail division, you will have up-to-date information on the market area.

Leasing space in a new or existing project is crucial to developers since rentals are their primary source of income and profit. To establish working relationships with developers, you need to have experience with the leasing side of the business. It will give you the opportunity to be out among the customers, to gain firsthand knowledge of available sites and changes in your area and to sharpen your skill in analyzing property and assessing real estate potential. In your first year as a retail salesperson, about 75 percent of your time will probably be devoted to leasing satellite and existing space. This percentage will undoubtedly change as you acquire more expertise with the development side and as you decide whether you can serve best the developer or the user.

This chapter will outline the various types of developers and describe how they operate. The material will suggest ways of obtaining information on growth patterns and projections to help you anticipate the services required by developers.

TYPES OF DEVELOPERS

Developers can generally be classed in two categories: equity developers and non-equity developers. The primary difference between the two is their investment stance in a project.

Equity developers enter into a project with the intention of holding and increasing their share of the ownership for long-term appreciation, equity build-up and increased cash flow. Because of their ownership role in a project, such developers are more concerned with the quality of a center's architectural treatment and the financial qualifications of the tenants.

Nonequity developers (also know as "merchant builders") build shopping centers and other projects with the objective of selling them.

In some cases, the cash flow on a project can yield more money to the owner than to the developer because of the valuation of the land, the percentages of the cash flow each is to receive, and because the owner's return is preferred. In a 50–50 joint venture, this is undesirable for the shorted party. Take, for example, a project that yields $190,000 in cash flow. The partners agree that the owner's preferred return is based on 10 percent of the land value and the developer's cut is the same, provided the funds are available. After the initial proceeds are distributed, both parties receive equal amounts of any remaining profits.

Let's now assume the land is valued at $1 million. Notice that the owner's preferred return of 10 percent would yield the owner an initial $100,000, leaving the developer with the remaining $90,000 of the $190,000 cash flow. Since this is an unbalanced return for 50–50 partners, the owner and developer might agree to lower the valuation of the land until the earnings splits yield both partners the same proportion of the cash flow. In our example, the land value could (or would) be lowered to $900,000. Notice that the owner now gets his preferred return of 10 percent, or $90,000. The developer also gets $90,000, leaving $10,000 in cash flow, which they split equally. Thus, by re-valuing the land, each party receives $95,000.

Because their involvement is short-term, nonequity developers may have to provide tenants with some assurances on project quality.

Developers who are involved in more than one project and are perhaps financially stretched might be unable to maintain a total equity stance and could choose a middle course. They may sell off larger portions of the center and agree to build to suit for a major user such as a bank. The bank parcel, along with the residual site area on which satellite shops would be constructed, would give developers substantial holdings in the development.

Retailers of substantial size may build shopping centers themselves, using their store as the anchor tenants. Such developers are concerned with operating profitable centers whose tenants will complement their stores.

JOINT VENTURE

Developers who cannot or do not wish to purchase land for development may choose to enter into a joint venture transaction. A *joint venture* is a partnership agreement, typically between a landowner and a developer, in which each has something to contribute and something to gain. The owner's contribution is the land. Many owners who have held land for a number of years cannot afford to sell outright because the proceeds would be heavily taxed. Developing the land, however, provides a depreciation tax shelter and the possibility of receiving a good return. The developer's contribution lies in improving the land, that is, providing the expertise to put together a shopping center development.

The owner agrees to accept a certain percentage return based on a negotiated value of the land (called a *preferred return*). When the center is completed and occupied, the first amount from the cash flow equal to that percentage is paid to the landowner. An equal amount, if available, is then paid to the developer. Remember, the owner's return is not guaranteed but *preferred*. This means that the owner is paid first from the proceeds of the venture, up to the determined percentage. If the cash flow is less than this percentage, the owner will be paid the maximum amount of money that is available.

Implementing the Joint Venture

To begin the transaction, the owner and the developer enter into an escrow agreement. The owner will not contribute the land to the partnership until the developer has the survey, the financing commitment, letters of intent from major tenants or signed leases. Only then does the owner convey title through escrow to the joint venture. The most difficult stage of the negotiation is between these two points since the owner will not turn over title to the land until it is absolutely certain the venture will go forward. For the developer, the most important stage involves getting commitments from the major tenants, which are needed to ensure adequate funding for the project.

A 50–50 Partnership

The procedure outlined above represents one way of structuring a joint venture. However, an owner who is willing to share in the risks as well as the rewards might form a *50–50 partnership*. In this case, the owner will contribute the land, forgoing the preferred return, and sign a construction loan with the developer for half of the projected income from the property. The advantage to this arrangement is that as the property matures there will be additional income from the rents. The owner chooses to share in the anticipated profit increase by relinquishing a low-risk return.

Ground Lease Versus Joint Venture

Instead of entering into a joint venture, a landowner might prefer a *ground lease* transaction, leasing the land for development (for further discussion of ground leasing, see the chapter on types of transactions). However, rent from a ground lease is considered ordinary income and would not provide owners with a tax shelter—one of the major attractions of a joint venture. With a ground lease, the owner states that the property is worth a certain amount and that a specific percentage return is expected on that stated value. With a joint venture, the amount of return is directly related to the risk the owner takes.

Payment of Commission

A broker receives the joint venture formation fee based on the price of the land contribution. The joint venture entity pays the commission; you will usually receive your fee at the time the escrow forms the joint venture, i.e., at the time the land is conveyed in escrow from the owner to the partnership.

You would most likely be involved first with the property owner, who would agree to pay you a commission in the event that you successfully complete a sales transaction, a lease or a joint venture. Ordinarily, the joint venture is not the first approach that you would take with an owner. However, if this turns out to be the most viable approach to the property, you will need to convince the owner that your choice is the best one. This may require some persuasion, particularly if the owner has held the land for a long time and fears the risks involved in such a venture.

When the owner has agreed to the transaction, make sure the developer understands that the joint venture entity pays your commission. This means that the developer and the property owner are each responsible for half.

Other Types of Joint Ventures

There are two other types of joint ventures: The developer may enter into a partnership with (1) a financial institution (lender) or (2) a major tenant, such as a supermarket. In both cases, the arrangements usually involve large developments. With the first type, a developer will tie up a large piece of property and bring in a financial institution as a partner, most commonly referred to as an *equity partner.*

In the second type of transaction a major tenant will initiate the project by asking a developer to locate an appropriate site for a store. The tenant will agree to form a joint venture partnership and provide the necessary financing. The developer will be responsible for the actual construction and development of the shopping center.

DEVELOPMENT FOR A FEE

A less common type of development structuring is one in which a developer (equity or nonequity) agrees to develop a shopping center project as a service to the landowner. In exchange for the expertise rendered, the developer would receive a negotiated fee from the landowner.

Development for a fee is a less popular method because it requires as much time and effort as traditional methods of development but does not carry the benefits that otherwise accrue to the developers.

GET TO KNOW THE DEVELOPERS

In drawing up an inventory of developers for your area, you should know the program and the reputation of each one: their strong and weak points, the type and quality of the projects they have done, their development posture, whether they are equity or nonequity developers or whether they will offer their services on a flat fee schedule. Collect site plans from the different developers and make a study of the space available in their projects.

In the real estate market, many developers rely heavily on brokers. A good-sized developer will probably have a leasing agent on the staff whose sole responsibility is to get the space rented. This person can be an excellent contact. For example, you may have a client whose requirements will be met by existing or proposed space in a developer's center. A leasing agent can help you locate the appropriate space and work out a lease agreement for your client.

An excellent way to become acquainted with developers is to attend local and national meetings of the International Council of Shopping Centers. Your presence there indicates to a developer that you are an active member of the brokerage community, one who is aggressive in seeking information and contacts.

When initiating contact with developers, be sure to meet with them at their place of business. Use the telephone only for follow-up.

Working with Developers

You should know something of the protocol expected in dealing with developers. Do not, for example, shop for the best offer from developers by presenting the same property to several different prospects at the same time. Take a property to one developer and make it clear that you consider him or her the best candidate for this particular piece of property. If developers know you are shopping for the highest price, they are unlikely to make a serious, competitive offer for the property.

A similar problem can develop when you have more than one developer bidding on a project. Each may want to know what the competition is doing. This is a delicate matter. You want to remain on good terms with each developer, yet you must protect the confidence of each. No broker can serve several masters.

If you are already working with a big developer and another calls to ask you to handle a transaction, make sure there are no conflicts in the categories you have covered. If you are already committed in one area, let the second developer know you cannot work exclusively for his or her firm in the same area. You avoid any misunderstandings, and the developer will not become annoyed if you call only once a month rather than twice a week.

Maintaining good relationships with developers is very important. In Southern California, for example, only a handful of people are responsible for 80 percent of the commercial retail development. If you antagonize one developer, the word may reach others, and it will be difficult to restore your credibility.

Commission Agreements

In every transaction, you should draw up a letter of agreement between you and the developer, stipulating the amount of your commission and a schedule for payment. These transactions usually involve large amounts of money, and your efforts will be rewarded only if you receive a commission. Commission agreements, which guarantee your fee, are discussed in detail in the chapter on forms.

Knowing the Market

Besides knowing the program and reputation of each developer in your area, you should also be aware of local laws and zoning ordinances, current tax and rental rates, and building requirements and regulations. You can obtain this information from civic organizations, the local chamber of commerce and municipal agencies responsible for zoning and redevelopment. You can gauge the future state of the market by asking municipal organizations where new development is being considered.

CONCLUSION

You can earn a substantial income from commissions by successfully working through transactions with developers. Remember, in working with sophisticated professionals, you must maintain a high level of credibility. You have to keep on top of the market, which requires constant research, analysis and evaluation. Be ready to draw upon all your experience in leasing space. Ask questions of more experienced salespeople, and keep in mind that you will learn much from the developers themselves as you begin to work with them.

Exercise A

1. What are the advantages and disadvantages to landowners of ground leases and joint ventures?
2. What is the difference between an equity and a nonequity developer?
3. How is the commission paid in a joint venture transaction?
4. What is meant by preferred return and residual return in the context of a joint venture?
5. How should the issue of commissions be handled when you decide to work with a developer?
6. What should you know about developers besides the kinds of projects they undertake?
7. Explain what developers might do if they wished to maintain a partial equity position in a development.

Answer A

1. *The advantage to landowners of a joint venture is that they avoid tax obligations that may be incurred from selling the land outright. The disadvantage is that the owner's return is not guaranteed. The advantage to landowners of a ground lease is that they retain ownership of the land. The disadvantage is that rent received may be considered ordinary income.*
2. *Equity developers build centers with the objective of holding them and benefitting from long-term appreciation. Nonequity developers build centers with the objective of selling them in the short-term.*
3. *In a joint venture, the commission amount is typically paid by the joint venture entity, based on the price of the land.*
4. *A preferred return is the return that is paid first from the proceeds of a joint venture to investors as a return on their investment. A residual return is the return paid from the remaining available monies.*
5. *When you decide to work with a developer be sure to draw up a letter of agreement between you and the developer stipulating the amount of your commission and a schedule for payment.*
6. *In addition to the types of projects each developer undertakes, you should know their reputations, their development postures, whether they are equity or nonequity developers, and their strong and weak points.*
7. *Developers wishing to maintain a partial equity position in a development might form a joint venture or a 50–50 partnership.*

15

Leasing and Building to Suit

INTRODUCTION

This chapter presents a discussion of several areas with which you are already somewhat familiar. Leasing, as it is examined here, pertains primarily to small shop leasing, which could be in either a freestanding building or satellite shops in a shopping center. Apply your knowledge of tenant qualification and tenant control as you read through this section. The material on national chain tenants explains what you should know about a chain's operation and requirements before you approach their real estate representative, and why property control is such an important issue. The build-to-suit transaction was treated briefly in the chapter titled *Types of Transactions*. Here you will find the detailed information you will need in each phase of a build-to-suit transaction. Following this section is an economic profile (pro forma) of a build-to-suit for a national chain tenant. The pro forma will give you an opportunity to examine the economics of such a project in an actual case. The basic format will, of course, change with time and and location.

SMALL SHOP LEASING

From the earlier chapter that touched on the subject of leasing, you should know the advantages of becoming proficient in this area. Not only is this a primary learning experience for you in the investment aspects of property, but the many contacts you make with tenants and owners create a present and potential inventory. In seeking either tenant prospects or available space, you will have talked with and qualified many real estate customers. You will have made yourself known to the users and originators of retail space. You can develop many leads through conversations with people who may not be thinking of relocating or expanding their stores at present. They may mention other retailers who have space needs or may themselves be in need of your services at a future time. If you are looking for a retailer to fill a particular space, the chances are very good, that through your many contacts, you will find tenants with requirements for other types of space than the one you are trying to fill. Whether their needs are immediate or for the near future, you may be able to initiate another transaction.

From a financial point of view, small shop leasing can provide you with a steady income. If you build up strong inventory and tenant listings, especially in your first two years in the retail division, you can be assured of a regular income as you work toward the goal of larger commissions.

Retail Space

You will want to know what spaces are available for leasing. It will be profitable for you to spend some times inventorying existing neighborhood shopping centers and convenience centers that are located in high-impact areas. As you well know, location is the cardinal rule of success in commercial real estate. A freestanding space located in a high-profile retail area, such as across from a community shopping center, will have strong drawing power. If a 10,000 square-foot convenience center had a 2,000 square-foot vacancy, it would be worth while to try to get an exclusive listing on it because it would be attractive space for any number of tenants.

Remember that being selective in the type of space you go after will be more profitable than considering any and every availability. You want to increase your chances of success by controlling desirable space and managing your time wisely. The first chapter discussed the advantages of restricting your inventory to spaces over 1,000 square feet. The rationale for this is that leasing small space takes about as much time as that required for a larger shop, though your commissions are much less.

Retail Tenants

When you are leasing space for a developer or owner of a shopping center, what kinds of tenants will you be looking for? The key to any successful lease transaction is the financial strength of the tenant. Financially well-qualified tenants will be the most acceptable to a landlord because they will provide a secure income for the center. Start with high-quality tenants: national chains, regional stores and strong local tenants. Get a copy of the tenant's financial statement as part of your qualification. A developer will want to have that information. It will save you time—and possibly embarrassment or a commission loss—if you ask for such data up front.

A developer can probably tell you very specifically what kind of net worth is needed from a tenant. The landlord will want to know, for example, whether a tenant has sufficient cash to outfit the store properly and operate for 12 to 16 months on his or her own resources. The tenant's assets or cash on hand represent staying power. This is a most important consideration for the landlord.

You will find, however, that no one rule determines a tenant's acceptability. A landlord may be willing to discount the tenant's net worth if the business would draw considerable traffic to the center. The advantages the tenant brings to the center in terms of tenant mix may also be the deciding factor. These considerations may override financial weakness on the part of the prospective tenant.

Tenant Mix

You should know what type of tenant mix the developer would like to have for the space you are trying to lease. Sit down with the developer and talk this through before you begin to submit lease proposals. Based on your understanding of the desired mix, you can identify the users you will want and can start canvassing them. If a dry cleaner is needed for the space next to the supermarket, compile a list of prospective tenants for that use and make contacts. If a retailer with a use deemed undesirable for the center calls you, you can simply tell this person that the developer has determined that this use would be incompatible with the proposed tenant mix. Be diplomatic. Tenant mix is a crucial element of a development, particularly for an equity developer who is interested in long-range quality income. Know the requirements and avoid submitting proposals to the landlord as they come in without regard for the kinds of use they represent.

Follow-up

Make it a point to keep in touch with tenants for whom you have found locations. Write a note to yourself in your monthly reminder file to contact tenants six months or a year after their transactions are completed. Loyalty to real estate salespeople does not usually run high. If you maintain your contacts by regular follow-up, however, you may get repeat business from these tenants. But remember, you have to take the initiative.

NATIONAL CHAINS

A developer whose major concern is to get dependable income from a shopping center may go for a ratio as high as three national tenants for each local tenant. These financially strong users, such as department stores, supermarkets and financial institutions, are responsible for the heaviest traffic in a center. They are so important to a shopping center's stability and growth that the economic feasibility of a proposed center is not assured until a developer has at least a commitment from one or more national tenants.

Researching the site location needs, growth patterns and potential of these users and making contacts with their real estate representatives can yield highly profitable multiple transactions. The site and building needs of national tenants are usually very specific. You will need to know both the square footage and dimensions of one of the buildings of a national tenant. For example, a fast-food operation typically has narrow buildings and limited frontage, while a furniture store usually requires a rectangular building with more frontage than depth.

When the site needs for a typical retail store are estimated, the land area is usually related to the building area on a three-to-one ratio. For every square foot of building, three additional square feet of land are required. This relationship does not hold true, however, for certain national chain users. Since many fast-food restaurants, banks and savings and loans have drive-through facilities, their parking needs might be reduced.

Before you call on the real estate representative of a national chain, do some research into the number and locations of their existing outlets. This information, along with whatever details you can learn about the chain's expansion plans, will probably give you clues about location gaps. If you determine that one or more additional outlets are wanted, you will need to provide basic information concerning location preferences and the alternatives that can be considered in situating. Can the chain rehabilitate or remodel an existing building to suit its needs? Will it buy land and construct its own building? Or does a build to suit or ground lease seem to be the best route to take?

If your goal is working with a national chain on its local site location, be aware that the most important question will concern property control. Obtaining an exclusive listing on a piece of property is the most significant element of any real estate transaction, but the first question that a national chain will ask is, "Do you control the site?" The company may not even want to look at a site until it knows the listing situation. If you cannot get an exclusive with the owner or landlord and no one else controls the property, try for a short-term listing position. Tell the owner that you are not interested in an exclusive for a broad marketing of the property, but that you want to present it to a specific user. The owner will probably want to keep his or her options open to be able to take advantage of the best offer that comes along. Explain that you will need to tie up the property for only 30 to 60 days. If you obtain an offer to purchase or lease from the tenant, the owner will then give you an exclusive. Essentially, you should try to control the property in any reasonable way you can. When you do business with a national tenant, there is always the strong possibility of multiple transactions.

Multi-market Tenants

Once you have successfully completed a transaction with a national chain you should explore the possibility of representing that tenant in other markets. There are several advantages and disadvantages to representing a tenant exclusively for a number of locations.

Advantages:

1. In acting as an exclusive representative of the tenant you become more knowledgeable about his or her other needs.

2. You have a better opportunity to save the tenant time and money. For example, due to your increased understanding of the tenant, you are better able to pre-negotiate points for him or her.

3. You learn to analyze sites more effectively from the tenant's point of view.

4. Representing a tenant helps you to establish relationships with developers more quickly.

5. You receive information on properties not otherwise available.

6. It helps you to build a track record and credentials.

Disadvantages:

1. Tenants are difficult to control.

2. You are not able to focus your efforts on one geographic area.

3. There is a high turnover rate among site representatives, the people you'll be generally working with.

4. A tenant's strategy may frequently change due to circumstances beyond your control, such as the economy, mergers, acquisitions, the cost of capital, etc.

5. By representing one tenant on a national basis, you must spend a great deal of time interviewing and selecting local brokers to work with, since you will be entering markets you are not familiar with.

6. Working with one tenant may preclude working with others, particularly competitors.

Nonetheless, representing a tenant in multi-markets can be an extremely rewarding direction for you to take. You must weigh a number of factors: your professional preference—representing tenants or property; the quality of national tenant you would represent; your own career development; the dollar potential; and the condition of the market—underbuilt or overbuilt.

Exercise A

1. Why is it important to know the dimensions and the square footage requirements of a national chain tenant's building?

2. What is the key to any successful lease transaction? Why?

3. If an owner is reluctant to give you an exclusive listing on a piece of property that you want to present to a chain tenant, how might you handle the situation?

4. Why might the three-to-one site ratio not apply to certain chain tenants?

Answer A

1. The dimensions may vary according to the type of user. A fast-food operation has narrow buildings and limited frontage, while a furniture store requires a rectangular building with more frontage than depth.

2. *The financial strength of the tenant is the key. The landlord must know whether the tenant has sufficient assets to stay with the business until it begins to turn a profit.*

3. *You can tell the owner that you do not want an exclusive, but merely wish to present the property to a specific user. Explain that you will tie up the property for only 30 to 60 days, and ask that you be given an exclusive if you obtain an offer to purchase or lease.*

4. *The three-to-one ratio might not apply to certain users, such as fast-food restaurants and banks that have drive-through facilities and, therefore, reduced parking requirements.*

BUILDING TO SUIT

The build-to-suit situation is similar to other commercial and industrial real estate transactions in that it involves bringing together a tenant with specific needs and a landlord with something specific to offer. The stages are very similar in each case.

1. The tenant is qualified first to determine his or her needs, then to see if he or she is a prospect for a build to suit.

2. A preliminary meeting is set up to discuss the tenant's particular needs with a developer.

3. The developer, broker, contractor, architect and lender develop a proposal and rental quotation.

4. The proposal is presented to the tenant.

The main difference between the build to suit and other commercial and industrial real estate transactions is that the landlord offers custom building according to the tenant's specific needs. The disadvantage in the build-to-suit transaction is that it is more time-consuming for all parties, including the broker. Since there are more steps in the transaction, there are more opportunities for the transaction to fall through. On the other hand, since the lease involved in this situation will be for a longer period of time than the average retail lease, the commission will be appreciably greater.

Factors other than the need for a specific building might be involved in the tenant's decision to have a building custom built. For example, the tenant might require extra space for parking, or extra land for future expansion. Location is always an important factor in determining the desirability and use of the land. Site selection factors would include such variables as land cost, availability of utilities and transportation facilities, zoning and building codes, taxes and police and fire protection.

Retail custom building often involves chain retailers who are interested mainly in location. In such a situation, the retailer often has plans and specifications already drawn up based on a standardized prototype used in existing stores within the chain. This particular situation presents the fewest difficulties, since the tenant knows what he or she wants.

Tenant Qualification

The most important role of the salesperson in the build-to-suit situation is to determine if the tenant really needs a custom-built building or if existing space may be modified instead. Several important factors must be considered in making that determination.

You must first learn the tenant's requirements. As indicated in the chapter on tenant qualification, this means finding out who in the company has the authority to make decisions regarding leases and purchases and what the company's real estate needs and financial capabilities are. You must learn both present requirements and future plans, and integrate these into an overall picture of the company's needs. Even if the tenant company knows something about what it wants, it may not be familiar with specifications that are used to determine physical needs.

Second, the broker surveys the market. The broker should have a complete inventory of property available, select those properties suitable for the tenant and present them. (See the chapter on showing property.)

The tenant involved in a build-to-suit transaction will usually be a strong regional or local company with specific needs. (National and international companies usually have real estate divisions that use local brokers only for site selection. They can, however, be build-to-suit prospects.) Frequently, you will be dealing with the president of the company, who may be vitally interested in every phase, and whose office may be in the new premises.

Tenant qualification is a very important step in determining build-to-suit qualifications. If you haven't analyzed your tenant's needs at this point, you might find out that he or she can't afford or don't want a new, custom-built building after all. You have wasted the developer's time and money as well as your own.

Preliminary Meeting

After you have qualified the tenant, your next responsibility is to arrange a preliminary meeting which involves:

1. writing a complete description of the tenant's requirements and financial strength
2. arranging to meet with a developer who can handle the project

The choice of a proper developer is one justification for your commission. From your inventory of developers, select a developer with a proven track record who can draw up a proposal in a relatively short period of time and adhere to cost estimates and time schedules. You should be able to list three names for your tenant, in order of priority, according to these characteristics.

Avoid shopping around for proposals when selecting a developer. If developers realize you are doing this, they will be less likely to make a serious offer. Developers will be as serious about your tenant as you are about them.

A similar problem arises when you do have more than a single developer proposing a project. Each will want some clue about what the competition is doing. This is a delicate matter to handle. You want to be on good terms with the developers, yet you must remember that you can't serve two masters.

An obvious and basic consideration in selecting a developer is choosing one who is willing to pay the commission once the work has been done. Usually a large amount of money is involved in these transactions, and your efforts will be rewarded only if you work with a developer you can count on. In every instance, you should always draw up a letter of agreement between yourself and the developer, stipulating the amount and time of payment of the commission. This should be done even before you disclose the name of your tenant.

At this stage of the transaction, the tenant may want a strict estimate of the future rental cost. Since this is still an unknown quantity, strive to avoid any specific quotation. If the tenant insists, you can show him or her similar properties in the area, while indicating that these do not fit the tenant's exact specifications. You might explain that rent is a function of cost, and neither you nor the developer will have a good handle on costs until getting into exact specifications with an engineer, architect, contractor and lender.

Or the tenant might ask what formula will be used to determine the rental price. Explain that you have to talk to your lender to get information on the type of loan available—which won't be known until the lender has information on the tenant, as well as the complete cost breakdown. Thus, you have legitimate reasons for not giving specific rental information at this time.

Proposal Preparation and Presentation

After you have determined the tenant's needs and financial abilities and have arranged a preliminary meeting between the tenant and the developer, you begin to work with both parties on the actual proposal. Time is now a major factor—the developer must be prepared to draw up a proposal of costs over several months (or years) in a short period of time. Again, this is a stage where your choice of developers is crucial. You need a fast, yet reliable contractor who can have an architect draw up a site plan, building layout and line drawing within a week to ten days on the average project. The builder must develop a cost analysis of the plan, talk to a lender, estimate total costs and come up with a quote on rental prices.

The elements involved in deciding upon a rent quote include:

1. *Land at present market value.* The developer may already own the land.

2. *Building costs.* A good developer should be able to estimate the cost of construction over a given period of time, including architectural fees and site work.

3. *Real estate commission.* This is agreed upon with the broker before the tenant is introduced.

4. *Interim (indirect) costs.* These include:
   - interest on the land during construction
   - taxes on the land during construction
   - financial costs, including points
   - interest on construction loans
   - insurance on the job
   - bonding, if necessary
5. *Contingency costs.* During construction, the tenant will sometimes change some specification for any of a number of reasons, ranging from changes in insurance safety regulations to personality disputes over offices. The developer and the tenant must agree that the rental will be a function of the final cost after such changes have been made.

Once these cost elements have been determined, the developer arrives at a rental calculation, based on the total cost compared to the return that he or she expects on equity. This calculation includes such variable factors as real estate taxes, insurance, and future maintenance and modernization costs.

Other contingencies that you might advise the developer to include in the rent quotation are that it be:

1. subject to approval of final plans and specifications by both parties
2. subject to approval of lease form by both parties
3. subject to approval of financing for the tenant

Having arrived at the total cost calculation and rental quotation, the developer arranges for a presentation to your tenant. Here, too, your understanding of and sensitivity to the tenant is very important. When all the factors have been packaged for presentation, you must be able to judge the tenant's response.

A quick or superficial presentation may give the tenant the impression that you are not really dealing with him or her seriously or paying attention to the specific details the tenant thinks are important—the reasons why the tenant chose to have the facilities custom-built in the first place.

A whole show of maps, charts, plans, drawings, and diagrams, on the other hand, might be overwhelming, giving the tenant the feeling that he or she may be getting into something too complex or expensive.

Once the proposal has been made, the tenant must decide whether he or she really wants to enter into the transaction. If you have done a good job of determining the tenant's needs and capabilities, and matched them with a developer who can deliver, this decision should be a formality. However, it is still crucial in determining whether or not the transaction will actually be carried out (and whether you get a commission). Once the two parties have agreed to go ahead with the deal, your major responsibility is over. You still have the obligation to ensure that communication between the tenant and the developer continues during the project and to help keep the transaction moving forward.

You may be of service to your tenant in presenting the developer's formal proposal to the tenant's company. Even when you have been working with the company's president, there may well be accountants and other advisors involved. Here the tenant can be of assistance, for your role in this area should be left to his or her discretion. The tenant may need your help in handling technical questions, or may just want moral support. On the other hand, you might be seen as an outsider with something to sell, or an intruder into an internal decision making process.

The Salesperson's Role

Once the formal proposal has been accepted and a lease form has been signed, the salesperson generally bows out of the transaction. However, in some cases, you may be involved in checking to see that lines of communication are kept open and that the transaction continues to move forward. Legally, you have done your job once the lease is signed, but in reality you are not finished until the tenant moves into the building. Your role, therefore, can vary from merely finding a suitable site and developer for a tenant to coordinating a whole project until the tenant occupies the building. Obviously, you should collect a larger commission for the latter service.

As has been discussed, the build-to-suit lease is an unusual situation that generally means more work and personal involvement for the broker. Whether or not you should take on this type of transaction depends on objective decisions about time and effort and personal decisions regarding your individual interests and abilities.

The Tenant's Role

The primary role of tenants is to learn their own needs and financial capabilities so that they can share them fully with you and the developer. This involves a survey of their present facilities, plans for expansion and reasons for moving. Occasionally, a tenant will find that it really isn't in his or her best interest to move at the present time, much less to get involved with a custom-built structure. It is your responsibility to point out the disadvantages of a move as well as the advantages. If you advise tenants unwisely, they're going to think of you and your firm every time they drive up to the building or have to cope with another problem that you could have helped them to avoid.

Exercise B

Answer the following questions.

1. In a build-to-suit, what are the typical stages involved in bringing together a tenant with specific needs and a landowner who has something specific to offer?

CHAPTER 15 / Leasing and Building To Suit   209

2. List factors that would lead a tenant to decide on a build to suit.

3. What criteria should be considered in selecting a developer for a build to suit?

4. What are three important functions of the salesperson in the build-to-suit transaction?

5. On what is the developer's rental calculation based?

6. List the factors involved in deciding on a rental quotation.

7. What expenses are considered interim costs?

8. What if the tenant, in the preliminary stages, asks for the formula to be used in determining the rental quotation?

9. What might you do if the tenant insists on a strict estimate of future rental?

10. At what point in the build-to-suit transaction is the salesperson's major responsibility over? What are the remaining responsibilities?

Answer B

1. *(a) The tenant's needs are qualified to determine if the tenant is indeed a build-to-suit prospect.*
    (b) A preliminary meeting is set up with a developer to discuss the tenant's particular needs.
    (c) The developer, together with the broker, contractor, architect and lender, prepares a proposal and rental quotation.

2. *Such factors would most likely include needs for custom building, extra parking facilities, extra land for future expansion and a specific location.*

3. *A developer with a proven track record must be selected, one who can draw up a proposal in a relatively short period of time and can accurately make and adhere to cost estimates and time schedules.*

4. *The salesperson's three main responsibilities are (a) qualifying the tenant in terms of decision making authority in the company, real estate needs, and financial capability; (b) arranging a preliminary meeting with a developer; and (c) working with the tenant and the developer on the actual proposal.*

5. *The rental calculation is based on the total cost compared to the return that he or she expects on equity.*

6. *The factors involved in deciding on a rental quotation are: (a) present market value of land; (b) building costs; (c) requirements of the real estate commission; (d) interim (indirect) costs; and (e) contingency costs.*

7. *Interim costs include: (a) interest on the land during construction; (b) taxes on the land during construction; (c) financial costs, including points; (d) interest on construction loans; (e) insurance on the job; and (f) bonding, if necessary.*

8. *You have legitimate reasons for not giving specific rental information at this time. Explain that you have to obtain information*

from your lender about the type of loan available, which won't be known until the lender has information on the tenant, and a complete cost breakdown.

9. *While avoiding any specific quotations, you might show the tenant similar properties in the area for comparison. Indicate that these do not meet the tenant's specifications as well as the other property. Explain that rent is a function of cost, which cannot be judged accurately without going into exact specifications with an engineer, architect, contractor, and lender.*

10. *Once an agreement has been reached between the two parties to proceed with the deal, the salesperson's major responsibility has been fulfilled. But the salesperson is still obligated to see that communication between the tenant and the developer continues during the project and to assist whenever problems arise.*

SUPERMARKET PRO FORMA (BUILD-TO-SUIT)

A pro forma, which simply means "according to form," is an economic guideline. It refers here to a projected operating statement outlining the financial advantages or disadvantages of a given project. You can use a pro forma to demonstrate the visibility of a development through an economic profile detailing the development's costs and the return on the investment. In other words, what is the total anticipated income from the proposed construction?

The pro forma on the next page is an economic profile on a build to suit for a freestanding building. As you read through the description of this pro forma, you may wish to compare it with the shopping center pro formas in the next chapter.

The total site area for the supermarket is 140,000 square feet, assuming a three-to-one ratio of land to building area. At $2.50 per square foot, the total land value is $350,000.

From the information on land match, one year at 12.5 percent, we can assume that this is not a piece of property that the owner has held for years. Rather, it is likely that the developer, knowing that the supermarket chain wanted a 35,000 square foot store at a certain location, tied up the property for the express purpose of building to suit this chain. The developer probably went to his or her financial institution for a land draw at 12.5 percent for one year, which comes to $70,000.

The financing costs are estimated at 14.5 percent times eight months times one-half. Since this project involves only a single building for one tenant, the construction period will be shorter than for a shopping center. The construction loan is not taken down at one time, but in periodic draws over a length of time averaging one-half the time of the construction period. In this case, the cost of construction financing is 14.5 percent annual interest, the construction period is eight months, and the effective interest period is one-half of that time.

The total land cost, $560,000, and the total development cost, $1,474,850, are converted to rent by applying to these figures the determined percentage return, which gives the annual return on the investment. The typical return on a build-to-suit for a freestanding building

FIGURE 15.1 Build-to-Suit Pro Forma

35,000 SQUARE FOOT SUPERMARKET

NEC MAIN STREET AND CENTRAL ROAD

CAPITOL, CALIFORNIA

LAND:

140,000 square feet at $4/square foot	$ 560,000
(Land to building ratio 3:1 = 25% coverage)	

DEVELOPMENT:

	Building	(35,000 square feet at $27/square foot)	$ 945,000
	Site work	(140,000 square feet at $2/square foot)	280,000
	A and E	(35,000 square feet at $1.50/square foot)	52,500
	Commission	(35,000 square feet at $1.25/square foot)	43,750
	Financing:	Land carry (12½%, 1 year)	70,000
		Construction ($1,321,250 × 14½% × 8 mos. × ½)	63,800
		Loan points (1½ on construction)	19,800

TOTAL DEVELOPMENT COSTS: $1,474,850

INCOME (Triple Net)

	Land:	($560,000 at 10%)	$ 56,000
	Improvements:	($1,475,230 at 12.81%)	188,977
			$ 188,928

Annual Rent	$ 244,977
Rent per square foot (annually)	$ 7

used to be ten percent to the land and a 12 percent return on the development costs. These standards have changed, however, due to the recent increases in the cost of financing. Now, each build-to-suit must be analyzed on an individual basis using the currently available cost-of-money figure for the given market area. Thus, although the return on land remains at the ten percent figure, the return on improvements depends on what financing the developer can obtain. In this transaction, the return on the land value is ten percent, which yields $56,000. Since the landowner is dealing with a major supermarket, a financially strong and highly desirable tenant that will probably attract other users to adjacent property, favorable leasing conditions are being extended. Another type of tenant might conceivably be asked to pay more rent to ensure a higher return. The total development cost of $1,474,850 is converted to rent at 12.81 percent, which represents the best available loan constant. The total annual rental of $244,928, divided by the size of the store, 35,000 square feet, costs the supermarket $7 per square foot per year.

16

Shopping Center Development

INTRODUCTION

Although the development of a large shopping center is certainly a highly complex undertaking, there is a logical sequence of steps involved from the initiation of the site search through the completion of construction. Some of these procedures, such as locating the appropriate site, collecting the data on demographics and zoning, tracking down leads and qualifying prospective tenants, are already familiar to you from preceding chapters. Others, which have not yet been discussed in any detail, touch upon the financing and valuation of a development.

This chapter will give you an overview of the types of shopping centers and of the general path that is followed in actualizing a project. It will also provide a more detailed account of the financial intricacies that enter into the development of a large center: estimating the income from the center, arranging for the permanent and construction loans and establishing the pro forma statement. At the end of the chapter, a sample pro forma will be analyzed to help you understand the items to consider when scrutinizing a proposed development for feasibility.

The following section is a discussion of types of shopping centers. The chapter on local developers gave some basic information about size requirements and transactions in which banks, restaurants and theaters are typically involved. Refer to that information to integrate it with the following outline. Remember, you will absorb facts more effectively if you continually relate one subject to another as you progress through the manual.

TYPES OF CENTERS

There are five categories of shopping centers:

1. convenience
2. neighborhood
3. community
4. regional
5. specialty
6. superregional
7. off-price

The definitions of the category may be based on size or, where size alone is not the distinguishing feature, on the types of users located in a center.

Convenience centers are small, anywhere from one-half acre to four acres, with between 5,000 and 40,000 square feet of gross leasable area (GLA). They usually accommodate a convenience market, a dry cleaner, a convenience-oriented user, a liquor store and a laundromat. This was the first type of shopping facility located in neighborhoods. Because of the limited land area, stores are often constructed with common walls in a strip facing the street. Hence, the slang term "strip centers." It is preferable, particularly when discussing convenience centers with governmental agencies, to refer to them not as strip centers but as convenience centers.

Neighborhood centers are the most active site developments that you will be involved in. Such centers are usually anchored by a major supermarket and often by a chain drugstore as well. Land requirement is between five and ten acres, with 50,000 to 100,000 square feet of GLA. The approval process and completion of construction will be considerably longer than for the convenience center, primarily because of the major tenant approvals. To a large extent, the majors will dictate the layout of your site plan, which will, in turn, affect the economics of the transaction by virtue of the number of pads and square footage of small shops that the majors will permit.

Community shopping centers are somewhat smaller than regional centers and are usually anchored by a supermarket, a junior department store, a drugstore and a variety store. The land area is from 15 to 20 acres, with about 150,000 to 200,000 square feet of GLA. The tenant mix, in addition to the service types found in convenience and neighborhood centers, will include a good variety of soft-goods and hard-goods tenants.

Regional centers have as their primary tenants several large department stores and require a land area of 80 to 100 acres, with from 800,000 to more than one million square feet of GLA. The most common type of construction today is the enclosed air-conditioned mall. Every conceivable type of retail and service user can be located within the center.

Specialty centers vary in size depending on the site and the strength of the market. They may have a GLA as small as 10,000 square feet or as large as 200,000 square feet. They do not have a major anchor tenant and are typified by the small, gift-oriented tenant. The largest occupant might be a 10,000-square-feet dinner house.

The "theme center," where a certain motif or style is used in the architectural treatment (for instance, the Cape Cod or western look), is really a type of specialty center.

Another type of center that is gaining popularity is the promotional or "promo" center. The word categorizes only the type of tenants that occupy the space. They are high visibility tenants—radio, television, and stereo stores—that rely on heavy advertising to do extremely high-volume business. These users usually do not pay percentage rents, because of the amount of money they spend on advertising to draw traffic to the center. If percentage rents are paid, they are significantly lower than in neighborhood centers.

Some specialty centers are "specialty" only in terms of use. These might be home improvement centers that would include furniture, drapery, floor covering and lighting stores. Another category would be an auto center for such things as car stereos, auto glass, transmission repairs and mufflers.

Superregional centers are generally anchored by three or more full-line department stores and are built on 50 to 165 acres with one to two million square feet of GLA. Usually, a minimum of a half-million people are needed in their trade area.

Off-price centers handle discount merchandise and are located on major highways or arteries with two to three and up to five anchor tenants in 30,000-square-foot to 100,000-square-foot stores. The site itself covers a quarter-million to a half-million square feet of land. Tenants are comprised of both soft-good and hard-good retailers.

STEPS INVOLVED IN DEVELOPMENT

The first stage is the search for an appropriate location. Each potential site is considered in terms of its suitability for a shopping center. A market survey is made to ascertain the need for and viability of a development. The survey includes a demographic study covering population, mean income, customer demand, buying habits, the rate of growth in the area, new construction and market potential.

The owners of the most likely properties are then contacted to learn whether their land is available, the price, and the terms under which they would be willing to sell. When the choice has been narrowed to one piece of available property, the developer will secure an option on the site.

Next, an architect prepares a simple plot plan showing the proposed layout of the center. This plan is a rough draft identifying the location and size of the parcel and defining the placement of building pad areas. Since the major tenants will be consulted on certain features of the construction, the finer details will be filled in later.

The feasibility of the development is not assured until a commitment has been received from at least one major anchor tenant. Then site plans are presented to the real estate department of a national or chain tenant that has expressed interest in opening another outlet in the selected location. If that company determines that the site meets its requirements, a letter of intent stating its interest and the conditions of its tenancy is prepared.

It is usually desirable to obtain a letter of intent from more than one major user. If the first national tenant you have contacted is a supermarket, it will usually require cotenancy with a drugstore. The interest of a drugstore chain is generally assured by the supermarket's commitment.

The tenant mix for the residual space in the center is the next consideration. Relying on personal contacts, leads, cold calling and a sign on the property, you will work on locating tenants for the pads and satellite shops. After prospective tenants have been found, the process of qualifying their needs, requirements, and financial strength is carried out. Once the construction begins it is easier to lease space, and by the time the center nears completion most of the space will be leased.

At this stage, the developer will secure the financing commitment. This cannot be accomplished until the income from the proposed center can be estimated from the finalized leases. Lenders will be particularly interested in the financial qualification of the anchor tenants. In many instances, the income from the national tenants will pay the expenses of operation and service the debt, while the smaller, local tenants will provide the developer's profit. An acceptable income from the center is usually assured if approximately 65 percent of the space is leased to national tenants and 35 percent to regional and local tenants. The type of permanent financing instrument the developer obtains is a function of the rapidly changing financing market and whatever he or she can negotiate that best suits his or her needs. (see the chapter titled *Financing*)

In the final planning stages, the requirements of each tenant are made known through the terms of the lease, and the architect completes the final plans for the center. When all of the preceding steps have been accomplished, the developer is ready to conclude the purchase of the property in accordance with the terms provided in the option.

REHABILITATION

As a professional retail salesperson, you should be on the lookout not only for development opportunities, but for rehabilitation opportunities as well. Rehabilitation of an existing center has a number of unique concerns.

Strategy

When purchasing a center to rehabilitate, a buyer must cover some specific areas in the sales contract. These include:

1. lease approval rights for new leases
2. the state of existing leases (particularly with regard to exclusives within the leases, any default provisions, expiration dates and options to renew)
3. a review of the structural elements of the center, especially the condition of the roof, the parking lot and the lighting

4. prorations (rents through the date of closing, arrearages—who gets credit for collection, security deposits, tax and insurance and leasing commissions)

Items that also need to be addressed include:

1. a review and evaluation of all service contracts
2. setting up ownership with the utility company
3. reviewing all existing plans and specifications for the center

Leasing. The first area to consider in rehabilitation is leasing. Working with the owner, you must help establish the desired tenant mix. For example, has the center failed in the past due to an insufficient anchor tenant? Is the tenant mix appropriate to the income level of the area it is located in? As part of this evaluation, you must consider the existing tenants. Are there short-term adjustments you can make with them to improve their contribution to the center without violating any provision in their lease? You must also evaluate the effect that existing tenants' departure from the center would have. When you have thoroughly analyzed the tenants currently in the center in respect to your desired mix, you should have a clear picture of those tenants to target in your marketing efforts.

You will find that attracting and keeping tenants while the property is being physically rehabilitated can be a challenge. Since their business will be disrupted due to construction, you may want to consider some creative lease structures, such as a percentage-only lease.

During Rehabilitation

In the construction phase itself, the owner has a number of concerns that you should be aware of. The major concern is keeping existing tenants profitable and enthusiastic about the rehabilitation during what can be trying times. This problem can be addressed somewhat by the time of year the construction takes place. Obviously, construction that occurs during the holiday shopping season will have a negative effect on the tenants. Also, every effort should be made to limit actual physical barriers during rehabilitation and to keep the center looking as undisturbed as possible.

You will make the greatest contribution to the rehabilitation process by having a thorough understanding of the market, appropriate tenant mixes, what other centers are doing in the area and what tenants are doing in the area. In this way you can advise the developer on how to structure the center and keep losses to a minimum while developing the center to its full potential.

The Pro Forma

The pro forma, as discussed in the previous chapter, is an operating statement for projecting the costs of a development and the expected return on the investment. When you become familiar with the basic concept of a pro forma, which may vary in length from one to several pages depending on how detailed the breakdown of information is, you will eventually be able to pencil in the appropriate data and know when the figures are reasonable. The figures in a pro forma are based on market values and current interest rates, or they are functions of percentages representing, in many instances, rule-of-thumb relationships between figures. The pro forma takes the guesswork out of estimating the worth of income property by showing the developer the bottom line on the operating statement—that is, the return on the money invested.

To prepare for the analysis of the sample pro forma at the end of this chapter, read through the following section on capital cost and income definitions.

CAPITAL COST AND INCOME DEFINITIONS

The following is a list of terms used to describe development expenses.

On-site and Off-site Costs

On-site costs include preparing the site for the construction of buildings. They cover import and export of soil. If the land has to be levelled, this means exporting dirt. If the property falls away from the street, dirt must be imported to the site. Streets on the site, parking space, landscaping and lighting are all on-site costs.

Off-site costs are developer's expenses associated with bringing street improvements and utilities to the property line. If the city or county has reserved a portion of the purchased property for a street dedication or for widening an existing highway or boulevard, the developer would be responsible for adding a curb, gutter or sidewalk. If the sewer line is in the middle of the street and is not brought to the property line, the required extra length would be an off-site cost for which the developer would be responsible.

When developers purchase property, they will try to purchase it on a net rather than a gross acreage basis. If a condition of developing the property is improving the street to 55 feet, leaving 20 feet for dedication, developers will not want to purchase land that is useless to them. They will ask the seller to reduce the price of the property based on a net useable square footage. The seller will then dedicate to the municipality that portion of the property scheduled for street improvement. He or she may or may not be reimbursed for it.

Direct and Indirect Costs

Direct costs, also referred to as hard costs, are those associated with building construction and improvement. They do not cover landscaping expenses.

Indirect, or *soft, costs* include architectural and engineering fees, financing, the cost of carrying the land during the construction period and commissions. Anything not directly related to construction and improvement would be considered an indirect cost.

Calculating Income

Several terms and formulas are used to calculate income from the development in terms of yield and percentage of return.

Scheduled gross income refers to the amount of income that will be collected when all spaces in the center are occupied; in other words, the total income from the GLA. This figure, less an allowance for vacancies and management, before debt service, gives the net operating income (NOI). (Since all leases are net, the only deductions for operating expenses would be a vacancy allowance and management fee.)

The projected operating expenses are determined and shown with the real property taxes and insurance. In today's market, expenses will be absolutely minimum because the developer will usually accept only absolute net leases. An absolute net, or net-net-net, lease means that the tenant is paying all the costs: taxes, maintenance of the common areas and insurance. In fact, most leases are now quadruple net, since the tenant also pays a proportional share of roof and structural maintenance.

When the debt service, that is, the total annual payment of principal and interest on the loan, is subtracted from the net operating income, the resulting figure is the *cash flow,* also called the *net spendable income.* These progressive calculations can be presented in a simplified outline:

1. scheduled gross income less vacancy rate and management = net operating income

2. net operating income less debt service = cash flow

A developer will be especially interested in the *cash yield* and *total gain* figures. To arrive at the anticipated total gain on a development, add the *gain in equity,* which is the amortized payment on the debt less interest, to the cash flow:

3. amortized debt payment less interest = gain in equity

4. gain in equity plus cash flow = total gain (yield)

The relationship, in terms of yield, between the amount invested in the property and the cash flow will give the *cash-on-cash yield:*

5. cash flow divided by investment = cash-on-cash yield

Once the net operating income is established, the value of the property may be calculated by the *capitalization of the net operating income.* The value is determined by applying a percentage rate that represents the relationship between the property and the income that it produces. An approximate sales price can be established by applying the capitalization rate, which will vary according to current market values and the type of property involved.

Financing the Development

The developer prepares the pro forma statement of the proposed development. The income information in the statement is taken from the executed leases or pro forma rents. The vacancy factor and management are deducted. If a developer has a true quadruple net lease, the lender will usually have no difficulty accepting 100 percent of the income that is shown on the pro forma.

The lending institution then analyzes the income and the quality of the leases. The value of the development is assessed by capitalizing the net operating income at a determined percentage factor to arrive at an economic value, which is usually more conservative than the market value. The amount of the mortgage will be a percentage of that value, varying from 50 to 75 percent, depending on the type of development and the security of the loan. The rate of interest and the terms of the loan are usually influenced by the type and quality of the development. Reducing the cost of money is an important factor in the overall cost of the development. A developer will want to negotiate the best interest rate available on the longest terms possible to lower the loan constant to a point where the maximum amount of cash flow can be shown.

Permanent and Construction Loans

The permanent loan is arranged before construction is ever started on the project. Obtaining the construction loan is contingent upon the commitment to the permanent loan. The amount of the construction loan is included in the permanent loan. The lender of the permanent loan will not necessarily be the same institution that grants the construction loan.

The take-out on the permanent loan is, in theory, at the end of the construction period. The permanent lender pays the construction lender the amount of the construction loan. Essentially, when the lender funds the permanent loan, the construction loan is wiped out. A developer will not want to start drawing on the permanent loan until the income from rentals starts coming in. If the draw on the loan begins before this time, the loan payments will have to be carried out of pocket.

The projected income from the development and the cost of the land are taken into consideration in estimating the maximum permanent loan. The amount of the construction loan is a function of the direct and indirect costs of construction.

The cost on the money for construction financing is usually roughly figured by dividing in half the interest that would accrue over a 12-month period. If $2,500,000 were borrowed at 13 percent, the interest over a 12-month period would be $325,000. However, the loan is taken down in stages as the money is needed to pay the expenses of construction. Therefore, after dividing the total interest of $325,000 by 12 for a monthly cost of $27,000, this last figure is divided by the number of months during which the developer actually drew on the loan. If it took only seven months to build the project, the total cost on the money would be $189,000, calculated by multiplying $27,000 by the seven months. As a rule of thumb, whatever the construction period is, the interest implication is usually roughly half of what the total interest amount on the money would be. For further details on financing, see the chapter titled *Development Financing*.

ANALYSIS OF A SAMPLE PRO FORMA

Figure 16.1 is a sample pro forma for a shopping center development. Study it as you read through this point-by-point analysis. Apply the information from the preceding section to the specific figures of the pro forma. Some of the items in the pro forma are self-evident; others will require the application of income calculation and financing principles.

Land

The figures pertaining to the land are written in as the total acreage and are the total number of square feet multiplied by the purchase price per square foot. In this case, 261,360 square feet at $4 per square foot equals a total land cost of $1,045,440.

Sales

This nonequity developer is trying to reduce the basis in the land as effectively as possible by selling major portions of the center to a market, a bank and a fast-food restaurant. The developer will hope to close four escrows at the same time: his land purchase and the sales to the market, bank and fast-food restaurant. The net result of that transaction, after paying a sales commission of five percent, or $54,000, is a $19,440 land cost.

Total sale (market, bank, fast food):	$ 1,080,000
Less land purchase:	−1,045,440
	34,560
Less commission:	− 54,000
Developer's basis in remaining land:	$ 19,440

In addition, the developer has a residual site area of 73,360 square feet on which to build 18,340 square feet of shops. The building area is figured as 25 percent of the total site area. The square footage figures for the market, bank and fast-food restaurant assume the three-to-one ratio of site area to building size; for example, the market site given above is 140,000 square feet, four times the size of the building. The developer is selling a parcel that includes the land under the building and the land necessary to support the user's share of the common area.

Development Costs (Shops)

Building and site work. These are the costs associated with constructing the 18,340 square feet of satellite shops. At $30 per square foot, the

FIGURE 16.1

SHOPPING CENTER
PRO FORMA
NON EQUITY

LAND		
(6 acres = 261,360 square feet at $4.00/square foot)		$1,045,440
SALES (To Tenants)		
(1) Market	140,000 square feet at $4.00/square foot	(560,000)
(2) Bank	28,000 square feet at $10.00/square foot	(280,000)
(3) Fast Food	20,000 square feet at $12.00/square foot	(240,000)
Commissions on Sales at 5%		54,000
Remaining Land	73,360 square feet	19,440
DEVELOPMENT COSTS (Shops)		
(a) Building	(18,340 square feet at $30/square foot)	550,200
(b) Site Work	(73,360 square feet at $2/square foot)	146,720
(c) A & E	(18,340 square feet at $1.50/square foot)	27,510
(d) Leasing	(18,340 square feet at $2.50/square foot)	45,850
(e) Financing	[(a) + (b) + (c) + (d)] × 14½ × 8 mos. × ½ plus 1½ points	48,970
(f) Contingency	(18,340 square feet at $2/square foot)	36,680
TOTAL DEVELOPMENT COSTS		885,930
LAND COSTS		19,440
TOTAL PROJECT COSTS		875,370
ANNUAL NET INCOME	18,340 square feet at $11.40	$ 209,076
	Less Expenses (8%)	(16,726)
	Net Operating Income	$ 192,350
LOAN	($192,350 ÷ .1281 ÷ 1.25) = $1,200,000	
DEBT SERVICE	(at 12.81K)	153,720
CASH FLOW		38,630
GROSS SALES PRICE		
Down Payment	$ 550,000 (cash flow capped at 7%)	
Loan	1,200,000	1,750,000
Less Project Costs		(875,370)
Less Commissions at 5%		(87,500)
POTENTIAL PROFIT		$ 787,130

total building construction figure is $550,200. The figure on the site work, at $2 per square foot, or $146,720, would include both on-site and off-site expenses. If there is anything unusual with respect to the on-site and off-site expenses, this will be brought out separately in the pro forma.

A & E. This is the standard abbreviation for architectural and engineering costs. In this example, we have fixed A & E to $1.50 per square foot of building. If you have no knowledge of what actual A & E costs would run on a project, five percent of the total building and site work can be used as a conservative estimate.

Leasing. This item refers to the leasing commissions on 18,340 square feet leased at a commission rate of $2.50 per square foot. More and more brokers are quoting a flat rate per square foot, rather than a graduated commission schedule. While the graduated scale encourages brokers to work on long-term leases, it can also be counterproductive. A retailer who wants only a five-year lease may be pushed to the bottom of the list because the broker's commission will not be as high as it would be with a longer lease. The flat fee per square foot motivates you to qualify each tenant based on individual abilities to merchandise in that location, as opposed to whether the tenant wants a lease of short, medium, or long term.

Financing costs. Financing costs include interest expenses plus points for financing construction costs and land. Construction costs ((a)–(d) on the pro forma) financed include building, site work, A & E, and leasing costs. The formulas for deriving the financing costs are:

$$\text{Construction:} \quad \frac{(a+b+c+d) \times 14.5\% \text{ interest} \times \text{time period}}{2} + \text{points}$$

$$\text{Land:} \quad ((\text{loan amount}) \times \text{rate} \times \text{time period}) + \text{points}$$

In our example, the land was not financed, and the construction costs to be financed are $770,280. From our equation, the financing cost on this amount is 14.5% interest times eight months, or two-thirds of a year, divided by two, plus 1.5 points. Thus:

$$\frac{(\$770,280 \times 14.5\% \times 67\% \text{ of one year})}{2} + 1.5\% \times 770,280$$

or

$$\$37,416 + \$11,554 = \$48,970$$

Contingency. This covers a vacancy factor and any variants in the site work or building construction. Where there is a significant amount of satellite leasing, there may be no way of knowing for certain what the vacancy factor will be. A rule of thumb, however, is to use five percent as a reasonable vacancy factor. If you have very precise information on what the total costs will be, you can pencil in a very light contingency factor of perhaps two percent or three percent.

Total development costs. This is simply the total of the development expenses for the shops, plus the $19,440 remaining land cost from the sale of the major pads—giving a total project cost of $875,370.

Annual Income and Net Operating Income

Annual income is the gross income generated from leases, for example, the $11.40 per square foot rental rate times the 18,340 feet of satellite space. The rental rate must take into consideration competitive rental rates for similar shops which will be in effect when the shops are available for occupancy.

Net operating income (NOI) is the annual income minus vacancy allowances and operating expenses. Since retail leases are usually net (tenant pays pro rata share of taxes, insurance, and common area maintenance charges), operating expenses are limited to management fees. In our example, the vacancy estimate is five percent of annual income, and management, three percent.

Loan, Debt Service and Cash Flow

From a loan commitment of $1,200,000 at 12.5 percent over 30 years, there is an annual constant (debt service) of 12.81 percent, or $153,720. This means that once the property is constructed and occupied, the owner's cash flow, after debt service, will be $38,630.

Net operating income:	$192,350
Less debt service:	153,720
Cash flow:	$38,630

Gross Sales Price

The loan figure of $1,200,000 is based on the economic value of the property, which is the estimated amount at which the property can be expected to sell in the current market, or the amount at which the $192,350 income from the property can be sold.

The selling price in this pro forma was calculated by capitalizing the cash flow at seven percent ($38,630 ÷ 7% = $550,000) which becomes the down payment added to the loan ($550,000 + $1,200,000 = $1,750,000). Seven percent reflects the current market for return on cash invested.

CONCLUSION

The purpose of the pro forma analysis was to help you develop the ability to dissect a piece of property on the spot, to be able to sit down with a client and get an immediate feel for whether the property is reasonably priced or overpriced. If you have a clear idea of how the basic calculations are made, what the relationships among the figures are, and how the figures in different relationships to each other yield various kinds of economic data for the investor, you should have little difficulty presenting a sensible project on a piece of property.

Exercise A

On the following page is a short equity developer pro forma. In this case, there are no sales of pads in the center; the profit is a function solely of the income from the leased space. Compare this operating statement with the nonequity pro forma.

1. How is the "equity required" calculated from the information given in the pro forma?
2. What two figures are used to calculate the 15.5 percent return to the investor?
3. How is the debt service calculated?

Answer A

1. To determine the "equity returned," the loan amount of $4,000,000 is subtracted from the total development costs of $4,496,680 giving a required equity of $496,680.
2. The figures used to calculate the percentage return to the investor are the cash flow and the equity required: the cash flow ($76,850) represents 15.5 percent of the equity required.
3. The debt service, or annual constant, is calculated from the loan commitment of $4,000,000 at 12.5 percent over 30 years.

Exercise B

1. What two figures are used to determine the cash flow from a development?
2. What are the two ways of computing the leasing commission for a development? What is the advantage of each?
3. What two factors does a lender take into consideration in figuring the maximum permanent loan?
4. How is the cost on the money for a construction loan usually figured? Why?
5. Are the permanent loan and the construction loan two separate loans? Explain.

THE NAPKIN PRO FORMA

In the previous section you examined the equity and nonequity pro forma in full-length form. These pro formas presented cost, income and return figures for the developer in detail. They provided a projection of

FIGURE 16.2

SHOPPING CENTER
PRO FORMA
EQUITY

LAND		
(6 acres = 261,360 square feet at $4/square foot)		$1,045,440
DEVELOPMENT COSTS		
(a) Market Building	(35,000 square feet at $27/square foot)	945,000
(b) Bank	(7,000 square feet at $70/square foot)	490,000
(c) Fast Food	(3,500 square feet at $60/square foot)	210,000
(d) Shops	(18,340 square feet at $30/square foot)	550,200
(e) Site Work	(261,360 square feet at $2/square foot)	522,720
(f) A & E	(63,840 square feet at $1.50/square foot)	95,760
(g) Leasing:	Market at $1.25/square foot	43,750
	Bank at 3% and 2%	41,580
	Fast Food at 3% and 2%	26,775
	Shops at $2.50/square foot)	45,850
(h) Financing:	Land carry (12 1/2%, 1 year)	130,680
	Construction loan (a) through (g) × 14 1/2% × 8 months × 1/2	144,350
	Loan points (1 1/2 construction, 1 1/2 permanent)	104,575
(i) Contingency:		100,000
TOTAL DEVELOPMENT COSTS		$3,451,240
TOTAL PROJECT COSTS		$4,496,680
ANNUAL INCOME	Market at $7.00/square foot	245,000
	Bank at $13.20/square foot	92,400
	Fast Food at $17/square foot	59,500
	Shops at $11.40/square foot	209,076
		$ 605,976
LESS EXPENSES	5% vacancy (shops only)	(10,454)
	3% management (shops only)	(6,272)
NET OPERATING INCOME		$ 489,250
LOAN	($575,950 ÷ .1281 ÷ 1.15) = $4,000,000	
ANNUAL DEBT SERVICE		$ 512,400
CASH FLOW		$ 76,850
EQUITY REQUIRED		$ 496,680
RETURN ON EQUITY (cash on cash)		15.5%
OVERALL RETURN ON CASH		13.1%

the developer's return assuming certain income and cost figures were realized. As you study the pro formas you begin to see that the cost, income and return figures are very much a function of one another. *Return* is determined by income in relation to development costs. To a large degree, *income* can be determined by figuring a return on development costs. And to a degree, *development costs* are limited by the project's income and the developer's needed return. Diagramatically you have an interrelated triangle:

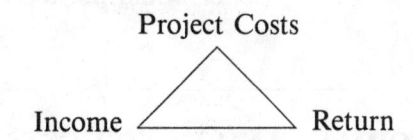

Project Costs

Income   Return

The interrelationships of costs, income and return enable the developer to look at a project's feasibility fairly quickly in what is called a "napkin" pro forma (so named because the calculations can be done on the face of a napkin). With a few calculations, the napkin pro forma can tell you any of the following:

1. what the developer's return will be assuming costs and income are known

2. what the project costs must be assuming the rents are known and a given return must be achieved

3. what the rents must be assuming the costs and return are known

In short, the napkin pro forma is a calculation that solves for any of the elements in the above triangle assuming the two other points in the triangle are known.

In actual practice, costs, income and return are influenced by outside factors other than the elements in the triangle. For example, development costs are known to fall into a certain range because experience has shown that construction and other costs are usually a certain amount per square foot. Similarly, rent levels are determined by the market and not just the project's capitalized costs. And finally, return is influenced by other investment return rates such as the yield on bonds, CDs and mutual funds. So what you have in the napkin pro forma are three interrelated factors that are also affected by outside influences. Given this situation, the rent, cost and return figures may or may not fit together.

Let's take an example. Assume a developer wants to make 12 percent on his project and that the going rate for space is $12 to $13 per foot. A $15 rental would therefore not be acceptable. Finally, let's say land and development costs were $90 per building foot. Now the question is, under these circumstances, will the venture be profitable enough?

The napkin pro forma will tell you the answer quickly. Here is the pro forma's formula:

$$(\text{developer's return}) (\%) \times (\text{project costs}) \leq \text{net rent}$$

The formal states that when you multiply the developer's return times the project's costs you get a necessary net rent figure (after expenses). Or, stated differently, the net rent figure must be greater than or equal to the developer's required return on development costs. That is the napkin pro forma. So let's see how our example fits together, assuming net rent is 90 percent of gross rent.

12% return ($90 sq. ft. costs) ≤ $12.50 average net rent ($90 sq. ft. costs)

$10.80 ≤ $11.25

The formula shows that indeed the project is feasible, at least on paper. The developer can exceed his or her required return under these market conditions because the rent levels are sufficiently high. If market rents were $10 gross, however, the numbers would not fit, as the developer would not receive the desired return over project costs.

NAPKIN PRO FORMAS AND LAND COSTS

Among the income and cost items in the pro forma, the cost of the land typically becomes the factor that determines a project's feasibility. Rents and development costs are fairly fixed in retail development, and any developer will typically have a minimum investment return figure. So the land cost is the only remaining variable in the equation which can vary significantly. Therefore, the most typical napkin pro forma will solve for what the land cost must be to make a project feasible. In other words, the developer will say, "I can do the project if I can buy the land for $X per square foot."

You as the salesperson must be able to use the napkin pro forma to illustrate that a center can be built on that land for $X of land cost per square foot or, if the land cost is firmly fixed, that a center can be built there at all.

SETTING UP THE NAPKIN PRO FORMA

The key to doing quick, napkin pro formas is converting all cost and rental figures to building square feet. That allows you to add apples and apples as opposed to apples and oranges. To illustrate, refer to the equity pro forma on page 226. You'll recall that in that example, the ratio between land footage and building footage is 3:1. Thus, to convert cost figures to costs per building foot, you *multiply all costs stated in land footage times four.* This multiplication restates costs per square foot of land in terms of cost per square foot of building.

For example, the land cost in the pro forma in figure 16.2 is about $1,000,000 for six acres, or about $4 per square foot of land. To convert the land cost to a cost per square foot of building, multiply $4 times four. The land cost in *building feet* is now $16 per square foot.

Continue through the development cost items (b-i) and convert all costs stated in land feet or as land dollar figures into costs per square foot of building. To do this, remember that total building square footage is one-fourth of the land square footage, or 63,840 square feet. Thus you have:

Land	$16.00	sq. ft. of building
Construction ($2,195,000 ÷ 63,840)	$34.40	"

Site work	$ 8.00	"
A & E	$ 1.50	"
Leasing ($157,955 ÷ 63,840)	$ 2.47	"
Financing (approx.)	$ 6.00	"
Contingency (approx.)	$ 1.50	"
Total Project costs	$69.87	sq. ft. of building
Total rent	$ 9.23	"

When you think of costs in terms of building square footage, you can plug the numbers back into the original formula:

$$\text{Income} \div \text{total project costs} = \text{return}$$

$$\text{Return} = \frac{\$9.23}{\$69.87} = 13.2\%$$

In doing these pro formas, experienced people already know the more fixed cost and income items. For example, a developer knows rough building costs per square foot on any given type of building. He also knows that site work, A & E and leasing will come in at a certain cost per square foot, which can be expressed per square foot of building. Finally, he knows the rent levels for given types of retailers and roughly what the rent will be when the center opens. So this is the equation he will typically set up to find the land cost:

$$\text{Land costs} \leq \frac{\text{Rent}}{\text{Return}} - \text{Development costs}$$

Using an example, let's say the developer sees a two-acre site as a prospective site for a ranch market. He knows the market building will cost $40 per square foot to build, and that other, soft costs, total another $10 per building square foot. He further knows that when the store opens, the maximum rent he'll get is $8 per foot after expenses. Needing a 13 percent return then, what must the maximum cost of land be? (Remember we must keep the relationship intact between costs per land foot and costs per building foot.)

$$\text{Land costs (bldg. foot)} \leq \frac{\$8.00}{.13} - \$50/\text{bldg. foot.}$$

Land (bldg. foot) ≤ $61.54 − $50 or $11.54
Land per foot ≤ $11.54 ÷ 4
Land per foot ≤ $2.88

Thus, to make this sample project feasible, the developer quickly calculates that the land must be purchased for $2.88 per foot or less.

SUMMARY

The napkin pro forma is the equity developer's short-cut way to calculate a project's feasibility using the variables of rent, project costs and investment return. By using the equation:

$$\text{Return} \times \text{project costs} \leq \text{net rent}$$

and "crunching" the numbers in dollars-per building foot, the developer can determine

- whether a project is feasible given certain cost, rent and return figures, or
- what a given variable such as land cost must be in order to make the project feasible.

Exercise C

Assume you see a vacant parcel of land advertised at $5 per foot. The site is ideal for a 40,000 foot retail center. You know a developer who will build the center if he can achieve a 14 percent return on costs. If the current market is $12 per foot, what must the development costs be to make the project feasible?

Answer C

development costs ≤ Rent ÷ return−land costs
development costs ≤ $85.71−$20 (bldg. feet)
development costs ≤ $65.71

Exercise D

What would the developer's return be given the following project were built:

    8 acres @ $4.50/foot
    construction: $3,484,800
    building ratio: 3.1
    site work: $156,816
    soft cost: $11/bldg. foot
    gross rent: $849,420
    vacancy and expenses: 9 percent

Answer D

land = $18/bldg. foot
construction = $40/foot
site work = $1.80/foot
soft cost = $11/foot
net rent = $8.87/foot
return = $8.87 ÷ 70.80
return = $12.53 percent

17

Development Financing

INTRODUCTION

This chapter will take a closer look at how financing affects both a shopping center's economic feasibility and how the center is finally developed. We will begin by examining what forms of development financing are available to the developer, and the mechanics of these alternatives. Then we will refocus on the retail development process and how financing influences and defines this process on a step-by-step basis. In studying this chapter you will get an insider's view of how developers think, how they gauge a center's feasibility and how they manipulate financing to develop an opportunity.

WHY KNOW ABOUT DEVELOPMENT FINANCING?

All retail developments require land, construction and debt or equity financing. The developer must tap our economy's capital markets for the financial resources needed to carry out any proposed project.

Since retail brokers and salespeople work closely with developers, it is necessary to be knowledgeable about financing a deal, not just in terms of mortgages and interest rates, but in terms of how financing influences the development process itself.

Real estate financing underwent a major upheaval in the late 1970s. Conventional financing methods were radically transformed by high interest rates, high inflation and a very volatile money supply. As financing methods changed, so did traditional development methods change as well. What may have once been a good development opportunity became an infeasible one. The "easy deals" became very scarce. The developer had to look much more closely at prospective developments because the margin of profitability had become much narrower.

Given the high cost of funds in the new financing environment, many developers were forced out of debt-financed developments. The developers, in effect, had to put up their own money to make a deal. "Equity financing" became the standard as opposed to the friendly lender underwriting the developer's risks.

As the developer was forced into the painful process of financial "re-education," so was the successful salesperson required to understand what was happening. Contemporary retail developers have experienced major changes, and those who remain are very wary of easy deals. In turn, the day of the naive salesperson is ending. Now you must know financing alternatives. You must know how a project can be debt financed and whether a project will necessitate equity partners, given the developer's own limited equity resources. Similarly, you must know whether there is room for the developer to provide his or her services or whether a deal is so tight that the retailer will have to build the outlet alone.

To a large degree, the role of the salesperson in the retail development process is the same: to identify development opportunities within the retail salesperson's territory for the developer to exploit. However, changes in financing no longer allow room for simplistic site presentations and demographic feasibility studies. In the contemporary scene, salespeople must develop the ability to:

1. find holes in retail coverage
2. know sites
3. have prospective tenants
4. analyze the numbers for feasibility, including current financing costs and methods

Finally, you must know how the contemporary developer thinks. There are inevitably good development deals to be made in today's market, as well as ways to finance those deals. The key, however, is knowing what the developer goes through to determine feasibility in the context of the current financing market. The salesperson who can figure out an acceptable return to the developer using current financing rates and methods will be successful in the new development market. The feasibility of a project still depends on quality of the tenants, location, land and construction costs, rent levels and investment requirements. Those factors haven't changed. What has changed is the nature of financing, which is why financing is the final consideration in determining if and how a project can be done.

FINANCING DEFINED

To understand what financing is you first have to get away from the notion that financing consists of a loan. That is only one form of financing, called debt financing. A better definition of financing is "any method of obtaining capital from one source to apply to something else." In our context, financing is *obtaining capital from a capital source for application to the retail development project.*

Types of Development Financing

Generally, commercial real estate financing falls into two categories: *debt financing* and *equity financing*. Debt financing is the traditional method of borrowing capital via the loan. A lender provides capital to the developer in exchange for the developer's promise to pay (promissory note) and security (deed of trust on subject property). Equity financing, on the other hand, is capital provided to the developer in exchange for an ownership position in the project and a share of the project cash flow, which represents an acceptable rate of return on the invested capital. In short, debt financing is renting funds, while equity financing is obtaining funds by giving up a share of the ownership.

The equity partner receives a *preferred* return from the project's income stream as return on his or her capital. Preferred return means that the equity partner receives proceeds from operations prior to the developer-partner. In addition, the equity partner shares in the property's appreciation and equity build-up.

Let's take a closer look at debt and equity financing. Then we'll apply these financing approaches to the steps in the development process.

Debt Financing Alternatives

In previous chapters you learned about the phases of financing in the retail development process. To review, these are:

1. the land loan
2. the construction loan
3. the interim loan (if necessary)
4. the permanent loan

There are several types of loans used in these funding phases. These loans are:

Land loans. In financing the land, the developer will typically borrow from his or her credit line or set up a land draw account.

If the developer uses his or her line of credit, the lender will advance funds for the purchase, typically, on an amortized or interest-only loan at the prime rate plus one point.

If the developer obtains a land draw account, he or she will put an amount down on the land and the lender will finance the balance at prime plus one and one-half to two percent. In many instances, the land will not be financed at all as the developer will purchase the land outright for cash.

Construction loans. Construction loans are interest-only loans to finance the hard and soft costs of the project's construction. Construction loan amounts are advanced as they are needed during construction, and the developer only pays interest on the loan amounts as they are advanced. The typical loan origination fee for this type of loan ranges from one to two points.

The collateral for construction loans is the land and, to a limited degree, the improvements. Banks and savings and loan associations are the primary sources of construction financing. Construction loan rates are higher than interim or permanent loan rates.

Interim loans. Interim loans are loans to developers from conventional lenders which are used to cover property carrying costs during the period between the completion of construction and the placement of permanent financing. Interim loans are needed whenever during this time period there is a financial drain on the developer's resources while contingencies are being satisfied or permanent financing is finalized. Oftentimes the construction lender will simply convert the construction loan to an interim loan if the payments on the former have been kept current. Interim loan rates are less than construction loan rates but more than permanent loan rates. In addition, the developer is usually charged points for the interim loan, which has a typical term of two to five years.

Permanent Financing

Permanent financing is the long-term debt instrument placed on a project that cancels out all other existing financing on the project. Typically, sources of permanent financing are insurance companies, pension funds and other nonbank financial institutions. If the economics allow it, developers will typically prefer to obtain permanent financing on a project, rather than go into the equity markets for capital.

The three types of permanent loans most often used are (1) the fixed rate, fully amortized loan, (2) the adjustable rate mortgage and (3) the participating mortgage.

The *fixed rate, fully amortized loan* is the most desirable form of permanent debt financing because its payments are constant and predictable throughout the loan term. This enables the developer to make an accurate projection of expenses and investment return. However, the fixed-rate mortgage is more expensive than an adjustable rate loan because the lender must absorb all the risks that interest rates may rise dramatically during the loan term. When this happens, the lender stands to lose money because the cost of funds exceeds the income from the fixed rate loans.

The *adjustable rate mortgage (ARM)* is a long-term (up to 40 years) amortizing loan with an interest rate that may fluctuate over the life of the loan. Each ARM's interest rate is tied to movements in various financial indexes such as the interest rate on T-bills. If T-bill yields go up, the ARM's interest rate goes up, and vice versa. The adjustability of the loan rate shifts much of the inflationary risks of lending to the borrower. Since the borrower absorbs the impact of inflation, the interest rate on ARM's begins at one and one-half to two points below conventional fixed-rate loans.

The *participating mortgage* is a loan in which the interest rate has been discounted in exchange for an equity position in the development, plus a participation in the project's rent increase. For example, a lender may discount the coupon rate by two points in exchange for 25 percent of the equity in the property and 25 percent of all rent increases over the base year (the first year of the lease). The participating mortgage is a fixed-rate amortized loan that usually remains in place until the property is sold. Upon sale, the lender will receive 25 percent of the appreciation in addition to the loan balance.

The next page shows the basic types of loans involved in debt financing.

EQUITY FINANCING

Generally, there are three common types of equity financing: partnerships, syndications, and private placements.

Partnerships

The developer who cannot make a project work with debt financing will next try to raise capital through an equity partnership. The equity partner typically is a major life insurance company which will provide capital for the land and development costs of the retail project. In exchange for these funds, the equity partner negotiates an ownership interest and a preferred return on the project's net operating income. The equity partner additionally shares in the property's appreciation and other ownership benefits.

The equity partnership, or joint venture, is in force when the land is deeded to the developer and equity partner. **(Do not confuse this partnership, however, with the joint venture partnership between the developer and the landowner.** They are two distinctly different relationships.) Once land is deeded, the equity partner's cash is applied to the project's construction and leasing. Note that there is no "loan" involved, as the equity partner's funds cover the land and development costs.

Syndications

Real estate syndications raise equity capital for development projects by selling equity shares in a project to large numbers of investors. For example, a syndicator may offer shares worth $5,000 each to investors with a minimum investment requirement of 5 shares. Each of perhaps 1,000 investors then would invest $25,000 minimum to create a gross equity pool of $25,000,000. After the syndicators pay commissions for raising the equity pool, the capital is applied to development projects. The investor then receives a proportionate share of ownership benefits from the projects acquired by the syndication. The retail developer can tap syndications as sources of equity capital for their developments just as they solicit the equity partner.

Private Placements

Private placements are a scaled-down form of syndication. They are put together, generally, to involve 35 or fewer investors in a specific develop-

FIGURE 17.1 Samples of Debt Financing

LOAN	TERMS, RATES, AMOUNT	PAYMENTS
Land: credit line	Prime + 1 point, interest only, no down: land price $500,000; prime rate 13%	$ 70,000/year
Land: draw account	Prime + 1-3/4 points, interest only, 20% down, e.g., land price, $500,000; prime rate 13%	$100,000 down $ 59,000/year
Construction	14 1/2%, interest only; 9 months, 1 point: construction cost $750,000	$ 40,781 interest $ 7,500 (points) $ 48,281 over 9 months
Interim	Convert above construction loan, 13 3/4% interest only, 3 years, 2 points, loan amount $750,000	$103,125 interest $ 15,000 (points) $118,125/year 1 $103,125/year 2, 3

PERMANENT FINANCING

Fixed-rate conventional mortgage	12 1/2%, 30 year amort., 1 1/2 points loan amount $1,200,000 (use loan tables to find annual loan constant)	$153,720 principal and interest $ 18,000 (points) $171,720/year 1 $153,720 thereafter
Adjustable Rate Mortgage (ARM)	2 points below fixed rate mortgage stated above, 30 year amort., 1 1/2 points; loan amount $1,200,000 (use loan table to find annual loan constant)	$131,760 principal and interest $ 18,000 (points) $149,760 /year 1 $131,760 until next adjustment
Participating mortgage	2 points less than fixed rate for 25% equity + 25% of rent increases; 10 1/2%, 30 year amort., 1 point loan amount $1,200,000; base year rent of $10/sq. ft., increases in 2nd year by 10%; building site 17,000 square feet	$131,760 principal and interest $ 12,000 (points) $143,760 total 1 year $131,760 principal and interest $ 4,250 rent increase $136,010 total year 2

ment project. Private placements generally are not required to meet securities registration requirements and are usually done on a local basis. Unlike large syndications, private placement allows the investor to be a part of a smaller investment group, and to be involved with a specific project.

Exercise A

Answer the questions below, then check your answers against the solutions provided.

1. Explain in a sentence how high interest rates in the debt financing of developments force developers out of debt markets and into equity financing markets?
2. It was stated that financing is not just getting a loan for some purpose. What then is financing?
3. What is preferred return?
4. There are four phases of debt financing during the development process. What are they?
5. When is interim financing used in the development process?
6. What is the most common source of long-term financing?
7. Why is a fixed-rate permanent loan more desirable than an adjustable loan? Why is it more expensive?
8. How is a participating mortgage similar to equity financing?
9. Distinguish an equity developer from equity financing. Can an equity developer use debt-financing?
10. How do private placements differ from syndications?
11. How does a joint venture with an equity partner differ from a developer's joint venture with the landowner?

Answer A

1. *High debt service on permanent loans very often wiped out net operating income, eliminating any cash-on-cash return.*
2. *Financing is obtaining capital for a project from either debt or equity coverage.*
3. *Preferred return is the equity partner's claim to his or her share of the net operating income, payable to the partner before the developer receives his or her share.*
4. *The four phases are land, construction, interim and permanent financing.*
5. *Interim financing is used whenever a developer needs to finance carrying costs of a project between the time when construction is completed and the permanent loan is in place.*
6. *Insurance companies.*

7. *The fixed loan creates a predictable debt service that the developer can be assured will not increase. Fixed-rate loans cost more because they are riskier to lenders; should rates rise, they could lose money.*

8. *The developer had to give up 25 percent of the project's equity to the lender.*

9. *Equity developers want maximum ownership for long-term ownership benefits. This does not relate to equity financing, which describes a method of financing. The equity developer can debt-finance or equity-finance.*

10. *Private placements differ from syndications in the number of participating investors. Private placements must have fewer than 35 investors.*

11. *The joint venture with the equity partner entails purchasing the land from the landowner, whereas the developer-landowner joint venture entails a transfer of land ownership to the developer-landowner partnership.*

FINANCING AND THE DEVELOPMENT PROCESS

In this section we will walk through the steps of development and illustrate how financing affects the developer's thinking and his development alternatives.

You may recall that developers can be classified as either equity or nonequity developers. Do not confuse these categories with the debt or equity financing alternatives; they are unrelated. The equity developer retains ownership of the property for long-term ownership benefits. The non-equity developer, which is typically a large, publicly held company, sells off its ownership interest in order to show a profit to its shareholders.

For the most part, the development community consists of equity developers, perhaps 75 to 85 percent. For that reason we will focus the following discussion on the equity developer and how the equity developer finances the development. As the discussion progresses, refer to the equity pro forma on page 217 of the chapter called Shopping Center Development. We will use this pro forma as our sample equity development project.

Steps in Equity Development

The following pages review the steps the equity developer goes through to develop the retail shopping center and the decisions that are made at each juncture.

The first step in getting underway is "pencilling out" the project at a given site. At this point, the developer asks: How many square feet will be built? What kinds of tenants will occupy the project? What improvements will be made? What will the land and construction costs be? Estimates of rent, expenses, NOI, financing and cash flow are made.

Foremost in the developer's mind at this point is *maintaining maximum, or total, ownership in the project*. That is the objective of the equity developer, and he or she is going to exhaust every opportunity for total ownership before selecting other development avenues. To maintain ownership, the preferred method of development is *debt financing*. If the project can support permanent financing, it can be built with the developer retaining ownership. If the project won't support debt-financing, the developer has three alternatives—sell off some of the shops to cover part of the development cost, get a participating mortgage and give up 25 percent equity, or seek an equity partner and lose half of his or her ownership.

Can the Project Be Debt Financed?

The developer estimates the feasibility of debt financing the project by identifying how much permanent money can be loaned *based on the net operating income* and compares this amount to an estimate of total development costs. The difference between costs and loan amount is the equity he or she must contribute. If the equity amount required is more than he or she can afford, the project cannot be debt financed by a non-participating mortgage. Let's take a closer look at these assumptions and the calculations used to make this determination.

1. Deriving the loan amount:
    a. The developer knows he or she can get roughly 110 percent market rent from his or her tenants assuming a 10 percent rent increase between now and the tenant's future occupancy.
    b. The developer estimates vacancy and expenses to get net operating income (NOI).
    c. The developer knows the lender will permit debt service to be 70 to 80 percent of NOI.
    d. Seventy to 80 percent of the amount of the NOI can be financed by a 30-year loan at a certain interest rate. The developer projects the going interest rate for the type of loan he or she will obtain (fixed, adjustable) and derives the loan amount using the annual debt constant.
2. Estimating development costs:
    a. The developer knows actual or rule-of-thumb costs per square foot for construction, leasing, site work, A & E and construction financing. These costs times the project's footage yields development costs.
    b. Land costs are figured by either using the owner's price or market value.
    c. The project cost will equal (a) + (b).
3. Comparing loan amount to costs:
   If the pro forma shows adequate coverage of project costs by the loan, the developer goes ahead with the next step in the debt financed development process. If there is clearly insufficient debt coverage for the amount of capital required, i.e., if the developer can't afford to put in the cash (equity) to bridge the gap between costs and financing, the developer may wish to consider the participating mortgage, selling some of the site to tenants, or finding the equity partner.

Step 1: Result: Insufficient Debt Coverage

Let's assume the developer's analysis produced the pro forma presented in the previous chapter. Referring to that pro forma, we'll also assume the developer only has $20,000 for an equity contribution. Reviewing the major alternatives, he or she can either:

1. sell sites to reduce the equity requirement
2. make a participating mortgage
3. find an equity partner

Sell sites. The developer could sell off the bank and the fast food market to reduce the equity requirement. If the bank and fast food store sold for $520,000, the developer would now have:

$2,500,000 development costs (approximate)

498,000 land costs ($1,045,440 − $520,000 commission)

$2,998,000 total project costs

The developer's new rent would be $454,000 and new NOI, $418,000. Using the same debt ratios, the new loan on the project would be $2,837,000. Comparing the loan with the total project costs, we see the developer needs to contribute $161,000 equity, which is within the budget of $200,000.

Obtain participating mortgage. The participating mortgage lessens the developer's equity requirement, but it in turn reduces the developer's profitability and ownership benefits. In our example, the developer would have to get a participating mortgage at 35 percent or more to debt finance the project successfully with only $200,000 in equity.

Find an equity partner. With some projects, it is obvious from the beginning that an equity partner must be found. If such is the case, the developer uses the equity partner's cash and splits ownership on a fifty-fifty basis. Once the project is completed, the equity partner receives the preferred return on the NOI much as a lender would have received the debt service payments.

Step 2: The Land Option and Option Period

Let's assume debt financing looks feasible. What the developer does now is tie up the proposed site through an option or escrow agreement. This gives the developer time to line up his financing and leasing commitments.

The land option itself states that, in effect, the developer will buy the land for $X per square foot, provided it is feasible to put up the shopping center. If the outlook seems to be poor, the developer will not close the land escrow or exercise the option. During the option period, many details must be taken care of including obtaining:

1. the forward funding commitment (if interest rates are going up)
2. commitments to lease from credit tenants

3. permits (building)
4. zoning clearances
5. title reports

The developer also sets up his or her land draw account or line of credit to purchase the property.

The loan commitment and major tenant commitments are the most important items to secure once the land option is established. Of these, the developer goes after the major credit tenants first. This is because the lender wants to see that a significant share of the debt service is covered by major credit tenants.

Letters of intent and rent levels. The tenant commitment to lease is likewise contingent on numerous factors such as the rent, the date of completion, construction financing and construction specifications. Of these, it is important to note that the rent the tenant intends to pay is governed by market values, not development costs. The intent letter will state a rent range. If the developer tries to justify higher rents as a function of development costs and high loan constants, the tenant may opt out. For the developer, the rent may be computed by determining the market rate of return on the established land value and adding the loan constant rate of return on the improvement:

Rent = 10% of land value + (improvement cost × loan constant)

For example, calculate rent for a supermarket given the following assumptions:

size: 35,000 square feet
land value: $450,000
cost of improvements: $1,405,000
amortized loan constant on improvements: .1281

$$\text{rent} = (\$450,000 \times 10\%) + (\$1,405,000 \times .1281)$$
$$= \$45,000 + \$180,000$$
total rent = $225,000/year

If $6.43 per square feet a year exceeds attainable rents in the local marketplace, the developer must make a decision on whether to subsidize this tenant, or to terminate current negotiations and attempt to find a tenant that can justify this rental payment.

The permanent loan commitment. If interest rates are increasing, the developer is well-advised to secure the loan commitment if the leasing commitments are in hand. If interest rates are falling, the developer might want to wait until later on in the construction stage for the loan commitment. Some construction lenders will require a permanent or "takeout" commitment prior to funding a construction loan to further insure that the loan will be repaid on time.

Loan commitments reserve a specific amount of capital at a stated interest rate for a limited period of time. The cost to the developer varies, but is generally two or three percentage points of the funds committed. Like letters of intent, loan commitments are subject to numerous conditions. Among these are:

1. that the tenants follow through on their commitments
2. that certain leasing goals must be achieved before the permanent loan is funded. Additionally, the initial funding may be partially reduced by a percentage of the entire commitment (known as a "holdback") until such time as leasing is completed or at 95 percent.

Other option period activities. Before the end of the land option or escrow period, the developer also must line up his or her minor credit tenants, have the plans prepared and begin to line up the construction loan. It is not, however, necessary to have the permanent or construction loan commitments before closing on the land.

During the land option period, the developer must:

1. set up a land draw account or credit line for land purchase.
2. line up major credit leases.
3. get a forward funding commitment (if desired).
4. satisfy other land option conditions, letters of intent conditions.
5. obtain preliminary plans of drawing.
6. line up other tenants.
7. line up construction loan.

Step 3: The Construction Period

Assuming the land option conditions are met, the developer purchases the land through the land draw or his or her credit line. Once the land is purchased, time is of the essence. At this point, the developer is within 60 to 90 days of construction.

The first task now is finalizing the construction loan and bidding and scheduling the construction. Once this is done the developer turns once again to the question of debt versus equity financing. His or her analysis of this question is now based on a lot more facts and real costs as opposed to the pro forma with its estimates and assumptions. The contracting bids are in, the construction costs are rapidly becoming known, the rent pledges are in and a certain percent of the property is leased.

To decide on equity versus debt financing, the developer now looks at two things: the available equity and the projected cash flow. If the center is only 60-percent leased, the combination of debt service on the land and the construction loan can begin to drain what the developer had earmarked for equity. If actual construction costs exceed the construction loan, the developer is again going back into his or her pocketbook. If the final debt coverage of the permanent loan cannot absorb costs as expected, the developer has to increase the equity commitment.

Before and during construction the developer weighs actual costs against actual income and takes a final look at the debt financing alternatives. If they prove to meet his or her equity limitations, or if cash flows can stay one and one-half to two points above permanent debt service, the developer can arrange a permanent loan commitment. If the developer is not satisfied with after-debt service return or the equity that he or she must put into the project, then he or she must investigate alternatives. Typically these include (1) reducing the equity requirement by selling a portion of the intended development or (2) seeking an equity partnership.

Exercise B

Answer the following questions, then compare your answers to the solutions provided.

1. Why does the equity developer try to exhaust all debt financing alternatives before resorting to equity financing methods?
2. How does the equity developer determine whether he or she can debt finance a project?
3. How does the developer estimate how much permanent funding he or she can get on a project?
4. Why would a developer sell off portions of the center to some of its tenants?
5. What essential tasks occur during the land option period?
6. What essential tasks are done after the land is purchased?

Answer B

1. *The equity developer tries to exhaust all debt financing alternatives before resorting to equity financing in order to maintain maximum ownership of the project.*
2. *The developer determines whether a project can be debt financed by comparing the net operating income with the projects' debt service. To debt finance, there must be sufficient cash flow after debt service.*
3. *The developer estimates how much permanent funding he or she can get by going through the following steps:*
   a. Estimating rent income at time of occupancy
   b. Subtracting an estimate of vacancy and expenses from (a)
   c. Taking 70–80 percent of NOI as the maximum amount subject to debt service; given an interest rate and terms for this amount, the loan can be identified using loan constants (loan amount = amount subject to debt service ÷ constant annual percent)
4. *The developer would sell portions of the center to lower the project's equity and/or debt service requirements. Selling some of the footage reduces the amount of footage the developer must purchase and finance.*
5. *The essential tasks during the land option period are:*
   a. arranging for major credit tenant leasing
   b. getting a forward funding commitment (which can occur later)
   c. setting up land financing
   d. preparing drawings
   e. satisfying other conditions

  f. beginning to line up construction loan
  g. arranging for minor credit tenant leasing
6. *After the land is bought, the developer:*
  a. finalizes construction financing
  b. completes construction
  c. completes/continues minor tenant leasing
  d. finalizes permanent financing or obtains an equity partner

18

Tenant Representation

INTRODUCTION

Exclusive tenant representation is an approach to retail leasing in which the salesperson represents a tenant exclusively in moving to new space or renegotiating a lease in a current location.

YOUR ROLE

As an exclusive representative of the tenant, your first responsibility is to qualify the tenant and learn his or her requirements. You can do this by visiting the current space, considering alternative layouts, determining location preferences and financial parameters and understanding the business's long-term growth plans.

The second step in servicing your tenant is to find the space that matches the needs you defined above. This involves getting up-to-date information on landlord's terms, doing an economic and functional analysis for the tenant and touring suitable locations.

After locating the right space for the tenant, you will be responsible for negotiating on his or her behalf. For more information refer to the chapter titled *Negotiation*.

Your role does not end with the successful negotiation of a transaction. As a tenant representative, you should also monitor the progress of the build-out for the tenant and keep in touch during the move itself. The service you offer includes being available to the tenant throughout the process of the relocation, not just until you've received your commission.

USING AN EXCLUSIVE REPRESENTATIVE

The Tenant's Perspective

A tenant receives several advantages by using an exclusive broker, including:

1. management of the relocation process by the salesperson
2. market expertise
3. best use of the tenant's time and money
4. negotiating expertise on the tenant's behalf
5. a single point of contact

As we discussed before, the role of the salesperson who exclusively represents a tenant begins with gathering market information and continues until the tenant is located in a new space or has a new lease in an existing space. The salesperson's role includes:

1. defining the tenant's requirements
2. conducting market research
3. completing an investigation of suitable sites
4. obtaining requests for proposals from landlords
5. completing lease negotiations
6. providing coordination, as needed, for phones, furniture, etc.
7. providing coordination, as needed, with a space planner
8. maintaining contact with the tenant throughout construction and occupancy

Your market expertise ensures that the tenant will see all sites that meet his or her needs. Through you, the tenant also will be provided with complete market information. Only by understanding the market and all alternatives will the tenant be able to make an informed decision.

A tenant's time is best spent on business. Your time is best spent in completing the real estate transaction. By doing the legwork needed in a move, you can free up the tenant to continue his or her business as usual.

In negotiations, knowledge is power. Your expertise in the real estate market will give your tenant a more powerful position in negotiations, contribute to his or her peace of mind and enable him or her to receive the best possible lease. Because you represent the tenant, and not the site, the tenant can rest assured that you have his or her best interest in mind. You will not be swayed by the fact that one possible location for the tenant is a center for which you have a listing. The tenant will receive unbiased information.

Finally, by working with one broker, the tenant is assured of saving time and energy. Not only does the tenant avoid having to speak with a number of different people, he or she is also assured of consistent, quality information. Each property will be considered without bias or duplication by a number of brokers. The tenant has one individual to hold responsible for his or her successful move.

The Landlord's Perspective

When the tenant is using an exclusive broker, the landlord can benefit as well. These benefits include your expertise on and qualification of the tenant's requirements, a lesser chance of commission disputes over who controls the tenant and a single point of contact who will follow through on all aspects of the transaction with the tenant.

THE TENANT REPRESENTATION AGREEMENT

The chapter titled *Forms and Legal Documents* includes a tenant representation agreement. However, it may be difficult to obtain a tenant's signature on such a document. An alternative is a tenant representation letter, a sample of which follows.

While this letter outlines the same responsibilities for both you and the tenant, the tone is more informal than the agreement. You must use your own judgment and your knowledge of the tenant to determine which he or she would find more acceptable. The most important thing is to obtain some commitment from the tenant in writing. Otherwise, you could spend a substantial amount of time working on the need with no commission to show in the end. You cannot afford to speculate with your time on a tenant who will not commit to you.

CONCLUSION

You may find the commissions from exclusive tenant representation to be very lucrative. This is particularly true in an overbuilt market, where space is numerous and tenants are more scarce. Try obtaining the exclusive right to represent on cold calls. Then determine for yourself what mix of business—site representation or tenant representation—is best for you and in your marketplace.

FIGURE 18.1 Sample Tenant Representation Letter

February 17, 1988

John Doe
XYZ Company
123 Commercial Avenue
Hometown, ST 55555

Dear John;

This letter confirms our discussion today regarding your firm's desire to relocate your store from your present location.

Grubb & Ellis Company will serve as your exclusive representative for the purpose of locating new retail space. While coordinating with you, Grubb & Ellis will be responsible for the following:

1. locating suitable buildings per specifications as determined by XYZ Company

2. providing materials and consultations to aid in evaluating various sites

3. negotiating the transaction on your behalf

4. following up to ensure that your move is successfully completed

Unless we agree otherwise, Grubb & Ellis will be paid all brokerage fees by the seller/lessor. It is agreed that all solicitation, presentations or other direct contacts to you will be handled by Grubb & Ellis.

This agreement may be cancelled by either party upon twenty-four (24) hours' written notice of intent to cancel.

If the foregoing is acceptable, please indicate your acceptance where indicated below, keeping one copy for your files and returning the original to Grubb & Ellis Company.

I look forward to the opportunity to serve you and assure you that I will aggressively perform in order to meet your objectives.

Sincerely,

Jane Smith
Office Marketing Division

APPROVED AND ACCEPTED FOR XYZ COMPANY:

By: _____

Date: _____

19

Negotiation

INTRODUCTION

A real estate transaction begins when you find a potential tenant. It ends with a signed lease or sale agreement and a commission for you. The middle part of the transaction is the process of negotiation–that is, the process of bringing owner and lessee or buyer together to mutually satisfactory terms.

Negotiation is a complex art that can be mastered through study and practice. This chapter can help you understand the importance of negotiation in developing a transaction, learn some negotiating techniques and appreciate the problems in the process.

Beyond this chapter it is up to you. Read books, role-play with other salespeople or your sales manager and observe more experienced brokers in your company. Analyze each negotiation situation in which you participate to discover which techniques worked, which ones didn't and why. Then build on the successful ones.

YOUR ROLE

You, the salesperson, represent the best interests of both the seller/lessor and the buyer/lessee in a situation in which the parties' objectives appear to be mutually contradictory—one wishes to obtain the highest rental rate or sale price, the other wishes to obtain the lowest price or rate. Your task is to bring these opposing points of view together to a conclusion that is mutually satisfactory and beneficial. It is, therefore, vitally important that you make sure both parties with whom you deal understand that you have the best interests of both in mind and that all discussion and negotiation will be conducted above board.

If you are a skilled salesperson, you will make sure both the owner and tenant understand the steps of negotiation. You will sketch for each of them what probably will be accomplished at each stage. You will also set a timetable and will constantly check to see that, to the best of your ability, the schedule is met.

In most instances settlement represents a compromise. It is toward that compromise between the owner and tenant that you work, taking queries, proposals and responses back and forth until a transaction is agreed upon and the deal signed.

You, as negotiator, will generally keep the owner and tenant apart until the end. They might not even know each other's names until they get together to sign the final papers. Almost invariably, if the parties meet earlier, negotiations are unnecessarily prolonged, simply because egos and emotions get in the way. A tenant may appear to be trying to push the owner into a nonprofit or loss situation, or the owner may seem to be gouging or cheating the tenant.

Also, both the owner's and the tenant's attorneys should be excluded from negotiations until the appropriate time. As a salesperson, you work with the owner and tenant to reach a business agreement. The lawyer's role is to put that agreement into the appropriate legal language after you have negotiated it. When lawyers are involved too soon, the negotiating process is usually prolonged, or matters become so complicated that the transaction is ruptured and a deal is never made. Lawyers generally have no motivation to see a transaction successfully completed, because their compensation, unlike yours, is not dependent on a resolution. Therefore, the lawyer's task should be to tend to his or her client's best legal interests, not to negotiate business points. That is your role.

RULES FOR NEGOTIATION

Trust, Confidence and Control

You must quickly establish in every negotiation situation your role as negotiator and the fact that lawyers should enter the picture only when their legal services are needed. You, concurrently, must have thoroughly qualified both the owner and tenant, discovering what's really important to each of them and what each would be willing to trade off for more important things.

In a leasing situation, you will make sure the owner understands that you will bring only thoroughly qualified tenants—those serious about the building and about making a deal, and with the financial capability to uphold their end of an agreement. As to the tenant, you must make sure he or she understands the owner's need to make a profit, and that only by doing so will the owner be able to keep the building in good repair and fulfill the agreement. You must also inform the tenant about the owner's feeling on rental rates and modifications. In every situation, a number of items can be negotiated. On some, though, one of the parties will not budge. It is necessary that the tenant realize the areas in which the owner probably will be adamant and vice versa.

Two things are important in the foregoing discussion. One, you must present yourself as a person who knows his or her business and can really represent the interests of both parties. You also must control the situation at all times, for if control slips to either party, your deal is as good as lost. Keeping parties apart, seeing that lawyers stay out until negotiations are completed and explaining the steps in normal negotiating procedures are all means of taking and maintaining control. They also build confidence and trust in both the owner and tenant.

Promises

Although price is always an important factor, never assure a tenant that you can arrange a sale or a lease for a certain price. If you do, you're taking a chance that might cost you the deal, the commission and a great deal of wasted time.

If the owner is asking $5 a square foot to lease, do not tell your tenant that you can get the building for any figure below the asking price. The price is on the listing. It cannot be raised. Whether it is lowered depends principally upon whether price can be made a matter of negotiation. You must, however, remain noncommittal about what you think the owner will settle for, because you actually don't know. You will be doing your tenant an injustice and yourself a great disservice if you do commit yourself. If your tenant insists on making a bid below the asking price, after you have reviewed the qualities of the building in relationship to your tenant's needs, the current market, the building's location and other similar factors, you can only take this bid to the owner with the understanding that the owner may or may not accept it. You can always advise a tenant that the bid might be so low as to strike the owner as ridiculous and preclude a counteroffer. But you cannot and must not make up the tenant's mind. Above all, do not promise anything. The same holds true when discussing the tenant's position with the landlord. Remain noncommittal about the tenant's final offer on rental rate and concessions. Again, you don't actually know his or her bottom line. To guess at this is to do a disservice to all involved parties.

Some tenants, of course, will go into a market in which five dollars a square foot is the going rate and insist that they will go no higher than four dollars. In this case, you might try to find the tenant a four dollar building, but if the market is strong, your chances of success are slender. Conversely, a landlord may price a building too high for the marketplace. If you cannot convince the tenant or owner to be realistic, and he or she remains adamant, you are probably better off not to waste time with that tenant.

You must not commit yourself to other items besides price. Building modification is such an item. Your tenant might want extra doors, a sprinkler system and extra power, thinking that the owner should pay for the items. Indeed, under certain circumstances, the owner might concede to some modifications, but you don't know. If a tenant's or owner's requests are unrealistic, persuade him or her to modify or forgo at least some of them. Tell him or her that all you can do is try to negotiate a deal if he or she still wants you to, but you hold no real hope of success. Then, if you do succeed, he or she will be pleasantly surprised and pleased. On the other hand, relations will surely suffer if you promise something and then are unable to make good on your commitment.

Further, make no promises about length of contract, escalator clauses or options. All these might be matters for negotiation, but commitments to your tenant or owner on them might create difficulties.

In general, make no promises except to serve both party's best interests in a thorough and professional manner.

WHEN TO NEGOTIATE

When a tenant finds a building suited to his or her needs as it stands, what, if anything, needs negotiating?

Several factors might be involved in negotiating the price: The amount of pressure on an owner to sell or lease, the owner's view of a tenant's suitability, the amount of time the tenant has to find suitable space and the state of the market. How these factors affect a transaction depends entirely on the situation. How you persuasively nudge the owner and tenant to a closing depends on your understanding of them and the prevailing circumstances. Unless an offer is way out of line, it might be greeted with counteroffers.

Few offers cannot be sweetened. A longer lease period than originally contemplated might influence either the owner or tenant to move nearer to the other's price. Modification or escalation clauses in one party's favor might be influential. Option clauses, such as a renewal clause, might also be a factor in price negotiation.

Frequently you must help the tenant decide which building is best suited to his or her needs. You might, on occasion, arrange an inspection tour to highlight the buildings you previously concluded would be best. As you approach a building, you could tick off its features and benefits, indicating how well they match the tenant's needs. In this way, it is generally not difficult to get your tenant's agreement and move swiftly to an offer. At other times the tenant will have difficulty deciding between two or three buildings. In this case, list the pluses and minuses of each building side-by-side and go over them with your tenant, relating each building to the tenant's needs. The point is, if you have properly compiled a list of buildings to show a thoroughly qualified tenant, one of them should satisfy his or her needs.

If your tenant is not firm on a particular building, suggest that he or she make a contingency offer, stipulating it within ten or thirty days or some other period of time. A contingency offer, like a firm, unfettered offer, takes a property off the market for a stipulated time. While such an offer can be advantageous to your tenant, it must be a serious one, and your tenant must understand this.

In the case of a sale, one contingency of the offer might be that the buyer obtain a certain amount of mortgage money at a certain interest rate within a particular time limit. Avoid, however, having the deal hung up over a half or quarter percentage point and a few years difference in mortgage time. A tenant probably should not be in the market if a quarter of a percent interest makes a great difference to him or her. Write the stipulation as broadly as possible. If the tenant wishes 12 percent mortgage money, make 13 the limit so as to allow for a fraction over what he or she would like to have. If the buyer wants an 18-year mortgage, make the limit 20 to allow some leeway. If your buyer does not get the exact interest rate and years he or she wants, help determine how much extra might have to be paid and balance that against the advantages of having a building that suits the individual.

With either a sale or lease, a number of contingencies having to do with building modifications could be included in the offer. Among them might be the construction of special space, installation of more air conditioning, increased signage or installation of a different fire protection system.

Other contingencies might have to do with safety, power and drainage surveys. Such surveys would be completed within a certain time to determine the adequacy of these items for your tenant.

Will an owner accept contingencies, and if so how many? There is no blanket answer. Much depends on the market, the attractiveness of the building, the amount of action there has been on it, the owner's estimate of how good a deal he or she can make and similar factors. It is up to you to know your area, the market and the owners with whom you deal, in order to advise a tenant on the kinds and extent of possible contingencies.

PROCESS

Remember that the primary objective of negotiation is to arrive at a meeting of the minds, a transaction that is mutually agreeable to both buyer and seller or lessor and lessee.

You must complete several phases in order to conduct a successful negotiation:

- planning
- preparation
- compromise
- agreement

Planning

In entering a negotiation, be clear on what each party hopes to accomplish and keep in mind that your objective is a completed transaction.

As part of the planning process you must lay the rules for what is to follow in each phase of negotiations. Explain to both parties that you are the neutral intermediary. Also, explain the appropriate role of lawyers. The tenant and landlord must understand that the negotiation is not a matter of win or lose, but should be a "win-win" situation. Your role is to facilitate this.

Think through what information you will need to service both parties as professionally as possible. You must understand each person's viewpoint in order to assist in a meeting of the minds.

Preparation

Knowledge and planning are vital to a negotiation. You should ask yourself a number of questions and do your homework if you don't know the answers.

1. What is each party trying to accomplish?
2. What items are negotiable for each party? To what extent are these negotiable?
3. What are the non-negotiable points on each side? Why?
4. What role does each party expect to play in the negotiation? What do they expect your role to be?
5. What outside factors (financing situation, marketplace, etc.) could have a bearing on the negotiation?
6. What is each side's deadline for completion?
7. Have you qualified both parties completely (authority, financial ability and motivation)?

When you have answered these questions, you should be informed and ready to begin the negotiation process.

Compromise

Compromise is the process that allows a negotiation to progress. Without compromise you would become deadlocked.

To facilitate compromise, your role is to balance each party's needs with items each is willing to change or forfeit. Both sides must understand that they will have to make concessions. Your job is to maintain the credibility to realistically discuss each point. What is common or appropriate? Why or why not? The successful salesperson does not merely relay information between the two parties, he or she provides market expertise to balance and evaluate each position.

All concessions should be conveyed in person, not over the telephone. If you meet someone in person, you receive more information, clues and feedback on what is acceptable, and determine what pace and mood the negotiation is taking.

Sometimes negotiations reach a temporary deadlock. You must be able to judge if a time-out is needed. This could be time for either party to reflect, gather information or just cool off. Your judgment of each party's needs and emotions will tell you when you're better off taking a break than risking more serious damage. If there is a lapse in negotiations, you must remember to do three things. First, remind both parties why it's in their best interests to successfully complete the transaction. Second, summarize for each side the agreed upon items. Third, clarify the issues that still need to be resolved and set a time to restart the negotiations.

Agreement

When both parties have agreed upon a mutually satisfactory position and have put it in writing, you have successfully completed your role as negotiator.

By using your market expertise, knowledge of each party, and common sense, you should be able to facilitate a mutually satisfying transaction and provide a service that will encourage both landlord and tenant to use your services again in future transactions.

20

Safety and Environmental Issues

INTRODUCTION

Besides being familiar with the marketplace in general, as a retail salesperson, you are also responsible for knowledge of specific properties and safety issues. These issues are, of course, critical to the seller/lessor, the buyer/lessee and to you as the intermediary. Be aware of the fire and security arrangements for each property. Does the center have a silent alarm? What type of security personnel are employed? What type of sprinkler system is installed? Do past security or safety problems exist? In addition to these typical safety issues, also consider the presence of asbestos insulation or fireproofing, electrical transformers containing polychlorinated biphenyls (PCBs), underground storage tanks, and soil and groundwater contamination.

UNDERGROUND TANKS

Underground storage tanks present a potential liability for both buyer and seller. Federal law plays a small role in the regulation of underground tanks, but each state has individual legislation in this area. The most important thing for you, as a salesperson, to remember is that you have to determine from the owner if there is or has been a tank on the property and then to disclose that to the buyer/lessee. The process for discovery and disclosure will be discussed at greater length later in this section.

ASBESTOS

Concern about asbestos in commercial buildings is high. In fact, asbestos was the first material to be regulated by the Federal Occupational Safety and Health Administration. The government estimates that 20 percent of public and commercial buildings now contain asbestos.

Many building owners, concerned about liability for asbestos-related claims, have considered removing all asbestos materials in a building. However, the difficulty in removing asbestos can create even greater risk and liability.

Asbestos has been highly regulated in recent years. In 1973, regulations were passed banning the use of spray-applied asbestos materials as building insulation or fireproofing, except in equipment and machinery. Buildings that were built before this ban have a potential problem. The Environmental Protection Agency's regulations on asbestos apply to owners and operators of asbestos emission sources. This includes building owners. The face liability from a disclosure standpoint is in selling the property, and from a safety standpoint with regard to employees, tenants and maintenance workers.

POLYCHLORINATED BIPHENYLS

Polychlorinated Biphenyls, commonly known as PCBs, are present in electrical equipment, including capacitors and transformers. Many retail buildings have transformers located in basement or sidewalk vaults or on rooftops. Institutional light fixtures may also contain PCBs.

In 1979, the Environment Protection Agency placed restrictions on the use of equipment containing PCBs. Responsibility for compliance with these rules lies with both the owner and the operator of the equipment. The owner of the property on which the equipment is located also can be held responsible. This is significant because transformers owned by an electric utility are often located in or adjacent to the building they serve. Thus, a building owner who merely uses utility-owned transformers or owns the property on which they are located may be held liable for any personal injury or property damage resulting from the PCB. For example, building owners have in the past incurred significant costs for cleanup, personal injury and loss of business when transformers have caught on fire. In some cases the building may have to be closed for a number of years for cleanup.

SOIL AND GROUNDWATER CONTAMINATION

There are clear guidelines for the management of hazardous wastes. One fact to keep in mind is that hazardous waste is not limited to the obviously heavy industrial site. Light industry, mixed-use facilities, warehouses, distribution centers and parking lots can also be sources of hazardous waste. Under existing regulations a landowner may be liable for "unauthorized disposals" of hazardous waste on his or her property. This includes any discharge, spilling, dumping, pouring, emitting or leaking of waste. The Environmental Protection Agency may order a cleanup. A property owner may be responsible for cleanup costs regardless of whether he or she owned the property at the time of the release, knew about the contamination or negligently caused the contamination. Both the seller and the buyer may be subject to a cleanup order if a property is contaminated, regardless of who was directly responsible for the contamination. For example, if the buyer of a property does not clean up hazardous waste on the site, he or she is contributing to a disposal. No showing of fault is necessary to impose liability. The only issue is whether or not a hazardous substance has been released. Liability is joint; that is, each party may be liable for the entire cost of the cleanup. As you can imagine, this will most likely result in litigation between present and past owners and perhaps tenants. There have even been cases where a bank, because it had foreclosed on a mortgage, was considered the owner of a property and held liable for cleanup costs. In addition to cleanup costs, anyone who willfully violates or refuses to comply with an EPA cleanup order is subject to a fine of up to $5,000 for each day noncompliance continues.

Another aspect of hazardous waste that you must be familiar with is *border-zone legislation.* In some states this legislation limits the owner of property from developing the land for certain uses when his or her property is within a certain distance (typically 2,000 feet) of a hazardous waste disposal. Any restriction binds not only the landowner, but all lessees and successive owners as well.

As a retail salesperson you must remember that potential liabilities may be addressed in the sale or lease contract. Therefore, it is particularly important for you to have thoroughly investigated and disclosed the environmental history, condition, and use of a property prior to completion of a transaction.

YOUR RESPONSIBILITIES

Because liability for cleanup can be both expensive and retroactive, buyers, sellers, landlords and tenants must know whether there is any contamination and its nature and extent. Without such an assessment, sellers risk liability for wastes generated by successive owners or tenants. Buyers may be responsible for a seller's or tenant's contaminations and tenants may be liable for an owner's or prior tenant's contamination.

There are several steps that a responsible retail salesperson must take to investigate any possibility of contamination.

Physical Inspection

The first step in an investigation is a physical inspection. Although toxic waste often is not visible, it is still important to make as thorough a visual evaluation as possible. Among the things to look for on the property and the adjacent site are storage tanks, septic pools, storage drums, a dump site, landfill, any standing water, the drainage system, equipment/automotive service areas and discolored soil.

For retail users, the strongest likelihood of contamination exists in a site that was built from the 1950s to the 1970s, when asbestos insulation and ceiling tiles were used, a site that was formerly agricultural (due to the possible presence of pesticides), a site with landfill or electrical transformers, or any site adjacent to a property with any of these conditions.

Owner/Tenant Inquiry

Your next step is to ask the owner and perhaps the current tenant questions about safety issues. For example:

1. Is there any hazardous waste, asbestos or equipment containing PCBs that you know of on your site or any adjacent site?
2. What is the current use of the site?
3. What chemicals and equipment are involved in the current use?
4. What use did past owners and tenants conduct on this property?
5. What use did past owners and tenants conduct on any adjacent property?
6. What chemicals and equipment were involved in past uses of this property and any adjacent properties?
7. Has an environmental report or violation ever been filed on this site or an adjacent site? (You can check the Environmental Protection Agency National Priority List and Remedial Response Information System for additional information in this area.)
8. What waste disposal methods do the current owner or tenant use, and what methods have been used in the past?

All questions asked and information uncovered must be documented and disclosed.

Testing

Once you have made oral and written investigations, the seller, buyer or tenant may follow up testing both soil and groundwater. This should be done by an independent specialist.

If contamination is discovered, the testing company may recommend a variety of cleanup methods including capping, containment barriers, groundwater collection, pumping and treatment, excavation and removal, on-site treatment, incineration, and solidification.

Documentation

A number of steps can be taken to protect all parties to a transaction.

1. Do your homework. Thoroughly investigate the property, its history and its current use.

2. Document and disclose everything.
3. Use a restrictive covenant if necessary. A restrictive covenant restrains land uses that may cause harm, such as drilling, excavating and building.
4. Determine financial responsibility within the sales agreement. You may allocate costs associated with contamination known at the time of sale, costs associated with contamination existing at the time of sale but not discovered until later, costs associated with contamination caused by the buyer or successors and costs associated with contamination of uncertain origin. This will not limit the parties' obligation to the government or third parties. However, it will help them understand their obligations to each other.

SUMMARY

All parties in a transaction rely on your abilities to structure a transaction that is mutually beneficial to all parties. To fulfill this function you must be up-to-date in your knowledge of safety concerns and the specific property involved in the transaction, and you must be able to communicate that information to all parties concerned.

FIGURE 20.1 Exhibit A

Buyer's Draft for Purchase of Property

1. Seller's Covenants, warranties and representations: The covenants, warranties and representations contained in this paragraph 1 will be effective on the date hereof and at Closing and will survive Closing. Seller covenants, warrants and represents to Buyer, its successors and assigns that:

   (a) No litigation is pending or, to Seller's knowledge, proposed, threatened or anticipated with respect to the Seller, or with respect to any other matter affecting the Property or the operation thereof.

   (b) Prior to Closing, Seller shall, at its sole cost and expense, and subject to Buyer's reasonable satisfaction, maintain the Property in good repair and in the same condition as of the date of this Agreement, reasonable wear and tear excepted.

   (c) If Seller is notified of any legal proceedings instituted against the Property prior to Closing, Seller shall promptly give notice thereof to buyer.

   (d) To Seller's knowledge after due inquiry, no electrical transformers, fluorescent light fixtures with ballasts or other equipment containing PCBs are or were located on the Property at any time during or prior to Seller's ownership thereof.

   (e) To Seller's knowledge after due inquiry, no asbestos-containing materials were installed or exposed in the Property through demolition, renovation or otherwise, at any time or prior to Seller's ownership thereof.

   (f) To Seller's knowledge after due inquiry, no storage tanks for gasoline or any other substance are or were located on the Property at any time during or prior to Seller's ownership thereof.

   (g) The Property and Seller's operations concerning the Property are not in violation of any applicable federal, state or local statute, law or regulation, and no notice from any governmental body has been served upon Seller claiming any violation of any law, ordinance, code or regulation, or requiring or calling attention to the need for, any work, repairs, construction, alterations or installation on or in connection with the Property in order to comply with any laws, ordinances, codes or regulations, with which Seller has not compiled. If there are any such notices with which Seller has complied, Seller shall provide Buyer with copies thereof.

2. Release: Buyer expressly releases Seller from any and all liability arising from or connected with the condition of the Property which is discovered after Closing.

3. Indemnity: From and after Closing, Seller shall indemnify, defend and save harmless from all losses or damages resulting from injury to or death of any person and damage to the Property, and any fine, which is occasioned or arises out of any breach of warranty, representation or covenant of Seller under this agreement.

FIGURE 20.2 Exhibit B

Seller's Draft

1. Conditions Precedent: Buyer shall have no obligation to purchase the Property from seller hereunder unless at Closing each and every representation and warranty and covenant contained in paragraph 2 below shall be true and correct on the date of Closing. If any representation, warranty or covenant contained in paragraph 2 below is not true and correct on the date of Closing, Buyer shall elect either to terminate this Agreement or to waive the condition and purchase the Property, and such election shall be Buyer's sole remedy.

2. Seller's Covenants, Warranties and Representations. Seller covenants, warrants and represents to Buyer, its successors and assigns that:

   (a) No litigation, and no governmental, administrative or regulatory act or proceeding is pending or, to Seller's knowledge, proposed, threatened or anticipated with respect to the Seller, or with respect to any other matter affecting the Property or the operation thereof.

   (b) Prior to Closing, Seller shall, at its sole cost and expense, and subject to Buyer's satisfaction, maintain the Property in good repair and in the same condition as of the date of this Agreement, reasonable wear and tear excepted.

   (c) If Seller is notified of any legal or governmental or administrative act or proceeding instituted against the Property prior to Closing, Seller shall promptly give notice thereof to Buyer.

   (d) To Seller's knowledge, no asbestos-containing materials were installed in the Property at any time during Seller's ownership thereof. (Include details of any asbestos that was found.)

   (e) To Seller's knowledge, all electrical transformers and equipment on the Property are shown in the Building Plans furnished to Buyer.

   (f) To Seller's knowledge, no storage tanks for gasoline or any other substance are or were located on the Property at any time during or prior to Seller's ownership thereof.

   (g) To Seller's knowledge, the Property and Seller's operations concerning the Property are not in violation of any applicable federal, state or local statute, law or regulation, and no notice from any governmental body has been served upon Seller claiming any violation of any law, ordinance, code or regulation, or requiring or calling attention to the need for any work, repairs, construction, alterations or installation on or in connection with the Property in order to comply with any laws, ordinances, codes or regulations, with which Seller has not complied. If there are any such notices with which Seller has compiled, Seller shall provide Buyer with copies thereof.

3. "To Seller's Knowledge" defined: "To Seller's knowledge" means to the actual, but not constructive, knowledge of (name) (title). Buyer has had full opportunity to inspect the Property and examine Seller's records, and Buyer agrees that Seller has no duty to make any investigation as to the matters warranted and represented in paragraph 2 above.

4. Release: From and after Closing, Buyer hereby waives, releases, remises, acquits and forever discharges Seller, its directors, officers, shareholders, employees and agents, and their respective heirs, successors, personal representatives and or administrative proceedings, claims, demands, actual damages, punitive damages, losses, costs, liabilities, interest, attorneys' fees and expenses of whatever kind and nature, in law or in equity, known or unknown, which Buyer ever had, now has, hereafter can, shall or may have to acquire or possess or arising out of or in any way connected with directly or indirectly out of, or in any way connected with, based upon, arising out of, (i) Seller's use, maintenance, ownership and operation of the Property prior to Closing, or (ii) the condition, status, quality, nature, contamination or environmental state of the Property.

It is the intention of this agreement that any and all responsibilities and obligations of Seller, and any and all rights or claims of Buyer, its successors and assigns and affiliated entities, arising by virtue of the physical or environmental condition of the Property are by this release provision declared null and void and of no present or future effect as to such parties. Buyer agrees to waive the benefits of Section _____ if the Civil Code of the state of _____ , which provides as follows:

"A general release does not extend to claims which the creditor does not know or suspect to exist in his favor at the time of executing the release, which if known by him must have materially affected his settlement with the debtor."

5. Indemnify: Buyer shall, to the maximum extent permitted by law:

   (a) Save, defend, indemnify and hold harmless (herein collectively called "To Indemnify"), Seller, its directors, officers, shareholders, employees and agents, and their respective heirs, successors, personal representatives and assigns (herein collectively called "Indemnified Parties") from and against any and all suits, actions, legal or administrative proceedings, claims, demands, actual damages, fines, punitive damages, losses, costs, liabilities, interest, attorneys' fees (including any such fees and expenses incurred in enforcing this indemnity) (herein collectively called "Damages") resulting from, arising out of or in any way connected with injury to or the death of any person (including, without limitation, any Indemnified Party) or physical damage to property of any kind wherever located and by whomever owned (including, without limitation, that of any Indemnified Party) arising out of or in any way connected with Seller's ownership or use of the Property, including, but not limited to, any such injury, death, damage, or loss arising out of the negligence of the Indemnified Parties.

FIGURE 20.3 Exhibit C

Seller's "As Is" Provision

Acceptance of Property "As Is": Buyer acknowledges and agrees that the Property is to be sold and conveyed to, and accepted by Buyer, in an "as is" condition with all faults. Buyer has investigated and has knowledge of operative or proposed investigated and has knowledge of operative or proposed governmental laws and regulations (including, but not limited to, zoning, environmental and land use laws and regulations) to which the Property is or may be subject and accepts the Property upon the basis of its review and determination of the applicability and effect of such laws and regulations. Buyer acknowledges that the Property has been used for the production of widgets for many years, and that such production involves the use of solvents and other chemicals. Buyer acknowledges the existence of storage tanks for gasoline on the Property. Buyer acknowledges the use of raw land on the Property for Parking. Buyer acknowledges the existence of asbestos insulation and PCB-laden electrical equipment on the Property. Buyer acknowledges that as a result of such uses and conditions, physical changes, including gasoline and chemical seepage, may have occurred on the Property. Buyer acknowledges that it is entering into this agreement on the basis of Buyer's own investigation of the physical and environmental conditions of the Property, including subsurface conditions, and conditions may not have been revealed by its own investigation. Buyer further acknowledges that Seller, its agents and employees and other persons acting on behalf of Seller have made no representation or warranty of any kind in connection with any matter relating to the condition, value, fitness, use or zoning of the Property upon which Buyer has relied directly or indirectly for any purpose. Buyer hereby waives, releases, remises, acquits and forever discharges Seller, Seller's employees, agents or any other person acting on behalf of Seller, of and from any claims, actions, causes of action, demands, rights, damages, costs, expenses or compensation whatsoever, direct or indirect, known or unknown, foreseen or unforseen, which Buyer now has or which may arise in the future on account of or in any way growing out of or connected with the physical condition of the Property or any law or regulation applicable thereto.

FIGURE 20.4 Exhibit D

Seller's Allocation of Testing Responsibility

1. Environmental Conditions: (a) Seller shall undertake at Seller's expense an investigation to determine the environmental condition of the Property, such review to be completed prior to termination of the Review Period. Such review shall include the sampling of soil and the drilling of observation wells at the locations specified in Exhibit 1 to this Agreement and such additional tests as Seller may reasonably deem necessary to determine the environmental condition of the Property. Buyer may participate in such review and shall have access to all information developed. Buyer agrees that the investigation outlined in Exhibit A represents a thorough and reasonable examination of the environmental conditions on the Property.

   (b) If the review pursuant to subparagraph 1(a) above identifies the existence of environmental conditions which may be subject to legal requirements for corrective action, Seller may terminate this Agreement.

FIGURE 20.5 Exhibit E

Seller's Disclosure of Written Information

Environmental Studies: Seller has provided Buyer with various environmental studies and reports conducted by independent contractors and various records of Seller concerning, relating to and affecting the Property which identify certain underground tanks, certain contamination of the soil and groundwater of the Property and other environmental information relating to the Property, and correspondence with various governmental entities concerning the Property and Buyer acknowledges having received the reports, records and correspondences that are identified on Exhibit A attached hereto. For reference purposes only, all such reports, records and correspondence identified on Exhibit A are referred to collectively as the "Reports." Seller does not warrant the accuracy of any information contained in the Reports.

FIGURE 20.6 Exhibit F

Buyer's Proposed Representations Regarding Operating Plant

Seller represents and warrants to Buyer that to Seller's knowledge:

(i) Plant A is used and operated in substantial compliance with applicable local, state and federal laws, ordinances, rules regulations and orders, and has all permits and authorizations required for its use and operation.

(ii) No material change has been made in the use or operation of Plant A, and no processes, materials or machinery have been introduced since (date) .

FIGURE 20.7 Exhibit G

Allocation of Costs

Post-Closing Corrective Action: If Buyer within (1) year following Closing, determines and demonstrates to Seller's reasonable satisfaction that environmental conditions subject to legal requirements for corrective action are present as a result of Seller's operations prior to Closing and that the presence of such conditions was unknown to Buyer before Closing, Buyer's sole remedy shall be to require Seller to correct or make arrangements for the correction of such conditions as are required by law.

FIGURE 20.8 Exhibit H

Seller's Indemnification of Buyer for Cleanup

1. Indemnity.

(a) From and after Closing, Seller shall indemnify, defend and save harmless Buyer from and against any and all losses, damages, liabilities, expenses (including reasonable attorney's fees), fines, penalties and costs arising out of the willful misconduct or negligence of Seller occurring during the exercise of the irrevocable license granted to it pursuant to paragraph _____ hereof.

(b) Seller's liability under the provisions of paragraph 1(a) is expressly conditioned upon Buyer furnishing Seller with prompt written notice of any matter of which Buyer receives actual notice which might give rise to liability on the part of Seller hereunder and Seller having control over the defense of any liability on its part hereunder, and over all negotiations relating to the settlement thereof; provided, however, that Seller shall keep Buyer advised on a reasonably regular basis of the progress thereof and Buyer shall have the right, at its expense, to participate in the defense.

(c) Notwithstanding the indemnity set forth in paragraph 1(a), under no circumstances shall Seller be liable to Buyer or any grantee of Buyer for any special or consequential losses or damages, including loss of use of profits, regardless of cause.

FIGURE 20.9 Exhibit I

Cost Splitting: Seller Partially Liable for Two Years

Seller shall indemnify and hold harmless Buyer, from and against eighty percent (80%) of the value of any Damages arising from any environmental contamination present at the Property as a result of Seller's operations prior to closing to the extent that such Damages in the aggregate exceed Five Hundred Thousand Dollars ($500,000); provided that such indemnity shall not extend to any demand for indemnification made more than two (2) years after closing.

FIGURE 20.10 Exhibit J

Seller's Proposed Restrictive Covenant

Restrictive Covenant: Buyer and Seller hereby agree that the deed delivered pursuant to this purchase and sale agreement will provide as follows:

WHEREAS, Conditions existing on the Property as a result of its use as a manufacturing facility for the processing of widgets make the Property unsuitable for certain uses, and

WHEREAS, The parties hereto desire and intend to restrict the use of the Property in the future so as to reduce the risk of injury or damage to persons and property as a result of the existing conditions,

Now Therefore, in consideration of the mutual promises of the parties hereto, each to the other as covenantor and covenantee, Buyer hereby covenants to Seller, which covenant shall be binding upon all successors in interest to the Property, that the Property or any portion thereof shall not be used for any purpose other than commercial manufacturing or industrial purposes only, at any time during a period of thirty (30) years from and after the date of recordation of this Deed. Said permitted commercial, manufacturing or industrial uses shall not include any agricultural use, any livestock raising or breeding use, any food processing uses, or any playground, sports, recreational, open space, public park, school or hospital uses, or any accessory or incidental use or uses thereto on the Property such as, but not limited to, residential uses of any density or nature whether permanent or temporary. If Buyer, or any successor in interest to the Property, shall cause or permit a breach of said covenant, Seller, or its successors and assigns, may enjoin such unpermitted use and seek other such relief to which it may be entitled.

The covenants contained herein are to run with the land and shall be binding on all parties and persons claiming under them. Buyer agrees that all the restrictions contained in this deed shall be inserted in full in all future deeds of the property covered by this deed.

21

Sale-Leasebacks

DEFINITION

A sale-leaseback is a transaction in which the owner/tenant of a property sells the property to a buyer and simultaneously leases the property back from the buyer.

The decision to do a sale-leaseback is an economic one. Most typically, it is to liquidate real estate equity for use elsewhere. Therefore, your first step as a salesperson when exploring this option with an owner/user is to complete a financial analysis.

ANALYSIS OF A SALE-LEASEBACK

In order to determine if a sale-leaseback makes economic sense, there are four basic questions you need to research.

1. What are the ownership costs for the property?
2. What would the lease costs be for the property?
3. What return could the owner/user receive from an alternative use of the money that is now real estate equity?
4. What are the tax implications of the transaction?

Obviously, the last question is one that demands the attention of the owner/user's tax specialist. However, you must weigh it as a consideration when presenting the sale-leaseback option.

THE PROCESS

There are six steps in the decision-making process for a sale-leaseback.

1. Identify the start date of the analysis and obtain the necessary information.
2. Add up the total ownership inflows and outflows over the ten year period on an after-tax basis.
3. Add up the total lease costs over the ten year period, after taxes.
4. Discount both cash flows at varying discount rates.
5. Compare discounted cost differentials to the client's internal yield returns.
6. Review the outcome with the client and the appropriate advisors (tax, etc.). Then let the client make the decision.

Identifying a Start Date and Obtaining Information

To provide a more accurate assessment of the situation, you will need to do a ten-year analysis using the present year as year one.

Your first step is to estimate how much net equity after tax the owner has invested in the property. To do this you must:

1. Estimate the current market value of the building.
2. Subtract out current loan balances.
3. Subtract out tax as if the owner were to sell today.

Example:

> Market value of property
> – Outstanding loan(s) balance(s)
> – Capital gains tax
> ─────────────────────────
> = Net equity after-tax

Now you have the owner's beginning investment amount as if he or she had bought the property today. Next you have to identify the income and expenses related to ownership. These include the operating costs, depreciation schedule, debt service, appreciation, tax affect and the cap rate for resale at the end of the term. This data will allow you to measure both inflows and outflows related to ownership over the ten-year period.

To analyze the sale-lease back side of the transaction, you assume the owner sold the property and executed a triple net lease. (In a triple net lease, the lessee assumes payment of all expenses associated with the eration of the property.) Next you identify conventional lease costs for a typical triple net tenant: the rent and expenses at current market rates, the increases per year and the tax consequences. You then have the outflow of the leasing side.

Ownership Inflows and Outflows

Once you have the needed data on ownership, you can compute the total cost of owning the building by adding the initial equity outlay to annual expense outlays and subtracting from that total the income from the resale of the property in year ten.

Example:

>   Net equity after-tax (example 1)
>   + Annual cash flows after-tax*
>   − Net resale value
>   = Total ownership costs

*To calculate the annual cash outflows after-tax take:

>   Income: (0)
>   − Expenses
>   = Net operating income (negative)
>   − Debt service
>   = Cash flow pre-tax
>
>   Net operating income
>   − Interest payments
>   − Depreciation
>   = Taxable income
>   × Tax bracket
>   = Taxable income/loss
>
>   Cash flow pre-tax
>   − Taxable loss
>   = Cash flow after-tax (annual net outflow, after-tax)

Leasing Outflows

Given that you have the necessary lease data, the occupancy expense in leasing the property is calculated as follows:

Example:

>   Triple net lease payments (annual outflows)
>   + Annual lease expenses
>   = Annual lease expense, pre-tax
>
>   Annual lease expense, pre-tax
>   × (1-tax bracket)
>   = Lease expense per year after tax

Discounting Ownership and Lease Cash Flows

Up to this point, you've assimilated ownership and leasing data and compiled both the total ownership and leasing costs over the analysis time period. Without introducing the time value of money, we could simply compare these two totals and see which is more costly, owning or renting. Unfortunately a dollar received in ten years is not worth as much as a dollar received today. More specifically, when the owner resells the building in year ten, the money received is worth less per dollar than the money invested in year one. Similarly, the lease costs in year ten do not have the same dollar value as lease costs in year one.

Whenever you have two cash streams involving varying outflows or inflows at different times over a ten-year period, there is no way you can compare the total value of each cash stream on an apple-to-apple basis. Only by selecting a discount rate and calculating the net present value of the cash streams can you compare their relative value dollar-for-dollar. Therefore the fourth step in the lease vs. buy model involves discounting occupancy costs into comparable, net present value terms.

Other Considerations

The sale-leaseback decision rests not only on a comparison of discounted lease and ownership costs, but also on how these costs relate to the business' internal investment yield on operations. For example, business capital may be put to better use in the business operation than in real estate equity. If the company is a widget-maker and the operating profits after-tax were 18 percent, the company probably wouldn't want millions tied up in real estate that only yielded ten percent. On the other hand, if the inflation rate were extremely low, the company may be better off owning than renting. In general, it is less costly to own at low discount rates and better to rent at high discount rates. Thus, for these and other reasons, it is necessary for the sale-leaseback analysis to consider a complete range of discount rates. It is important to determine the discount rate that the client feels best applies to his or her economic situation.

TYPES OF SALE-LEASEBACK

The examples given above deal with the most common type of sale-leaseback, that in which the land and building are sold and leased back. Other varieties of sale-leaseback are:

Land-only sale-leaseback. Used principally by developers, a land sale-leaseback is where the land component of the property is valued, sold and leased back to the owner while the ownership of the improvements remains unchanged. The developer typically executes a subordinated ground lease.

The reason for not selling and leasing back the improvements is that typically they have depreciation write-off potential. The developer gets the best of both worlds: The nondepreciable land payments are deducted via lease payments, the improvements are depreciated, and 100 percent of the land value has been liquidated.

Finally such arrangements are structured so the buyer/landlord is assured of clear title to land and improvements at the end of the lease term or upon default.

Exchange-leaseback. A complex transaction having several variations. The two basic types are:

(a) Where the seller/tenant trades the facility for a "like-kind" nonbusiness property and leases back the facility.

(b) Where the seller/tenant trades the facility for the lease itself.

In both cases the transactions are much more technical to structure and require extensive legal, financial and tax advice.

WHEN TO DISCUSS THE SALE-LEASEBACK OPTION

Obviously, because of the complicated and limited nature of doing a sale-leaseback, saying, "I'm John Jones of ABC Realty and I'm here to talk to you about doing a sale-leaseback" is not an effective opening on a cold call. However, there are several clues you can listen for in a cold call. These include comments such as:

1. "Real estate is not our problem. Our problem is capital."

2. "We're getting killed on taxes. We've taken most of our depreciation on this place and two-thirds of our debt service now in principal."

3. "We've got the best profit margin in the business. The problem is we need more facilities to accommodate our growth, and the banks don't like our balance sheet."

4. "We've considered selling, but leasing is always more expensive than owning."

5. "I'm considering refinancing this place so we can get our hands on more capital."

CONCLUSION

As you have seen, the sale-leaseback analysis and decision is an extremely complex one. You as a salesperson are not in a position to serve as sole advisor to a client in this matter. It is very important that he or she also involve financial, legal and tax advisors in the process. However, you can educate a client on the sale-leaseback option and the process for analysis.

Glossary

Adjustable rate mortgage (ARM). A long-term loan in which the lender may periodically adjust the interest rate based on a government index.

Amortization. The gradual repayment of debt by means of systematic, even payments of principal and/or interest over a set time period; at the end of the time period, there is a zero balance.

Anchor tenant. A "triple A" tenant, such as a large department or discount store or a nationally known chain, which forms the nucleus of a modern shopping center. The anchor tenant is the mainstay that draws the public and stabilizes the center by assuring a profitable operation for all the other tenants. Anchor tenants are usually sought out first by developers, and they are usually given favorable leases.

Annualized sales. Expanding on an annual basis: a procedure whereby taxable income from sales for a fractional year is multiplied by a fraction equal to 12 divided by the number of months in the shorter period. The resulting tax is then reduced by applying the same formula in reverse.

Architectural drawing. Includes all architectural contracts and drawings, such as plot plans, floor plans, elevations, sections, details, schedules and any architectural drawing that forms a part of the contract documents. Exceptions include mechanical, electrical, structural and special areas of concern normally performed by consultants to the architect or owner.

Assessed value. The value placed on land and building by a township or county assessor for use in levying real estate taxes.

Assignment. The transfer in writing of an interest in a lease, mortgage or other instrument. The assignor, or lessee, transfers the remainder of the term created by the lease, and the assignee becomes liable to the original lessor for rent. The assignor may or may not retain secondary liability for performance under the lease, depending upon the terms of the lease.

Assignment of lease. This type of assignment occurs when a tenant transfers all interest in a leasehold to another. This distinguishes it from a sublease, in which some portion of the lease is retained.

Base lease. A contract stating the minimum established requirements that are applicable to all tenants.

Basis points. There are 100 basis points in each percentage point. Thus, a loan interest rate 150 basis points over the prime rate would be prime rate plus 1.5 percent.

Building module. A unit of length and width by which the plan of a building can be standardized and which facilitates the design and layout of office space. The module places constraints on the size and shape of many of the elements of the physical systems. In contrast, buildings of a nonmodular design present many problems for initial design and subsequent alterations.

Building shell. The exterior walls and roof of a building together with a dirt floor and utilities "stubbed" to the premises.

Building standard. Specific construction standards that have been established by the owner and architect to achieve a uniform element of design throughout the building and establish a cost basis for fitting up charges and/or allowances. Such items may be changed only with approval of the building owner or the managing representative.

Build to suit. An agreement between a landlord and a new tenant whereby the landlord assumes the obligation of modifying the demised space to the tenant's specifications within the constraints of the building standards. The tenant takes possession when space is completed.

CCRs (covenants, conditions and restrictions). Legal documents recorded at the county level on every property which sets the terms for all matters affecting property usage.

Cancellation clause. A provision in a lease that confers upon one or both parties the right to terminate the lease upon the occurrence of the condition or contingency set forth in the said clause.

Capitalization. The process of ascertaining the value of a property by the use of a proper investment rate of return and the net income expected to be produced by the property. The formula of net annual income divided by proper capitalization rate is expressed: income ÷ rate = value.

Certificate of insurance. A certificate issued by an insurance company or its agent verifying that a certain insurance policy is in effect for stated amounts and coverages, and naming those insured.

Clear span. The amount of floor area clear of interference from columns.

Common area. Area used by two or more tenants or third parties and not under the control of any one tenant.

Common area maintenance. Maintenance of land or improvements that exist for the benefit of all tenants or property owners, such as shopping center parking lots, malls and so forth.

Community shopping center. Larger shopping center anchored by a junior department store and approximately 150,000 to 200,000 square feet in size on 15 to 20 acres. It may serve several populated areas and satisfy more than the basic needs provided for by small neighborhood centers.

Constant. A percentage which, when applied directly to the face value of a debt, develops the annual amount of money necessary to repay principal and interest over the full term of the loan.

Construction allowance. Landlord's contribution to the cost of construction and/or alteration necessary to prepare a space for a tenant's occupancy. This may be an established amount, or it may vary from one type of transaction to another.

Construction cost estimate. A figure submitted in advance of construction, not binding unless submitted as a bid. It is used to help a developer arrive at a decision concerning a proposed project.

Construction loan. A short-term or interim loan to cover the construction costs of a building or development project, with loan proceeds advanced periodically in the form of instruments or draws as the work progresses.

Contractor. An individual and/or firm used in performing work on construction projects. There are different classes of contractors, which are normally listed under the heading of subcontractors. The function of the subcontractor is to perform a particular task only under the direction and coordination of the general contractor, who takes on the responsibility of managing the project in accordance with the construction documents. The general contractor is normally selected through bidding procedures and is totally responsible for completion of the project in a skillful manner that is acceptable to both architect and owner. However, the general contractor may be preselected to handle all work within a particular project. This is usually the case for multi-story office buildings where the general contractor is the same for all tenant space construction. The contractor also could be contracted on a time-and-material basis, which may or may not have an upset maximum.

Convenience store. A store in a strip center, usually open long hours and specializing in "pick-up" food, drug and beverage items.

Cost approach. The process of estimating the value of a property by adding to the estimated land value the appraiser's estimate of the replacement cost of the building, less depreciation.

Cost-of-living increase. Increase reflected on the wholesale price index or the cost-of-living index, which can be national, regional or confined to a metropolitan area.

Debt coverage ratio. The ratio of net operating income to annual debt service.

Debt financing. Raising capital by borrowing from a lender.

Debt service. The amount of money needed to meet the periodic payments of principal and interest on a mortgage or debt which is being amortized.

Deed restrictions. Clauses in a deed limiting the future uses of the property. Deed restrictions may take many forms: They may limit the density of buildings, dictate the types of structures that can be erected, or prevent buildings from being used for specific purposes or from being used at all. Deed restrictions may impose a myriad of limitations and conditions.

Default. Failure to meet an obligation when due or to perform any provision of a lease, mortgage or other agreement.

Demised premises. Premises, or parts of real estate, in which an interest or estate has been transferred temporarily, such as an interest in real property conveyed in a lease.

Demography. The statistical science dealing with the distribution, density, vital statistics and characteristics of population.

Demolition clause. A clause within a lease denoting the fact that if or when the ground lease has expired, the building will be demolished per such clause. The lessor must notify the tenants within an established time of such condition.

Depreciation. Loss of value due to all causes. Depreciation includes (1) physical deterioration (ordinary wear and tear), (2) functional depreciation (see also *Obsolescence*) and (3) economic obsolescence (causes outside the property).

Design development. The process by which, upon approval of the schematic design, the architect proceeds with the development of the plans and elevations of the building. Drawings establishing all major elements and outline specifications are prepared. A revised statement of probable construction cost is usually made at such time.

Economic obsolescence. Impairment of desirability or useful life or loss in the use and value of property arising from economic forces outside the building or property, such as changes in optimum land use, legislative enactments that restrict or impair property rights and changes in supply-demand relationships.

Encumbrance. Any lien, such as a mortgage, tax or judgment lien. It can also be an easement, a restriction on the use of the land or an outstanding dower right that may diminish the value of the property.

Equity financing. Raising capital by granting an equity (ownership) interest in a given real estate project in exchange for the required capital.

Escalation clause. A clause in a contract providing for increases or decreases in rent payments in accordance with fluctuations of certain costs or expenses of the landlord. (Also called *Escalator Graded* or *Step-up clause*.)

Escrow. A written agreement between two or more parties providing that certain instruments or property be placed with a third party to be delivered to a designated person upon the fulfillment or performance of some act or condition.

Exclusive agency listing. A listing contract under which the owner appoints a real estate broker as the one exclusive agent for a designated period of time to sell the property on the owner's stated terms, and under which the owner agrees to pay the broker a commission. However, the owner reserves the right to sell without a commission to a prospect not introduced or claimed by the broker. (See *Exclusive right to sell*.)

Exclusive listing. A contract to sell property as an agent, whereby the agent is given the exclusive right to sell the property or is made the exclusive agent for its sale.

Exclusive right to sell. A listing contract under which the owner appoints a real estate broker as the exclusive agent for a designated term. The broker must sell or lease the property on the owner's stated terms, and the owner agrees to pay the broker a commission when the sale or lease is consummated.

Extended coverage policy. This extends protection to owners over the following general exceptions on the standard ALTA owner's policy. General exceptions referred to are (1) rights or claims of parties in possession not shown by public records; (2) encroachments, overlap boundary line disputes, and any matters that would be disclosed by an accurate survey of the property; (3) easements and claims of easements not shown by public records; (4) mechanics' liens not shown by public records and (5) taxes or special assessments that are not shown as existing liens by public records.

Field observation. Observation deemed necessary by the architect to ensure successful completion of the project. (Also called *on-site observation*.)

Fire rating bureau. A bureau whose functions include maintaining a complete set of files with state insurance departments that cover not only rating schedules, basis or key rates, and charges or credits applicable, but also rules and clauses affecting the rates and grading of the value of public fire protection.

Fire sprinkler system. An automatic fire-protection system that provides a flow of pressurized water from overhead nozzles when the temperature exceeds a predetermined level. The nozzles are fitted with plugs that melt at relatively low temperatures. There are two types of sprinkler systems (ordinary hazard and calculated system) the dry system, in which the water-supply pipes are filled with compressed air to hold the water behind the dry valve to prevent freezing, and the wet system, in which the water supply pipes are filled with water up to the nozzles.

Fire wall. A wall constructed of fireproof material, which is installed to check the spread of fire into other areas of a building or adjacent properties for one, two or four hours.

Fixtures. Personal property or improvements so attached to the land as to become part of the real property. The right of the tenant to remove fixtures may be given by stipulation in the lease or by separate written agreement between the parties.

Functional obsolescence. Defects in a building or structure that detract from its value or marketability. (See *Obsolescence.*)

Graduated lease. A lease that provides for specific increases or decreases in rent at definite times during the terms of the lease.

Gross income. The total of money received from income property of a business before operating expenses, taxes, depreciation, commissions, salaries, fees and other expenses are deducted.

Gross lease. A lease on property whereby the lessor is to pay all property charges and taxes regularly incurred through ownership. (See also *Net lease*)

Gross rent multiplier. A figure that, when used as a multiplier of the gross income of a property, produces an estimate of the property's value.

Ground lease. A lease, usually of long duration, of land to a tenant or developer who covenants to erect or has erected a building on the premises. The building is considered security for rentals. If the tenant defaults, the landlord may foreclose on the lease. (See *Subordinated ground lease.*)

HVAC. An abbreviation for heating, ventilating and air conditioning.

Income approach. The process of estimating the value of an income-producing property by capitalization of the annual net income expected to be produced by the property during its remaining useful life.

Installment contract. A contract for the sale of real estate wherein the purchase price is paid in installments over an extended period of time by the purchaser, who is in possession, and the seller retains title until final payment.

Interim financing. Short-term, temporary financing that is generally in effect during a building's construction or until a permanent, long-term loan can be obtained.

Interim loan. A short-term loan usually made during the construction period, often referred to as a construction loan. In modern usage, the interim loan describes a short-term loan put in place after construction, but prior to a permanent loan.

Interior Partitions. All types of interior non-load-bearing partitions that enclose or subdivide tenant space. May be of steel, wood, glass, masonry or combinations of these materials. Such partitions may be either movable or nonmovable, prefabricated or built on the job.

International Council of Shopping Centers (ICSC). A council based in New York City whose primary aim is the establishment of a forum where businesspeople in apparently competitive relationships can assemble to exchange helpful ideas and experiences resulting in the stability of the shopping center industry.

Land contract. A contract for the purchase of real estate on an installment basis. Upon payment of the last installment, the deed is delivered to the purchaser. (See *Installment contract.*)

Land lease. A ground lease; a contract for the possession and use of land.

Latent defect. A physical deficiency or construction defect not readily ascertainable from a reasonable inspection of the property, such as a defective septic tank or underground sewerage system or improper plumbing or electrical liner. (Also called *hidden defect.*)

Lease. A contract whereby, for a consideration (usually termed rent), one who is entitled to the possession of real property transfers such rights to another for life, for a term of years, month to month or at will.

Lease insurance. A lease guarantee policy that protects the landlord against a default in rental payments on the remaining portion of a lease. Used primarily in store and office leasing, it raises the credit position of the smaller tenant so he or she can obtain space that a landlord might otherwise reserve for a highly rated or national company. It acts as a relief for the tenant if financial difficulty prevents making the payments. The premium for such a policy is usually paid by the landlord. In apartment house leases, it insures against loss in rental payments in the event of a tenant's death.

Letter of intent. Based on the points agreed to orally in the negotiations, the written letter of intent, or lease proposal, sets out in detail the items on which agreement has been reached. When acknowledged in writing by the signatures of both parties, the document becomes legally binding on both. It can then be used as a basis for financial planning and for negotiating mortgage financing.

Lien. A right given by law to a creditor to have a debt or charge satisfied out of the property of the debtor. It applies to a particular piece or pieces of real or personal property.

Limited partnership. A partnership arrangement that limits certain of the partner's liability to the amount invested and also limits the profit he or she can make. A limited partner is not permitted to have a voice in the management.

Listing contract. An agreement between a landlord (as principal) and a licensed real estate broker (as agent) by which the broker is employed to sell the real estate on the landowner's terms within a given time, for which service the landlord agrees to pay a commission. (See *Open listing, Exclusive agency* and *Exclusive right to sell*.)

Loan constant. A method of calculating loan payments to express the payments in terms of percentage of the total loan. Given the rate of interest and the term of the loan, the percentage of the loan needed to repay it on a fully amortized basis may be ascertained.

Loan correspondent. A mortgage firm that services a mortgage held by an investor by sending notices to the mortgagor and making collections of principal, interest and reserves, and by remitting net principal and interest after deducting service fees.

Market data approach. The process of estimating the value of property through the examination and comparison of actual sales of comparable properties.

Market value. The highest price that a buyer who is ready, willing and able, but not compelled to buy, would pay, and the lowest price a seller who is ready, willing and able, but not compelled to sell, would accept.

Merchants' association. Localized association that promotes the general business interests of the merchants in the particular shopping center and conducts promotional programs, publicity, special events, cooperative advertising and other joint endeavors. Such associations are conducted as nonprofit organizations.

Month-to-month tenancy. A tenancy from month to month is generally created when no definite lease term is specified by the parties and the rent is payable monthly. Such a lease may be written or oral and can be terminated by either party at the end of any month. Otherwise, it is renewed automatically from month to month on the same terms.

Mortgage broker. An individual or company that obtains mortgages for others by finding lending institutions, insurance companies or private sources that will lend the money. Mortgage brokers sometimes service the account by making collections and handling disbursements.

Neighborhood shopping center. A relatively small group of stores devoted to the basic needs of the immediate neighborhood, anchored by a supermarket or drugstore on five to ten acres and generally between 50,000 and 120,000 square feet in size.

Net lease. Lease under which the tenant pays the agreed-upon rent plus utilities and taxes.

Net-net lease. Lease under which the tenant pays the agreed-upon rent plus utilities, taxes, insurance and maintenance.

Net-net-net lease. Lease under which the tenant pays the agreed-upon rent plus all costs of maintenance and repair. (Also called *Triple net lease.*)

Net operating income. The sum derived after deductions from gross income for vacancy and expenses.

Obsolescence. Lessening of value due to being out of date as a result of changes in design and use: an element of depreciation.

Open listing. A listing contract under which the broker's commission is contingent upon the broker's producing a buyer before the property is sold by the owner or another broker.

Option. A contractual agreement giving one party the privilege of demanding, within a specific time, the carrying out of a transaction upon stipulated terms.

Overage. The percentage of the volume of business a retail store does over a specified time that goes to the landlord as additional rent.

Owners' policies. Designed to meet the normal title insurance needs of owners of real estate. The protection usually extends to the heirs at law or devisees of the property owner in the event of death and to the corporate successors of corporate owners.

Package. The assumption by a person or organization of responsibility under a single contract for the design and construction of a project to meet the specific requirements of another; the performance of certain initial development activities, such as market research, land evaluation, land acquisition, project design and concept, architecture, engineering, zoning and the obtaining of financing.

Parcel. A specified part of a larger tract of land; a lot. A description of the property setting forth the boundaries.

Parking ratio. The ratio of required parking spaces to the number of units or square footage area in an office, market or other building.

Partial release clause. A clause found in some mortgages and deeds providing for the release of a portion of the property when certain prescribed stipulations are met.

Participating mortgage. A mortgage in which the lender discounts the face interest rate on the mortgage in exchange for an equity position (ownership) in the project and participation in increases in net income over the base year.

Percent of gross. A leasing or lending arrangement whereby the lender or landlord receives a negotiated percentage of gross income of income-producing property.

Percentage lease. A lease in which the rental is based upon a percentage of the volume of sales. With the advent of discount houses, large chain stores and modern shopping centers, this has become an increasingly popular method of leasing.

Percentage of return to land. Return left after appraiser discounts the ratio of the land's anticipated value at the end of the improvement's economic life to its present-day worth.

Permanent loan. A long-term loan, typically ranging from 25 to 30 years. Modern permanent loans are amortized over 25 to 30 years, but often are "called" in 10 to 15 years.

Planned unit development (PUD). The PUD is "overlay" zoning that enables a developer to obtain a higher density (and sometimes a mixed use for commercial and industrial) than is permitted by the underlying zoning.

Points. Refers to percentage points charged by a lender for originating a loan or committing to originate a loan. A fee of one to two points is usual, and would mean that the fee is one percent to two percent of the amount you are borrowing.

Preferred return. The first cash flow dollars in a joint venture flow to a partner as a return on his "investment." This return is preferred but not guaranteed in the event of poor or zero cash flow.

Preliminary cost estimates. First estimates, which are recognized as ballpark figures and arrived at before detailed data have been made available to the estimator.

Preliminary costs. Expenditures that are made before the main project is begun, such as feasibility studies, subsoil exploration, financing commitments and the like.

Preliminary title report. A report on the condition of the title to a specific piece of property after an examination of the abstract has been made. It is issued by the title insurance company when the firm prepares to write a title guarantee policy; the commitment lists all details of the title examination that will be included in the final policy. It is used at a closing in place of the formal title policy.

Prime lease. A lease most desirable for a particular use; a lease that provides for a prime fee, for which the rent payable is exceptionally well secured by enhancement in the value of the land since the lease was made and/or by the value of improvements erected by the lessee.

Prime location. A choice property site; one ideally suited for a specific purpose.

Prime rate. The loan interest rate at which a bank will lend funds to its most solid, credit-worthy commercial customers.

Prime tenant. A tenant who occupies a great portion of the space available within a given building. The building may in addition be owned by such tenant.

Private placement. An offering of a real estate security that is exempt from registration with state and federal regulatory agencies because it does not involve a public offering. Private placements are for a specific property and usually involve less than 35 investors.

Pro forma. A preliminary financial statement compiled by the developer to determine the feasibility of building a project.

Procuring cause. "A broker will be regarded as the 'procuring cause' of a sale, so as to be entitled to commission, if his efforts are the foundation on which the negotiations resulting in a sale are begun." *Coles vs. Pattison,* 189 Okl. 160, 114 P. 2d 457, 458.

Protective covenants. (See *Deed restrictions.*)

Punch list. A list prepared by the architect, designer and owner, and formally submitted to the contractor. The list notes any deficiencies in the completed construction and ensures verification that such work has been accomplished in a good, workmanlike manner with respect to the contract documents.

Realtor®. A registered trademark term reserved for the sole use of active members of local boards of Realtors affiliated with the National Association of Realtors.

Recapture. A method used by many supermarkets in which they are able to pay their taxes out of overage rents that normally would go to the developer.

Reciprocal easement agreement (REA). Also known as a *common area agreement.* A document attached to a shopping center lease that is binding between the stores in that center and states that there will be reciprocal easements among all stores on the common areas such as the parking lot and sidewalks.

Regional shopping center. A large shopping center complex serving an extensive, well-populated area. Usually one or two major department stores form the nucleus, with 50 to 100 or more other stores, a post office, bank, theater, and other such facilities furnishing the public with goods and services. Such a center is generally 800,000 to over 1,000,000 square feet in size on 80 to 100 acres.

Release clause. Provision in a trust deed or mortgage to release portions of the property from the lien upon payment of an agreed amount of money. Subdividers are required to have these.

Rentable area. The importance of this subject dictates the following detailed definition. In the United States and Canada, there are three methods of measuring rentable area in office buildings. All three measure the total square footage.

1. International Association of Building Owners and Managers. From the inside of the outside wall (or in new buildings from the glass line) to the outside of the inside wall (or hall wall) and center to center on the division walls. Columns are included.

2. General Services Administration. Same as above except all columns, division walls, service closets, etc., are included. Net usable space only. In making leases to the federal government, this method must be used.

3. So-called New York Method. Space is measured right across the floor from glass line to glass line, subtracting only elevator shafts and stairwells. In the case of multiple occupancy on one floor, the common space, usable and nonusable, is apportioned among the tenants according to the size of their respective areas.

Replacement cost. The new cost of replacing the subject property with property having exactly the same utility and amenities.
Restriction. A limitation placed upon the use of property contained in the deed or other written instrument in the chain of title.
Return. Profit from an investment; the sum of money that a property brings after expenses are paid.
Sale and leaseback. A transaction in which the seller remains in occupancy by simultaneously signing a lease (usually of long duration) with the purchaser at the time of the sale. By doing so, the seller receives cash for the transaction, while the buyer is assured a tenant and thus a fixed return on the investment.
Sales contract. A contract containing the complete terms of the agreement between seller and buyer for the sale of a particular parcel or parcels of real estate.
Sandwich lease. The lease held by a nonpossessory lessee who has subleased the possessory interest to another.
Schematic design. A suggested plan, design or program of action resulting from the inspection of the site and conferences with the client concerning the building program. The client's needs and requirements are analyzed, zoning regulations and codes affecting the work are studied, and sketches and statements of probable construction costs are prepared for the owner's approval.
Settlement. The process at the closing of a sale of real estate negotiated by a real estate broker whereby the broker usually accounts to the principal for the earnest money deposit and deducts the commission and advances by use of a form of settlement statement.
Sinking fund. A gradually accumulated fund created to diminish a debt. At the end of a given period, the fund will have a sufficient amount, including interest earned, to replace the loss or satisfy the obligation that has fallen due.
Step-up clause. (See *Escalation clause*.)

Strip center. A small shopping center, usually containing a food market and/or drugstore or discount store and other small shops, located next to a major access route on a strip of land with parking in a band directly in front of the stores.

Subject to. The term meaning limited, qualified or subordinate to. When used in connection with mortgages, it refers to taking title to property having an existing mortgage without assuming personal liability for its payment. If liability is to be assumed, it must be so stated and agreed upon.

Sublease. A lease executed by the lessee of an estate to a third person, conveying the same estate for a shorter term, or a portion of the estate for the same or a shorter term. When the entire estate is sublet for the entire remainder of the term, it is called an *assignment*.

Subordinated ground lease. A ground lease in which the lessor (owner) places his or her right in relation to the structure subordinate to that of others, such as the holder of the construction loan or permanent mortgage. (See *Ground lease*.)

Subordination. When a lienholder, a lessee or one having an interest in or claim against personal or real property, places the interest behind that of another.

Subrogation. Replacing one person with another in regard to a legal right, interest or obligation; substitution such as an insured person transferring claim rights to the insurance carrier in return for direct payment of the loss.

Survey. The process of measuring land to determine its size, location and physical description; also, the map or plat showing the results of such survey.

Syndication. A combining of persons or firms to accomplish a joint venture of mutual interest.

Take-out commitment. A commitment by a lending institution to take over a short-term construction loan and issue a more permanent mortgage.

Tax rate (real estate). Generally quoted as so many dollars per $100 of assessed value, the general real estate tax is made up of the taxes levied on real estate by various governmental agencies and municipalities, such as the city, the county, school districts, park districts or other authorities.

Tenant improvements. Additions to the basic leased area (such as special fixtures) made by the tenant. The tenant must cover the fixtures by an agreement with the landlord or the fixtures will belong by law to the owner of the land. Trade fixtures can, however, be removed unless they have become "an integral part of the premises" by the manner in which they are fixed.

Tenant mix. The variety of tenants in a shopping center. This mix should be designed so that the different businesses will draw customers for each other.

Three-to-one ratio. A standard relationship of land site to building area: For every one square foot of building area, three square feet of land are required. This may vary somewhat depending on the user. (Also called *25 percent site coverage*.)

Title insurance policy. A policy insuring an owner or mortgagee against loss by reason of defects in the title to a parcel of real estate, other than those encumbrances, defects and matters that are specifically excluded by the policy.

Topography. Surface features of land, such as elevation, ridges, slope, contour.

Trade fixtures. Articles installed by a tenant under terms of a lease and removable by the tenant before the lease expires. These remain personal property; they are not true fixtures.

Traffic count. A count of cars passing a shopping center on major access routes, taken to determine prospective business.

Transfer tax. A levy on a deed transfer, signified by affixing stamps to the deed.

Volume per square foot. The method of estimating probable total construction cost by multiplying the adjusted gross building volume in square feet by a predetermined cost per unit of volume.

Waiver of lien. The intentional or voluntary relinquishment of the right to a mechanic's lien. It is routinely signed by contractors when they are paid for their work.

Work letter. That part of the lease outlining in detail all work that is to be done for the tenant by the landlord.

Wrap-around mortgage. A technique in which the lender assumes payment of the existing mortgage and gives a new, increased mortgage to the borrower at a higher interest rate. The new mortgage "wraps around" the existing one. With the trend in today's mortgage market toward rising interest rates and appreciated property values, wraparound mortgaging has gained increased acceptance.

Zoning ordinance. Exercise of policy power by a municipality in regulating and controlling the character and use of property.

Index

A
A & E, *see* Architectural and engineering costs
Accessibility, 168–70
Adjustable rate mortgage, 234
Advertising
 brochures, 144–49, 151–52
 classified, 144
 display, 144
 letters, 146, 149
 salesperson's function in, 149–50
Agency relationship, 78
Agreement, 254
Amortized debt payment, 219
Annual income, 224
Architectural and engineering costs, 223
Area
 assignment, 7–8
 description, 167–68
ARM, *see* Adjustable rate mortgage
Asbestos, 256
"As is" provision, 262
Assessor's map, 166–67

B
Banks, 187
Benefits, 100–103
Border-zone legislation, 257
Brochures, 144–49, 151–52
Broker's responsibility
 to buyer, 78–79
 to seller, 77–78
Broker's sign, *see* Signs

Building
 feet, 228
 -to-site ratio, 30
 work, 221, 223
Build to suit, 3, 38
 arrangements, 30
 generally, 204–5
 preliminary meeting, 205–6
 proposal, 206–8
 salesperson's role in, 208
 supermarket, 210–12
 tenant
  qualification, 205
  role in, 208
Business volume, 168
Buyer's draft for property purchase, 260

C
Canvassing, 18
Capital costs
 calculating income and, 219
 construction loans and, 220
 direct, 218–19
 financing and, 219–20
 indirect, 218–19
 off-site, 218
 on-site, 218
 permanent loans and, 220
Capitalization, 219
Cash
 flow, 219, 224, 269
 on cash yield, 219
 yield, 219

Chain tenants, 31, *see also* National chains
Chambers of commerce, 16
Classified advertising, 144
Cleanup indemnification, 264
Closing, 162
 transaction, 108–10
Clubs, 16
Cold calls, 2, 84–88, 90–94
Commercial space worksheet, 11
Commission, 2, 38, 206
 agreements, 50–52, 196
 payment and joint venture, 194
Community shopping centers, 214
Company selling, 103–5
Competition, 170
Compromise, 254
Construction
 exhibit, 62–63
 loans, 220, 233–34
 period, 242–43
Contingency, 223
 costs, 207
Convenience centers, 214
Cooperating broker, 78–79
Corporation site, 174
Cost
 allocation, 263
 splitting, 264
 see also various specific costs
Cotenants, 32
County proposed developments, 181
Criss-Cross Directories, 16
Custom-built, *see* Build to suit

285

D

Daily plan, 122, 125–26
Daily planner, 127
Decision making, 34–38
Debt financing, 233, 239
   samples, 236
Debt service, 224
Demographics, 32, 157
Desert General Corporation site, 174
Developers
   fee-based, 195
   getting to know, 195–96
   joint venture, 193–95
   types of, 192
Development
   costs, 221–23, 227
   for a fee, 195
   financing, 219–20
      defined, 232–35
      development process and, 238–44
      equity and, 235–38
      why, 231–32
   steps for shopping centers, 215–16
Direct costs, 218
Direct mail, 18
   programs, 17
Directories, 16
Disclaimer, 145–46
Disclosure of written information, 263
Discount
   stores, 31
   centers, 215
Discounting, 270
Display advertising, 144
Documentation, 258–59
Drill questions, 105–6
Drugstores, 31, 184
Dun & Bradstreet, 16, 35

E

Easy deals, 232
Environmental issues, 255–59
Environmental Protection Agency, 256–58
Equity
   developers, 192, 226
   development steps, 238–43
   financing, 233
      partnerships, 194, 235, 240
      private placements, 235–36
      syndications, 235
Escrow files, 129
Exchange-leaseback, 271
Exclusive
   agent, 42–43
   agreement, 52, 246–47
   authorization of lease, 72
   listings, 13
   marketing agreement, 23–26
   right to sublease, 65–68

F

Fast-food locations, 185
Features, 100–3
Fee-based development, 195
Fiduciary obligations, 77–78
Field representative, 36–37
50-50 partnership, 193–94
Financial
   capability, 34–38
   institutions, 30
   news, 16
   statement, 35, 38
Financing, 219–20, 231–44
   costs, 223
Fixed rate, fully amortized loan, 234
Folder, 17
Follow-up, 160–62, 201
   calls, 8
Forms
   commission agreement, 50–52
   construction exhibit, 62–63
   exclusive authorization of lease, 72
   exclusive right to sublease, 65–68
   income-expense summary, 73
   leases, 52–62
   offer to lease, 62, 64–65
   purchase agreement, 69–72
   tenant representation agreement, 47–49
"For sale," "for lease" signs, see Signs
Franchises, 35

G

Gain in equity, 219
GLA, see Gross leasable area
Goals
   long term, 114–16
   setting, 113–14
   short-term, 116–20
Gross
   leasable area, 214, 219
   lease, 52
   rent, 227
   selling price, 224
Ground lease, 4, 194
Groundwater contamination, 256–57

H

Handling objections, 107–8
Hard costs, see Direct costs
Hazardous waste, 256–57
Home improvements, 183
Hot spots, 7–8
Housing tracts, 182

I-J

Income, 227
   calculations, 219
   -expense summary, 73
   levels, 168
Indirect costs, 207, 218
Inserts, 17
Interim
   costs, 207
   loans, 234
International Council of Shopping Centers, 15, 195
Inventory system
   area assignment, 7–8
   commercial space worksheet, 11
   gathering information, 8–9
   land worksheet, 10
   listing agreements, 13
   property files, 12
   retail inventory system, 9
   time investment, 12
Investment sales, 4–5
Joint-venture, 235
   commissions, 194
   50-50 partnership, 193–94
   ground lease vs., 194
   implementing, 193
   transaction, 5

L

Land, 221
   costs, 228
   footage, 228
   loans, 233
   -only sale-leaseback, 270–71
   option, 240–41
   at present market value, 206
   sale, 3–4, 50
   worksheet, 10
Landlord's
   construction exhibit, 62–63
   perspective, 247
Lease
   clauses, 54, 62
   document, 53
   exclusive authorization of, 72
   gross, 52
   net, 53
   percentage rental, 52–53
   shopping center, 54–61
Leasing, 223
   existing space, 1–2
   national chains, 201–4
   new projects, 2
   out flow, 269–70
   small shop, 199–201
Legal documents, see Forms, various specific documents
Letters, 146, 149
   of intent, 241
Listing, 156
   agreements, 13
   contract, 2
   signs and, 140
   system, 16
Loan, 224
Local developers, see Developers
Local users, 157–58, 163
Location, 31–32
   visiting, 32, 34
Long-term control (of tenants)
   concentrating on more than one tenant, 42
   exclusive agent, 42–43
   in general, 41
   protecting tenants, 43–44
   working with other brokers, 44–45
Long-term goals, 114–16

M

Maps, 182–89
Mailing list, 146

Index

Market, 189
  knowledge, 196
  survey, 8-9
  value, 206
Marketing
  exclusive agreement, 23-26
  locating information, 15-17
  proposal, 17-18, 19-22
Monthly plan, 122
Monthly planner, 123
Multi-market tenants, 202-4

N

Napkin pro forma
  defined, 225-27
  land costs and, 227
  setting up, 227-29
National Association
  of REALTORS®, 79
National chains
  generally, 201-2
  multi-market tenants, 202-4
National users, 157-58
Negotiation
  process, 253-54
  rules for, 250-51
  when to do, 252-53
  your role in, 249-50
Neighborhood centers, 214
Net
  leases, 53, 219
  -net lease, 219
  -net-net lease, 219
  -net-net-net lease, 219
  operating income, 219, 224, 239
  rent, 227
  spendable income, 219
Newspapers, 16
NOI, *see* Net operating income
Nonequity developer, 192, 221-24

O

Objectives, *see* Goals
Offer to lease, 62, 64-65
Off-price centers, 215
Off-site
  costs, 218-19
  improvements, 167
One-mile radius developments, 177
Open listings, 13
Operating plant representations, 263
Option period, 240-41
Organization
  pending files, 126
  tickler files, 128-29
Owner, 158
  signs, *see* Signs
  -tenant inquiry, 258
Ownership inflows and outflows, 269

P

Participating mortgage, 234-35, 240
Partnerships, 235, *see also* Joint venture
PCBs, 256
Pending files, 126, 128
Percentage rental, 52-53

Permanent financing, 234-35
Permanent loan, 220
  commitment, 241-42
Physical inspection, 257-58
Planned unit development, 167
Planning, 253
Polychlorinated biphenyls, 256
Population density, 167
Preferred return, 193, 233
Preparation, 253-54
  for showing property
    generally, 155-56
    to local users, 157-58
    owner interaction, 158
    route, 156-57
Presentation, 158-60, 172-73
Principals only, 79
Private placements, 235-37
Pro forma, 210-12
  analysis of
    annual income, 224
    architectural and engineering
      costs, 223
    cash flow, 224
    contingency, 223
    debt service, 224
    development costs, 221, 223
    financing costs, 223
    gross sales price, 224
    land, 221
    leasing, 223
    loan, 224
    net operating income, 224
    sales, 221
  napkin, 225-29
  rehabilitation, 217-18
Project
  costs, 227
  signs, 137
Promises, 251
Promo centers, 215
Property
  files, 12
  purchase documents, 260-65
  for sale or lease by owner, 139
  site, 176
Proposal, 17
  preparation and presentation, 206-8
Pro rata share, 54
Prospects' needs, 98-100
PUD, *see* Planned unit development
Purchase, 4
  agreement, 69-71

R

Real estate specialist, 36
REALTORS®, 16
Recapture clause, 62
Referrals, 2, 17
Regional centers, 214
Regional users, 157-60
Rehabilitation
  during, 217
  leasing, 217
  pro forma, 217-18
  strategy, 216-17

Reinforcing statements, 104
Rent
  clause, 54
  schedules, 160-61
Rental
  adjustments clause, 54
  calculation, 207
Reporting (marking administration), 18
Representations, 263
Requisitions (for signs), 142
Restaurant News, 16
Restaurants, 31, 186
Restrictive covenant, 265
Retail
  awareness, 26
  -client requirements worksheet, 33
  inventory system, 9-12
  promotion, 143-53
  space, 200
  tenant requirement form
    demographics, 32
    location, 31-32
    tenant mix, 32
  tenants, 200-201
Retailers, 192
Retail Tenant Directory, 2, 15
Return, 227
Riders, 136-37
Right turns, 157
Route, 156-57

S

Safety issues, 255-59
Sale-leasebacks
  analysis of, 267-68
  definition of, 267-68
  process for, 268-70
  types of, 270-71
  when to discuss, 271
Sales, 221
  forecast, 168
Salesperson, 208
Savings and loans, 188
Scheduled gross income, 219
Security, 233
  deposit, 54
Seller's
  disclosure of written information, 263
  draft of property purchase, 261
  proposed restrictive covenant, 265
Selling
  right person, 106-7
  skills, 97-112
Service stations, 31
Shopping center
  development
    capital costs for, 218-20
    income of, 218-20
    napkin pro forma for, 225-30
    pro forma analysis, 221-25
    rehabilitation of, 216-18
    steps involved in, 215-16
    types of, 214-15
  lease, 55-61
Shopping Center World, 16
Short-term control, of tenants, 41

Short-term objectives, 116-19
Showing property
  follow up, 160-62
  to local users, 163
  preparation for, 155-58
  presentation of, 158-60
  when vacant, 162
Signs, 2, 17
  contents, 136-37
  generally, 135-36
  persuading owners for, 137-42
  requisitions for, 142
Site, 175
  availability, 170
  description, 166-67
  identification, 166-67
  improvements, 167
  presentation, 172-73
    area description, 167-70
  work, 221, 223
Small business, 35-36
Small shop leasing
  follow up, 201
  generally, 199-200
  retail
    space, 200
    tenants, 200-201
  tenant mix and, 201
Soft costs, *see* Indirect costs
Soil contamination, 256-57
Space needs
  chain tenants, 31
  discount stores, 31
  drugstores, 31
  financial institutions, 30
  restaurants, 31
  service stations, 31
  supermarkets, 31
  theaters, 30
Specialty centers, 214-15
Special-use permits, 157
Split commission, 37, 44
Start date, 268-69
Sublease
  exclusive right to, 65-68

Subleasing, 2
Subordination clause, 62
Subrogation, 54
Supermarket, 31
  pro forma, 210-12
Superregional centers, 215
Syndications, 235-36

T
Takeout, 220
  commitment, 241
Task, 98
Telephone
  procedures, 88-90
  techniques
    cold call strategies, 83-88
    effective procedures, 88-90
    practice, 90-94
Tenant, 208
  control
    in general, 40
    long term, 41-45
    short term, 41
  information, 32
  mix, 32, 201, 216
  multi-market, 202-4
  perspective, 246-47
  qualification, 155-56, 205
    building to site ratio, 30
    financial capability and decision
      making, 34-38
    getting information from tenant, 32
    overview of needs, 29-30
    retail-client requirements, 33
    retail tenant requirement form, 31-32
    space needs and transactions, 30-31
    tenant control, 40-45
    visiting location, 32, 34
  registration, 43-44
  representation, 245-48
    agreement, 47-49
    letter, 248
  retail, 200-201
Testing, 258, 262
Theaters, 30

Theme center, 215
Three-mile radius developments, 180
Tickler
  files, 128-29
  system, 120-22
Time investment, 12
Time management
  organization, 120, 126-29
  planning, 113-26
  skills for effective, 129-33
Title validity, 38
Total gain, 219
Traffic
  arteries, 166
  count, 157, 167-70
Transactions, 108-11
  build-to-suit, 3
  ground lease, 4
  investment sale, 4-5
  land sale, 3-4
  leasing existing space, 1-2
  leasing new projects, 2
  purchase, 4
  subleasing existing space, 2
Trust, confidence and control, 250-51
Two-mile radius developments, 178-79

U-Z
Underground tanks, 255
Use clause, 54
Utilities, 167
Vacant property, 162
Variances, 167
Waiver of subrogation clause, 54
The Wall Street Journal, 144
Weekly plan, 122
Weekly planner, 124
Wholly owned subsidiaries, 35
Yield, 219
Zoning 157
  variance, 167

NO POSTAGE
NECESSARY
IF MAILED
IN THE
UNITED STATES

BUSINESS REPLY MAIL
FIRST CLASS   PERMIT NO. 56502   CHICAGO, IL

POSTAGE WILL BE PAID BY ADDRESSEE

Real Estate Education Company
a division of Longman Financial Services Institute
520 North Dearborn Street
Chicago, Illinois 60610-4975

The Language of Real Estate
2nd Edition
John W. Reilly

ER CARD

ostage-Paid envelope today!

	Price	Total Amount
....	$19.95	_____
....	$19.95	_____
....	$19.95	_____
....	$19.95	_____
....	$19.95	_____
....	$34.95	_____
....	$34.95	_____
....	$34.95	_____
....	$22.95	_____
....	$31.95	_____
....	$38.95	_____
....	$31.95	_____
....	$32.95	_____
....	$10.95	_____
....	$13.95	_____
....	$24.95	_____
....	$22.95	_____
....	$22.95	_____
....	$18.95	_____
....	$18.95	_____
....	$10.95	_____
....	$10.95	_____
....	$29.95	_____
....	$16.95	_____
....	$16.95	_____
....	$13.95	_____
....	$19.95	_____
....	$17.95	_____
....	$19.95	_____
....	$14.95	_____
	Book Total	_____

ers shipped to AZ,
CO, CT, FL, IL, MI,
N, NJ, NY, TX, VA,
d WI must include
plicable sales tax.

Postage/Handling
0 + .50 postage
r each additional
book

TOTAL

REAL ESTATE EDUCATION COMPANY

PROPERTY MANAGEMENT, 3rd Edition,
by Robert C. Kyle, with Floyd M. Baird, RPA/SMA, Contributing Editor

The revised third edition presents management techniques for apartment buildings, co-ops, condominiums, office buildings, and commerical and industrial properties. Includes steps for creating a management plan and discussions of how to handle owner/tenant relations, leasing procedures, marketing space, and other problems. *Property Management's* popular, practical approach to management is enhanced by numerous sample forms, ads, and charts.

Key features added to the third edition:
- discussion of single family homes—how they differ from apartments, vacation homes, and timeshare properties
- section on trust relationships
- coverage of the "intelligent building," including maintenance of automation systems, telecommunications, and office automation
- discussion of industrial development incentives, including industrial revenue bonds, foreign trade zones, and others

Check box #10 on the order card. $34.95   Order Number 1551-10   copyright 1988

ESSENTIALS OF REAL ESTATE INVESTMENT, 3rd Edition,
by David Sirota

Completely updated and reorganized, the third edition provides the most timely treatment available of an area of real estate that is constantly changing. Effects of the 1986 Tax Reform Act on the real estate investment process and its applications are fully explained.

Third edition highlights include:
- financing and insurance topics consolidated into one chapter
- additional discussion of defaults and foreclosures
- updated coverage of S Corporations—*vis-a-vis* the Subchapter S Revision Act and 1986 Tax Reform Act
- explanation of how the Uniform Partnership Act controls partnerships

Check box #8 on the order card. $34.95   Order Number 1559-01   copyright 1988

REAL ESTATE BROKERAGE: A SUCCESS GUIDE, 2nd Edition,
by John E. Cyr and Joan m. Sobeck

Newly published in its second edition, this text sets the industry standard on opening and operating a real estate brokerage office. Revised and updated to reflect today's market, it features coverage of such timely topics as agency and the effects of the 1986 Tax Reform Act. Also included is a new chapter focusing on industry trends.

Key features of the second edition include:
- presentation of agency and the law
- discussion of one-appointment approach to obtaining listings (in addition to two-appointment method)
- changes resulting from the 1986 Tax Reform Act—revised income tax deductions related to brokers' expenses, effects on investor ownership, depreciation, maintenance, refinancing, and installment sales
- glossary

Check box #12 on the order card. $31.95   Order Number 1965-01   copyright 1988

AGENCY RELATIONSHIPS IN REAL ESTATE
By John W. Reilly

This timely book explains all of the real estate agent's basic relationships with buyers and sellers of real estate—including the hot topic of "dual agency"—in clearly written, nontechnical language. The text also fully discusses kinds of services offered to clients, as opposed to customers, as well as types of agency representation a broker may choose to offer. Practical information on how to avoid misrepresentations is also presented.

Agency Relationships in Real Estate features:
- extensive appendix on all U.S. cases involving agency
- in-text situations and examples that highlight and emphasize key points
- checklists that show the agent's responsibilities and obligations
- quiz and discussion questions that reinforce important concepts

Check box #19 on the order card. $22.95   Order Number 1560-08   copyright 1987

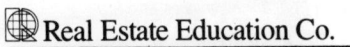

Real Estate Education Co.

LONGMAN
WHERE EXPERTS BEGIN